THE WORLD COURT AND THE CONTEMPORARY INTERNATIONAL LAW-MAKING PROCESS

By the same author

Books

Judicial Review in the English-Speaking World
Föderalismus und Bundesverfassungsrecht
Constitutionalism in Germany and the Federal Constitutional Court
Comparative Federalism. States' Rights and National Power
"Peaceful Coexistence" and Soviet-Western International Law
Federal Constitution-Making for a Multi-National World
International Law and World Revolution
Conflit idéologique et Ordre public mondial
The Illegal Diversion of Aircraft and International Law (The Hague Academy Lectures)
Parliamentary Privilege and the Broadcasting of Parliamentary Debates
The International Law of *Détente*. Arms Control, European Security, and East-West Cooperation

Books (as Editor)

Canadian Jurisprudence. The Civil Law and Common Law in Canada
Law, Foreign Policy, and the East-West *détente*
The Freedom of the Air (with M.A. Bradley)
New Frontiers in Space Law (with M.A. Bradley)
The International Law of Communications
Aerial Piracy and International Law
Federalism and Supreme Courts and the Integration of Legal Systems (with Pierre Pescatore)

THE WORLD COURT AND THE CONTEMPORARY INTERNATIONAL LAW-MAKING PROCESS

by

EDWARD McWHINNEY, Q.C.
Membre de l'Institut de Droit International

SIJTHOFF & NOORDHOFF 1979
Alphen aan den Rijn, The Netherlands

ISBN 90 286 0908 3

Printed in The Netherlands

TABLE OF CONTENTS

FOREWORD

The present study derives from special lectures given to the Faculty of Law of the Jagellonean University of Cracow and to the Polish Society of International Law, in Cracow in the Autumn of 1976; and from various other lectures forming parts of a Graduate course given in French in the *Institut du Droit de la Paix et du Développement*, in the Faculty of Law of the University of Nice, in the Spring semester, 1977.

I am deeply indebted to Professor Stanislaw E. Nahlik and to his colleagues and Faculty assistants and students at the Jagellonean University of Cracow; and to Professor René-Jean Dupuy, Director, and to Dr. Gisèle Ringeard, Secretary, of the *Institut* in the University of Nice, for the very warm welcome and hospitality extended to me during my stay with them, and also for the stimulating intellectual exchanges and criticisms in private and seminar discussions.

I am grateful to the Editors of the *Canadian Yearbook of International Law; Equality and Freedom (International and Comparative Jurisprudence)*; the *Hastings Constitutional Law Quarterly*; the *Syracuse Journal of International Law and Commerce*; and the *Zeitschrift für ausländisches öffentliches Recht und Völkerrecht*, for permission to draw upon studies that I have published in their Review in the past several years.

August, 1978

Edward McWhinney
Simon Fraser University, Vancouver.

Chapter I

INTRODUCTION: CLASSICAL INTERNATIONAL LAW SOURCES AND CONTEMPORARY INTERNATIONAL LAW-MAKING

The new International Law of our times[1] is at once a consequence of that Big Power, (East-West) *détente* that marked the ending of the post-war, Cold War era in international law and relations, and also a causal factor in that *détente's* further development and concretisation over the succeeding years.[2] It is, beyond that, a demonstration of that basic tenet of Sociological Jurisprudence of the necessary or inevitable symbiosis between Law and Society – the mutual and reciprocal interaction of positive law rules and of basic societal facts or conditions.

This new International Law is both the *corpus* of new substantive legal rules and norms created during the era of *détente* and after, and also the process – the actual institutions, instruments or procedures – by which those same legal rules and norms were established or recognised over that same time period. International Law, on this view, has never been a closed system of legal categories that jelled once and for all in some bygone era, but a dynamic, continually operating process of rejection or refinement of old rules; and the confirmation of new ones in supplement or replacement of the old.

To characterise this process of international law-making, overall, as being dialectical, is to eschew the traditionally-favoured United Nations designation of a "progressive development" of International Law. The phrase "progressive development" has a normative ambiguity inherent in it that has, no doubt, occasionally facilitated the obtaining of a voting consensus in the United Nations and in its various specialised arenas. But in a World Cummunity marked today not simply by a duality of main competing political ideologies such as existed in the Cold War era with its basically bipolar model of World Public Order, but by a plurality of different political, social, and economic systems, to talk, for scientific-legal purposes, of a "progressive development" of International Law is either to lend oneself to a conscious semantic confusion or else to engage, in the end, in professions of rival political faiths.

The term dialectical development seems more accurately to describe the competition and conflict, in concrete problem-situations, of the different basic societal interests that exist of *de facto* in the World Community today, and the different basic conceptions of World Public Order, or *Weltanschauungen*, from which those different interests ultimately derive. It also identifies the process of interaction and of mutual exchange and barter and compromise whereby, in the end, some of those competing societal interests will be preferred to others and some rejected altogether; with, more usually, most of the interests accommodated, in measure, after a degree of reciprocal give-and-take.

1. The Sources of International Law

The concept of a list, a more or less closed list, of categories of formal sources of International Law, is the product, essentially, of 19th century analytical positivism, with its emphasis on juridical formalism. It is reflected in the proclamation, in Article 38 of the Statute of the International Court of Justice, detailing the categories of legal rules to be applied by the Court in deciding disputes submitted to it:

(a) international conventions, whether general or particular, establishing rules expressly recognised by the contesting states;
(b) international custom, as evidence of a general practice accepted as law;
(c) the general priciples of law recognised by civilised nations;
(d) subject to the provisions of Article 59, judicial decisions and the teachings of the most highly qualified publicists of the various nations, as subsidiary means for the determination of rules of law.

Article 59 of the Court Statute, be it remembered, stipulates that the decision of the Court in any case – "has no binding force except between the parties and in respect of that particular case", thereby excluding any posibility of a Common Law-style doctrine of *stare decisis* or binding authority of the Court's own prior decisions in subsequent cases.

Classical International Law was, perhaps, excessively preoccupied with the quest for an ultimate, approved source for each legal rule. The notion of a legal community, it was argued, presupposed the existence of a legal sovereign, or at least sovereign authority: with legal rules being general commands issuing from the sovereign authority to the members of that community. Every claimed legal rule, therefore, to deserve the name of law must fit into at least one of the pre-determined *a priori* categories of such commands – into one of the sources. If not, it was not a valid legal rule.

The argument is, of course, a circular one; if the claimed proposition fits into one of the recognised sources, it must be a legal rule; and if it is a legal rule it must fit into one of the pre-ordained sources.

By contrast, the Legal Realist approach to the definition of law and to the establishing of whether or not a claimed proposition deserves the accolade of legal rule is to put emphasis on the facts rather than on the *a priori* legal categories. If all the interested parties accept a claimed rule as being law, it must be so without need for too much speculation as to whether or not the claimed rule fits into the pre-ordained categories; or, for that matter, without any occasion for anguished concern if it should turn out that the claimed rule does not. The legal principle prohibiting the orbiting of nuclear weapons in space vehicles was affirmed by the Soviet Union and the United States in joint declarations issued in 1963. The principle was subsequently written in as one of the specific provisions of the Space Treaty of 1967.[3] What, then, was the international legal status of the principle in the four years between its solemn affirmation by the only two parties with the necessary technological capacity to do anything about it, and its formal enshrinement in one of the recognised categories of sources of International Law, as proclaimed in Article 38 of the World Court Statute? It is not possible, on the facts, to deny that the principle was treated as fully binding on them in international law, during that time period, by the two main political protagonists.

The emphasis on a Law-as-Fact approach, with corresponding de-emphasis of juridical formalism and of the quest for an *a priori* category of legal sources into which a claimed legal rule can, somehow or other, be consigned, is part of the new Legal Realist conception of the international law-making process. In the same view, West Germany could be argued as being legally bound by the stipulations of the Geneva Convention of 1958 even though it had never ratified the Convention;[4] and France could certainly be held to its own unilateral declaration of intention not to resume high altitude nuclear testing[5], even though such declaration neither was concretised in treaty form nor came within the existing category of estoppel at international law.[6]

2. Dilemma of the Hierarchical Relation or Ranking *inter se* of the Different Sources

Classical International Law usually looked to its two main constituent legal elements – the Anglo-Saxon Common Law and the Continental European Civil Law – for any guidance as to primacy, in terms of their respective juridical origins or sources, as between two different, competing legal rules. Except for the greater weight given by the Common Law internal, municipal law systems to judicial decisions as such, flowing from Common Law doctrines of *stare decisis* and the binding authority of a legal decision, and for the Civil Law respect for *doctrines* (including, of course, the opinions of textwriters and judicial decisions [*jurisprudence*] under this rubric), Common Law and Civil Law-derived notions of the relative ranking of the different formal sources of International Law are not widely different, the practical synthesis of the two being reflected in Article 38 of the World Court Statute.

While recognising, of necessity, that statute (here Treaty) law breaks customary law to the extent of any inconsistency or contradiction between the two, Classical International Law, as applied by the West, has, as a matter of history, always given a dominant place to customary International Law, particularly long-established customary rules.

In international legal arenas like the United Nations and its specialised agencies and its specialised legal conferences, Western jurists have frequently been forced into a defensive position *vis-à-vis* the role of old custom, and have taken a correspondingly restrictive view of international legal codification conventions that purport to re-state the old law, where these conventions are adopted by something less than unanimity. There has also been a denial of the normative, law-making quality of United Nations General Assembly Resolutions except so far as these are simply declarations of, and reflect already existing, customary law. By contrast Western attitudes to the World Court and to its law-making *rôle*, have tended to be tied, since World War II, to the American-inspired "World Rule of Law" campaign for extending, among other thing, the Court's compulsory jurisdiction; but these essentially positive conceptions of the Court's position can no doubt be expected to be modified as the emerging new political majority among the judges of the Court, reflecting the Third World's interest in the Court and in the processes of election of its judges, shews a disposition to utilise the Court's quite considerable law-making potential in the service of the creation of the "new" international law.

In comparison to the West, the Soviet Union and the Soviet bloc countries have given prime emphasis to treaties in the international law-making process,[7] with a special exception designed to repudiate the so-called "unequal treaties" which are narrowly defined by Soviet jurists so as to apply, essentially, only to treaties made by the Soviet Union in the era of immediate post-October Revolution political-military weakness, and to analogous "Imperialist" treaties.[8] Customary international law, and here especially old custom, may not be automatically binding on "new" countries that have come into existence after the customary rule has emerged.[9] As for Resolutions of the United Nations General Assembly, recommendations of specialised International Organisations, and decisions of the International Court of Justice and of International arbitral tribunals, these are relegated to the status of "subsidiary" sources only; and, particularly in the case of U.N. General Assembly Resolutions, may be dependent, for their legal efficacy, upon the comprehensiveness, and also inter-systemic representativeness, of the voting majorities actually composing them.[10]

The Third World has not merely continued the emphasis, suggested by Soviet publicists, on *new* custom at the expense of the *old* custom in whose creation the Third World countries, if they have participated at all, have participated only notionally as members of erstwhile colonial Empires; but Third World countries have initiated a search for new arenas and new processes for international law-making in which the Third World numerical voting powers can be exercised to the full. This involves not merely the full use of the international codifying or general legal conference directed to the elaboration of multilateral conventions involving the re-statement and, in the process, re-formulation or re-writing altogether, of older, custom-based rules of international law; but the vigorous and imaginative recourse to law-making in the newer international arenas like the U.N. General Assembly and its Committees and the specialised U.N. agencies. The U.N. General Assembly Resolution begins to take on a declaratory, hortatory quality, under the impetus of Third World drafting and direction;[11] and in spite of the denials by Western jurists and publicists of any present law-making character, such Resolutions to an increasing extent in recent years come to acquire a sense of prophesy and of law-in-the-making. In strictly juridical terms, the U.N. General Assembly Resolutions on such key subjects as Decolonisation and Independence, on National ownership and control over natural resources, and on a new international economic order, may not be, in their immediate orgins, "hard" law; but, as "soft" law,[12] they have a habit of turning out to be the international law-in-action of today, and the "hard" law of tomorrow or the day after tomorrow. The U.N. General Assembly majorities that adopted those Resolutions have, in this sense, been demonstrated, in time, to have a keener sense of the "winds of change" in the World Community and the general movement and direction of World history than those established states that either opposed or abstained in the actual votes on the Resolutions, or else went along with them, reluctantly, in the final vote.

The new Third World majority in the United Nations General Assembly has only now, and most belatedly, begun to discover the potentialities of the World Court as an international law-making, policy-making arena; for it is only since the politically controversial, 8 to 7 majority decision of the Court in the *South West Africa* case in 1966,[13] that the Third World countries have in any conscious way tried to use their voting power in the General Assembly, (and to a rather less extent, of course, in the Security Council), to elect judges who might be expected to be disposed to create new law, as distinct from logically developing or re-stating the old. This process can only be said to have begun as yet; but, as it is extended and developed, we may reasonably expect to see a significant differentiation and departure of Third World attitudes to the World Court from both Soviet and Western-based approaches.

3. Contemporary Practical Problems of the Sources of International Law

The notion of sources of international law must be recognised today as a comprehensive term veiling three different conceptions – a creative process (how a rule emerges as law); the creative factors (the instruments and machinery of international law-making); and the end-product of those creative factors operating through the creative process (that is, the substantive legal rule itself).[14]

Putting to one side any consideration of the actual substantive rules emerging in this way, some major problems exist as to each of the conventionally-accepted categories of sources of International law.

(a) *Custom*

First, as to custom, and referring here now to "old" custom, what is the exact *rôle* of the consent of states, and particularly of new states that were not in existence, in independent, autonomous form, prior to the emergence of a claimed rule of customary international law? If one speaks of an implied consent, in the case of such new states, as, on pragmatic grounds, we no doubt should in spite of the legal fictional elements present in such a characterisation, how is such an implied consent to be negated by a new state, and negated by how many states, for such a claimed customary rule to lose its legal quality, both *vis-à-vis* the individual recusing state or states and also generally?

Again, and referring here to the time element inherent, as an indispensable element, in the formation of a rule of customary international law, just how much passage of time is actually requisite? It has been pointed out, correctly, that in certain of the newer areas of international law – if not the new international law, as such – the technological base of the problem is such that time has a habit of galloping: hence one can speak, only half satirically, of a sort of "instant" customary international law in the law of outer space. The space-time dimension, as such, occupies a peculiar importance in regard to the formation of rules of customary international law, for we are involved not merely with *time*, as with the application of the concept of *occupatio* in Eastern Greenland [15] or in the Spanish Sahara [16], but also with spatial notions, as, for example, the relevance, in determining the legal connotation today of *occupatio,* of Western-based, Roman-Law derived conceptions of an essentially static territorial possession, in the case of Islamic, nomadic peoples such as were to be found in the Western Sahara at the time of the Spanish arrival. [17]

The practice of States remains, of course, the key constituent element, in the emergence of any new rule of customary international law. The most interesting application of State practice in the contemporary era lies in the area of unilateral, initially non-licit, actions that are not effectively protested by other States and even by other States directly affected by them. Examples are, perhaps, the United States "Quarantine" action in the Cuban Missile crisis of October, 1962, which, though sought to be justified under other legal categories, undoubtedly amounted, in so far as it was effectively protested neither by the Soviet Union nor by other countries having maritime connections with Cuba, to an extension of the existing International Law of Pacific Blockade. [18] Further examples are to be found in the various unilateral national proclamations of a 200-mile Territorial Sea, or in the conclusion of a plethora of bilateral treaties between different countries with recitations to the same effect: presumably, in the absence, up to the present, of any broadly-based, multilateral convention on the Law of the Sea extending the boundaries of the existing, custom-based territorial sea, the effect, in juridical terms, is to create a new general custom, or at least a new gloss on the old custom, through a series of interlocking unilateral national declarations or bilateral arrangements. This innovatory, individual or bilateral initiative-based, mode of approach to the creation of new general norms of international law may be aided by an emerging trend in World Court jurisprudence, as evidenced in several recent judgments, to favor the granting of legal effect to unilateral declarations of State intention, even if these were not necessarily designed to have legal effect at the time they were originally made, or directed to the purposes of present conflicts. [19]

(b) *Treaties*

The larger questions involving Treaties as a source of International Law today go to the political difficulties and imperfections inherent in the treaty-making process in view of the increase in sheer numbers of participants, not less than in the ideological differences separating them.

The conflict between rival conceptions of World public order and also the challenge of societal change in the World Community are to be seen in the debate over the *rôle* and purpose of legal codification as achieved through a multilateral convention to be enacted by an international codification conference or even series of conferences as with the Law of the Sea. Is the legal codification treaty to be limited to a "restatement" of the old or pre-existing international customary law, with or without those comparatively modest, incremental extensions normally licensed through analogical extension of the old rules – grammatical or logical interpretation, according to Civil Law canons; or is it to take the pre-existing law simply as a point of departure for purposes of some sort of radical re-casting or novation of law? Third World countries, quite understandably, tend to press for a creative, legislative function for the international codifying treaty; where the post-industrial societies, both Western and Soviet, opt more generally for a more restricted, "restatement" only, function.

The increase in actual numbers of participants in international conferences consequent upon the expansion of the World Community and the opening of United Nations membership in the wake of the massive decolonisation and independence of the 1950s and 1960s, has had certain easily observable practical consequences and effects for such international conferences, that are not necessarily related to their subject matter. One such effect is the general attrition factor noticeable with so many international reunions called together for the purpose of drafting multilateral conventions: the gap between the number of States officially represented at a diplomatic conference and the number actually signing the draft Convention resulting from it; the further gap between the number of States signing the draft convention and the number then going on to take the further step of formally ratifying it; and, finally, the gap between formal signature and formal ratification on the one hand and the concrete, legislative and administrative inplementation of the treaty on the other.[20] The attrition factor is, of course, most marked in areas where the subject matter of the treaty may involve covert, non-publicised difficulties of an ideological character for certain governments that were, perhaps, persuaded mainly by the desire for a favourable public image abroad or other, similar considerations, to take part in the project of convention in the first place. The Tokyo, The Hague, and Montreal Conventions directed to the alleviation and control of aerial piracy come readily to mind. The non-fulfilment, to date, of various United Nations-based projects for a convention outlawing international terrorism may indicate simply that the conflict of values represented for many key participants by the subject matter of the proposed convention is too fundamental today to be veiled over, as yet, by further diplomatic conferences and the elaborate legal formulae flowing from them even where, as with the Tokyo Convention of 1963, for example, they do no more than re-state already existing customary international law-based norms.[21]

A further major question in regard to mutilateral conventions is how nearly universal they must become in their participants to achieve a general law-making effect, going beyond the States actually signing and ratifying them. At a certain point, do multilateral treaties become binding even on the non-signers and nonratifiers? In the International Court of Justice, there is, as already noted, judicial *dicta* in support of the proposition that West Germany is bound by the provisions of the Geneva Convention of 1958 even though never ratifying that Convention; the legal argument finds support on other grounds than an obligation *qua* Convention, however.[22] Going beyond that, is, for example, France, which was not a party to the Moscow Test Ban Treaty of 1963, bound by that Treaty's principles? According to the argument, by virtue of the overwhelming number and inter-systemic representativeness of the State adhesions to the Moscow Test Ban Treaty, its legal principles may be said to have entered into general international law. The issue was present in the *French Nuclear Tests* cases, but without any necessity to be disposed of in view of the essentially procedural, adjectival law-based nature of the final decision by the International Court. [23]

When we turn to bilateral treaties, the personality of the State participants in those treaties becomes all important. The juridical equality of States is a key principle in the "new" International Law, adumbrated, as such, in the Soviet-inspired Principles of Peaceful Coexistence and in the corresponding United Nations Declaration of Principles of Friendly Relations and Cooperation among States in accordance with the U.N. Charter [24]; but some States are clearly more important (or more equal) than others in the political influence or style leadership that they give to their own national treaty-making ventures. Viewed in terms of the international law-making process and the instruments of international law-making, the Soviet-U.S. bilateral treaty, or else the Soviet-U.S. jointly elaborated treaty draft which other States are free to adopt but not to alter in any significant way, have come to be decisive in the elaboration and refinement of the international law of the era of the *détente*. The Moscow Test Ban Treaty of August 1963, represents the archetype of this process of law-making on key international tension-issues – through joint initiative, usually expressed through Summit Meeting diplomacy – of the two erstwhile bloc leaders. [25] The Test Ban Treaty was conceived and authored by the Soviet Union and the United States, (with the participation of Great Britain), through Summit Meetings, and was then signed by these three States, and, only subsequent to their signatures, opened to other States for their official acceptance, without those other States, however, having either participated in the process of elaboration of the Treaty's terms or having the power to modify them. In the same vein, though perhaps more tactful in its at least surface deference to the sensibilities of the other, lesser or supporting powers, is the operational methodology applied for further developing the *détente* through the successive treaty-based measures directed towards nuclear disarmament and arms control, and to the security of territorial frontiers in Europe and of the post-World War II political-military settlement in general. The public arena for these later international law-making ventures is the general international conference, rather than the Summit Meeting *à deux*; and the chosen instrument is the multilateral treaty, and not the limited or bilateral treaty as the intermediate step to the more general accord as had been the case, for tactical reasons, with the Moscow Test Ban Treaty. Yet the close, working collaboration established between the Soviet and U.S. delegations to such general international conferences, the continuing exchange of drafts between their two delegations and the eventual approximation of their respective projects, was indispensable to the overall political progress in pursuit of *détente* maintained at these conferences; and to the concrete success actually achieved with particular initiatives like the Space Treaty of 1967, the Nuclear Non-Proliferation Treaty of 1968, the Treaty forbidding the emplacement of Nuclear Arms on the Sea-bed of 1971, the Treaty on the Manufacture and Stock-piling of Bacteriological Weapons of 1972, and the eventual Helsinki Accord of 1975. This was all part of the highly successful, problem-oriented, step-by-step approach to East-West *détente*; and in both its origins and also its succesful implementation it was undoubtedly assisted by the Western acceptance, *de facto*, of the Soviet preference for treaties as the prime source of international law today; and of the Soviet preferences, in actual treaty-making, for bilateral negotiation, if possible through secret diplomacy at Summit Meetings, as the indispensable *prior* step in the whole negotiating process. And outside the more general *détente* framework for which, once achieved, some more general World Community approval or ratification *ex post facto* is desirable, there is still a considerable area for Soviet–U.S. joint initiatives pursued, at this time, on a bilateral basis only: the Moscow Summit Meeting of May, 1972, and the so-called SALT I accord and ABM Treaty emerging from it, and the Vladivostock Summit Meeting of November, 1974, and the resultant SALT II document, are simply the most recent major examples in what has been a continuing process, over a decade and a half of *détente*.

(c) *Resolutions of the U.N. General Assembly*

U.N. General Assembly Resolutions are officially characterised, in Soviet legal doctrine, as subsidiary sources of international law. The Soviet attitude is deliberately conservative, more so, certainly, than *Soviet bloc* doctrine which is prepared to concede a law-making quality to such Resolutions where they are adapted unanimously, or at least have inter-systemic, tri-bloc (Soviet, Western and Third World) support in the General Assembly.

In Western juridical doctrine in the immediate aftermath of the euphoria of the 1951 Uniting for Peace Resolution of the U.N. General Assembly, Western political leaders and Western legal publicists tended to postulate a right, indeed a duty, on the part of the General Assembly to move affirmatively to "fill the gaps" in the Charter whenever necessary, constitutionally, in support of the General Assembly's peace-keeping responsibilities. The Uniting for Peace Resolution was adopted by an overwhelming majority (52 to 5, with 2 abstentions) in the then Western-dominated General Assembly. In the intervening years, with the more than doubling of U.N. membership in the wake of large-scale decolonisation and independence, the automatic pro-Western voting majority in the General Assembly has disappeared for all practical purposes; and with it the Western enthusiasm of yesteryear for the claimed plenary, legislative power of the General Assembly, leaving the traditionally more reserved Western view that such Resolutions have legal efficacy only when they are declaratory of pre-existing law.[26]

With the triumphant new anti-colonialist, anti-imperialist voting coalition installed in political control of the General Assembly, the General Assembly Resolution has become the prime instrument for the re-making of the old International Law in the image of the new Third World majority. There are some limitations to all this, of course: the Third World majority is not homogeneous for all purposes, and on a number of key issues, such as the energy crisis and even the concrete implementation of the new international economic order, there is no longer a complete congruence of interests as between, for example, the economically well-to-do oil producing and exporting countries and those Third World countries without major natural resources or raw materials within their territorial limits. The other limitations go to as yet unresolved doctrinal issues of just how, in analytical jurisprudential terms, to classify or categorise such Resolutions, assuming that they are law in the first place. What is clear, however, is that the largely hortatory propositions of yesterday contained in such Resolutions as those on de-colonisation, national ownership of natural resources, and the like, have really represented law-in-the-making in their execution and development, and now number among the accepted principles of the "new" International Law.

(d) *Decisions of the International Court of Justice*

The older, classical "European" legal community of the era of the League of Nations and of the Permanent Court of International Justice greatly favoured judicial settlement as a mode of international problem-solving, – no doubt, because of the essential identity of basic attitudes and political expectations on the part of the States principally involved in having recourse to the Court at that time. The interstitial judicial legislation necessarily involved in the judicial decision-making process presented, in consequence, no fears of any leap into the unknown in terms of the elaboration of new international law doctrine in the process of decision-making. The change from the League of Nations to the United Nations, and from the Permanent Court of International Justice to the present International Court of Justice brought a substantial and ever-continuing broadening of the representativeness of the Court and its judges, in keeping with the similar broadening of the representativeness of the United Nations itself; and this trend has been accentuated and accelerated since the 1966 decision of the International Court in the *South West Africa* cases, rendered by an 8 to 7 majority on the second, tie-breaking vote of the President of the Court.[27] In the wake of the very strong political reaction by Third World leaders against the *South West Africa* decision, there has been a tendency to much greater politicisation of the elections of judges to the Court, with corresponding long-range changes to be expected in the over-all philosophy of the Court and in its approach to judicial legislation. On that basis, and with the anticipated changes in the political composition of the Court majority as a result of a more active and interested Third World *rôle* in the judicial elections in the General Assembly and Security Council, it may be expected thet Western publicists who had been, earlier, favourably inclined to an activist, policy-making, legislating *rôle* for the Court, will become more cautious; and that, by the same token, the Third World countries who had been so suspicious of the old, allegedly conservative or reactionary Court, will look to it increasingly as another and favourable arena for developing new international law on an affirmative basis. Only the Soviet Union seems to remain consistent in terms of long-range institutional attitudes and expectations; and the restrictive Soviet approach that has characterised the post-War period, stemming from past Soviet empirical experience, and that has consistently denied any place for judicial legislation on the Court, can therefore be expected to continue to prevail with Soviet policy-makers.

In consequence of the fact that the Court, as a result of the staggered system of judicial elections, with a third, only, of the Court being renewed every three years, seems still in transition from the old, pre-1966, pre-*South West Africa* Court, to a newer, more consciously policy-oriented tribunal, the decisions of recent years have been characterised by mutiple opinion-writing – both dissenting and also special, concurring opinions, – with the doctrinal divisions among the individual judges so great that it is often very difficult to extract any common principle or *ratio decidendi*, even in matters decided by near unanimity in voting terms.

4. Main Trends in the International Law-Making Process Today

In an era of very rapid societal change in the World Community, it is inevitable that there should be corresponding pressures for rapid changes in the positive law international law, in measure with the societal change. What we have today is a plurality of sources of international law, both old sources and new ones, with the clear majority political preference in the United Nations being for the newer, "democratic" instruments of law-making like the U.N. General Assembly Resolution or the recommendations of specialised international organisations. There is a concomitant favouring, also, of newer, more informal modes of international law-making,[28] without too much regard for their conformity, or otherwise, to the old, pre-ordained, closed formal categories of sources established in the era of dominance of legal positivist thinking on international law. In Legal Realist vein, the question, now, is increasingly likely to be whether the parties regard themselves as being legally bound in concrete circumstances; rather than whether a claimed rule fits into one or other of the long-established legal categories. The doctrinal emphasis thus becomes one of Law as Fact,[29] in the constant tension today between stability and change in the World Community and in the positive law rules that are supposed to reflect basic societal conditions and demands in the World Community.

Looking, for the moment, only to those other (lesser) categories of sources listed, apart from treaties and custom and judicial decisions, in Article 38 of the World Court Statute, we find, understandably enough in a World Community characterised by a plurality of different social and economic systems, that "the general principles of law recognised by civilised nations" do not bulk too large in concrete problem-solving. Perhaps that is too much to expect, except in so far as, by imaginative excursus into comparative law, one can attempt to postulate as a sort of international *jus gentium* certain key principles common to all major legal systems. The quest at definition of the legal extensity of *jus cogens*, [30] – so far, a legal category without precise content – could take this form.

The "teachings of the most qualified publicists of the various nations", once a most prestigious form of legal authority in the era of that narrower, Western or European-based World Community, have been affected by the marked expansion of United Nations membership without a corresponding development, at the same time, of a *corpus* of non-European or non-European-derived doctrine, – on a quantitatively equivalent basis at least. The classical international law *doctrines* of the late 19th and early 20th centuries remain, thus, too narrow in their particular cultural roots and in their original socio-economic base, to retain their erstwhile prestige and legal authority. At the same time, the "publicists" – the law professors and legal text-writers – as a legal skill group, have been too generally touched by that *dédoublement fonctionnel*[31] involved in accepting legal briefs or acting as special legal adviser to their own national government in pursuit of national political interests: the legal publicists may therefore run the risk of being seen as *parti pris* and of losing in consequence that reputation for intellectual detachment and political neutrality that characterised the writings of the great text-writers in the classical, 19th century and early 20th century, era of international legal doctrine, with the proliferating new national yearbooks or journals of international law, by the same token, declining into exercises in legal particularism and in the propagation of parochial national legal interests. The publicists turned official governmental legal spokesman or apologist will, of course, continue to contribute importantly to the general international law-making process. The difference is that the contribution will no longer be *qua* publicist, with all the legal authority or prestige of the old *responsa prudentium*; but as part of the ordinary political-dialectical process of development of international law, where contending political protagonists try to maximise their contending national interests, with the final legal solution one of political accommodation or compromise among those interests. Is there a place for the independent legal scholar and jurist of yesteryear?[32]

Lastly, Equity, [33] which once seemed to offer hopes for a flexible expansion of old international law customary rules to meet new societal conditions, has tended to jell, as it did finally in English legal history, into a series of closed precedents, with the creative, innovatory possibilities limited to logical exegesis and not much more.

It is for reason of the very limited possibilities of utilisation of the conventional categories of sources for purpose of re-making the old international law that the Third World working majority in the United Nations General Assembly and the specialised agencies has begun to innovate so dramatically in terms of the instruments of international law-making. The "soft" law of the hortatory-style U.N. General Assembly Resolution has a habit of ending up eventually, as we have seen, as "hard" law, in terms of concrete follow-up action both by the Third World countries and also by other countries reacting defensively to the international pressure against them. The "wild" custom, originally created by unilateral State action interlocking with similar and reciprocal unilateral State action by other members of the World Community over a period of time – such as the original Pacific Coast Latin American States' proclamations of a 200-mile fishing zone, – starts as a species of particularised or localised, regional international law gloss on the general international law. It then becomes more generalised as other countries, outside the original region involved, begin to follow suit; and it acquires, in the process, a revisionist finality and becomes declaratory of new law. In the same way the consensus accord of an international legal conference that might otherwise sunder if submitted too soon to the harsh test of a formal, recorded vote on a definitive treaty draft, ripens, in its own time, into a new-style programmatic international law for the future. These have been the practical ways – processes, procedures – in which the new international law has tended so largely to emerge, as law-in-action, in response to the new forces in the World Community since the achievement of the Big Power *détente*.

Chapter II

JUDICIAL LAW-MAKING. JUDICIAL SELF-RESTRAINT AND JUDICIAL ACTIVISM: FROM SOUTH WEST AFRICA, SECOND PHASE, 1966,[1] TO NAMIBIA (SOUTH WEST AFRICA) 1971[2]

1. South West Africa, Second Phase 1966. Judicial Self-Restraint Applied

The International Court of Justice's judgment, in 1966, in *South West Africa, Second Phase*, is no doubt the politically most controversial opinion rendered by the present Court or by its predecessor, the old Permanent Court of International Justice. In the 1966 judgment, the Court, having already in 1962 decided by an 8 to 7 majority that it had jurisdiction to hear Ethiopian and Liberian complaints against South Africa,[3] split evenly, 7 to 7, and then decided by 8 to 7 on the second, tie-breaking vote of the President of the Court, that neither complainant state had standing to receive judgment in the matter. The *volte face* seemingly made by the Court, from its 1962 judgment to its 1966 judgment, as between a policy of judicial activism and interventionism in behalf of national self-determination in Southern Africa, and a policy of judicial self-restraint in regard to great political *causes célèbres,* aroused the ire of Third World spokesmen in the U.N. General Assembly and elsewhere. For the logical basis of the distinction sought to be made by the new, 1966 judicial majority from the earlier, 1962 judicial decision was such as might well baffle the ingenuity of the medieval Schoolmen, seemingly justifying the conclusion, in the eyes of the Court's political critics, that the new judicial majority had sought to invoke proceduralisms to mask a substantive, policy decision of a politically conservative or reactionary character.

Such criticisms are, of course, somewhat simplistic and tend to overlook or down-grade the historical continuity of the Court's essentially adjectival law-based approach and also the Court's insistence upon the establishment of a proper jurisdictional base as a prior condition to any ventures in judicial policy-making, of whatever nature. The charge, above all, that the Court, in *South West*

Africa, Second Phase, demonstrated itself as being a "European" or "White Man's" Court, is valid only in the particular sense that, in consequence of the built-in attrition factor in the constitutional processes of renewal of the Court membership – with a third, only, of the Court's judges having to submit themselves to re-election at each three year interval – the Court, in 1966, remained a predominantly European body, (both Western European and Communist Eastern European). The new Third World majority in the United Nations General Assembly, created in consequence of the large-scale decolonisation and independence in Asia and Africa from the 1960's onwards, had, in this respect, not yet succeeded, and perhaps not yet really tried, to translate its numerical voting power in Court elections in the General Assembly and the Security Council, into a Third World political majority on the Court.

The 1966 *South West Africa, Second Phase*, decision, on examination, reveals itself as not being noticeably polemical in character, and as not, in any case, containing radical differences as to basic philosophy of international law as between majority and minority judges, in spite of the closeness of the final 8 to 7 majority vote. The official Opinion of Court, appearing over the signature of the President, Sir Percy Spender, and declining jurisdiction to render judgement on the Ethiopian and Liberian complaints against South Africa, has, it must be said, ample precedent in the domestic jurisprudence of most legal systems, whether Common Law or Civil Law. Courts do have the right to avoid ruling on substantive legal issues by deciding on narrow procedural points. Judicial self-restraint is a recognized legal virtue in many countries, both Western and Communist, especially, one might suggest, where great political *causes célèbres* are involved that could more appropriately or conveniently be referred to the other, more directly and avowedly political, organs of community policy-making for favour of political problem-solving – in the case of the World Community, to the General Assembly and Security Council. The functional specialisation and differentiation of decision-making *rôles* represented, in rudimentary, triadic separation of powers form within the United Nations institutions, would, on this argument, have suggested a prior recourse by those activist elements in the United Nations dissatisfied with the racial situation in South Africa in general and with the continued South African control over South West Africa in particular, to the more overtly political arenas of the United Nations. This was, in fact, the course of action decided upon and then succesfully launched by the Third World opponents of South Africa, after their procedurally-based defeat in *South West Africa, Second Phase* in 1966. The U.N. General Assembly, on the resumption of its sessions, immediately after the *South West Africa, Second Phase* decision, voted in October, 1966, by 114 votes to 2, with 3 abstentions, in resolution 2145 (1966),[4] to declare the South African League of Nations-derived Mandate over South West Africa as terminated; and the General Assembly continues to be the main arena of Third World-based action against South Africa, to this day.

To return to the *South West Africa, Second Phase* judgment of 1966, the official Opinion of Court[5] accords, in its closely analytic reasoning and adjectival law orientation, with the best canons of the English Equity Bar, to which Judge-President Spender, who signed the Opinion on behalf of the Court, and also the British judge, Sir Gerald Fitzmaurice, who is understood to have played a major *rôle* in the drafting and elaboration of the Opinion, both belonged in terms of their professional training and experience and also their general philosophical orientation. Nor is the majority Opinion of Court ideological in any mid-1960's, vestigial Cold War sense: the Polish member of the Court, Judge Winiarski, joins with Judge-President Spender and the rest of the majority judges in the official Opinion of Court, and while the Soviet judge, Judge Koretsky, dissents,[6] he does so on the same deliberately restrained basis of technical, procedural, adjectival law argumentation as the Court majority. It is left to the American judge, Judge Jessup, in his Dissenting Opinion[7], to open up substantive issues of the legality or otherwise of governmentally-practised racial differentiation or discrimination, along the judicial activist, legislative, "policy" interpretation lines favoured by the United States Supreme Court since the President Franklin Roosevelt-inspired Court Revolution of 1937; when, by contrast, and again in American constitutional terms, the Court majority applies the special legal philosophy of judicial self-restraint and of the practical political limits to Court-based legislation or law-making generally associated with the late Mr. Justice Felix Frankfurter of the United States Supreme Court.

2. Namibia (South West Africa), 1971. The Preliminary, Procedural Issue Re-examined

The World Court had a further occasion to examine the South West Africa Mandate question in its Advisory Opinion, rendered in 1971, in *Legal consequences for States of the Continued Presence of South Africa in Namibia (South West Africa) notwithstanding*

Security Council Resolution 276 (1970).[8] The reference to the Court had been initiated by Security Council Resolution 284 (1970)[9] adopted in terms of Article 96 (1) of the United Nations Charter and Article 65 of the Court Statute, the preamble to the Security Council Resolution reciting that such an Advisory Opinion from the Court would be –

> "useful for the Security Council in its further consideration of the question of Namibia and in furtherance of the objectives the Council is seeking."

Before it could reach the substantive legal issues and, indeed, before it could exercise jurisdiction in the first place, the Court had to overcome some major preliminary, procedural issues. One of these concerned the legality of Security Council Resolution 284 (1970) itself, which had requested the Advisory Opinion from the Court: in the actual vote in the Security Council two of the permanent members of the Council had abstained [10], and it was contended that the Resolution had not, in consequence, been adopted by – "an affirmative vote of nine members including the concurring votes of the permanent members", as required by Article 27 (3) of the Charter for Security Council decisions on substantive matters. The Court, to dispose of this objection, took notice of the fact that Security Council practice, extending over a long period, showed that presidential rulings and the positions taken by members of the Council, particularly permanent members, had consistently and uniformly interpreted voluntary abstention by a permanent member as not constituting a bar to the adoption of the resolutions. [11]

A cognate objection, going to the validity of the Security Council vote, was that since the Namibia issue related to a dispute between South Africa and other members of the United Nations, South Africa should, in terms of Article 32 of the Charter, have been invited to – "participate, without vote, in the discussion relating to the dispute", preceding the actual Security Council vote. This objection was rejected by the Court on the argument that, while the language of Article 32 of the Charter was mandatory in relation to a "dispute", the Namibia question had not been placed on the Security Council agenda as a "dispute", but as a "situation". [12] The distinction here, with all respect, seems a purely verbal one, and in any case as precious a one as that relied upon by the Court majority in *South West Africa, Second Phase* in 1966 to distinguish and limit the earlier, 1962, Court majority holding on jurisdiction over the same issue. The Court majority did, however, in the present case, vote that the South African

Government had itself neglected to request the Security Council to treat the matter as a "dispute" for purposes of Article 32: "Having failed to raise the question at the appropriate time in the proper forum, it is not open to it to raise it before the Court at this stage".[13]

A rather more important objection, in this same context, was to the effect that quite apart from Article 32 of the Charter, the question now posed to the Court by the Security Council really related to an existing dispute between South Africa and other States, so that the present reference to the Court by the Security Council was simply an attempt to do indirectly by the Advisory Opinion route what could not be done directly by the contentious jurisdiction route since lacking the consent of one of the parties to the dispute – in this case, the key party, South Africa.[14] The leading authority invoked here in support of the Court's now declining jurisdiction was the old Permanent Court of International Justice's ruling in the *Estern Carelia* question in 1923.[15] But *Eastern Carelia* was promptly distinguished by the Court majority on the basis that, in *Eastern Carelia*, one of the States concerned, the Soviet Union, was not a Member of the League of Nations and did not appear before the Court; whereas, in the present case, South Africa was a Member of the United Nations and, as such, was – "bound by Article 96 of the Charter, which empowers the Security Council to request advisory opinions on any legal question."[16] This is, it may be suggested, rather an ingenious Common Law style of distinguishing earlier, inconvenient judicial precedents than a reflection of the general philosophy and reasoning of the old Permanent Court in *Eastern Carelia*, at the time of its decision in 1923. However, as the present Court now noted, South Africa had, in fact, participated in both the written and oral proceedings, and had also, while raising specific objections against the competence of the Court, addressed itself to the merits of the question.[17]

Related to the Court's disposition of this particular objection was its handling of the South African request to be allowed to appoint a judge *ad hoc* for purposes of the Court hearing of the Advisory Opinion reference.[18] The South African Government based its request to be allowed to name an *ad hoc* judge on the then existing Article 83 (now Article 89) of the Rules of Court, applying to advisory opinions requested "upon a legal question actually pending between two or more States," and permitting any party not already represented on the Court to choose a judge under Article 31 of the Court Statute. The Court disposed of the

South African request on the basis, narrowly, of its own "*prima facie* appreciation of the facts and the law", and its conclusion therefrom that there was no "legal question actually pending between two or more States" [19]; and the Court equally disposed of a South African request that, if the Court should not rule that South Africa was entitled to a judge *ad hoc, as a matter of right*, it should, nevertheless, exercise the discretion granted to it by Article 68 of the Court Statute and allow a judge *ad hoc* as a matter of grace. [20] These Court holdings [21] were, however, strongly contested within the Court, the decision to deny South Africa a judge *ad hoc*, as a matter of right, being contested by three of the judges (Judges Fitzmaurice, Gros, and Petrén [22]); and, as a matter of the discretionary power of the Court under Article 68 of the Court Statute, being contested by five of the judges (Judges Fitzmaurice, Gros, Petrén, Onyeama, and Dillard). [23] By the same token, the Court rejected individual South African objections to Judge-President Zafrullah Khan [24] and to Judges Padilla Nervo [25] and Morozov [26], based on Article 17(2) of the Court Statute [27] and these judges' past involvement in various activities, within the political organs of the United Nations, directed against South Africa, – in the terms of the official Opinion of Court,

> "statements made or other participation by the Members concerned, in their former capacity as representatives of their Governments, in United Nations organs which were dealing with matters concerning South West Africa ....; activities in United Nations organs of the Members concerned, prior to their election to the Court ....; participation of the Member concerned, prior to his election to the Court, in the formulation of Security Council resolution 246 (1968), which concerned the trial at Pretoria of thirty-seven South West Africans and which in its preamble took into account General Assembly resolution 2145 (XXI)." [28]

Yet while the Court's rejection of the objections to Judge-President Zafrullah Khan and to Judge Padilla Nervo was made unanimously, the Court vote to over-ride the South African objection to Judge Morozov of the Soviet Union was obtained only by a 10 to 4 vote. [29] Judge Fitzmaurice, in the Annex to his Dissenting Opinion to the official Opinion of Court specially devoted to what he characterized as "Preliminary and Incidental Matters" [30], starkly contrasted the Court's refusal to allow South Africa an *ad hoc* judge with its rejection of the South African challenge concerning the propriety of three regular judges of the Court sitting in the case: [31]

"In the light of the explanations as to this, given in the Opinion of the Court, it has now to be concluded that, outside the literal terms of Article 17, paragraph 2, of the Statute, no previous connection with the subject-matter of a case, however close, can prevent a judge from sitting, unless he himself elects as a matter of conscience not to do so." [32]

Judge Gros, in his Dissenting Opinion [33] to the official Opinion of Court was even more pointed on the issue of judicial disqualification:

"The Court's decision contradicts the principle, to which Article 17 of the Statute lends formal expression, that a Member must not participate in the decision of any case in which he has previously taken part in some other capacity. This Article, moreover, is an application of a generally accepted principle of judicial organisation deriving from an obvious concern for justice. The new interpretation which has been placed upon it cannot, therefore, be justified." [34]

It is difficult to avoid the conclusion that the Court majority in the *Namibia* Advisory Opinion in 1971 was reacting, in measure, to all the criticisms of *South West Africa, Second Phase* in 1966 to the effect that the Court had there tried to avoid the public opprobrium of rendering a politically unpopular substantive decision, by resorting to narrow proceduralisms as a means of evading the substantive law issues altogether. In *Namibia*, the Court majority seems to try to compensate, *ex post facto*, for the judicial self-restraint of *South West Africa, Second Phase* by treating the preliminary, procedural issues somewhat elliptically in its desire to reach the substantive issues quickly and without unnecessary hindrances. The minority judges in *Namibia* in 1971 are as legally persuasive on the necessity for a strict observance of all preliminary, jurisdictional issues as a pre-condition to any ruling on the substantive issues, as the judicial majority was in *South West Africa, Second Phase* in 1966. The intrinsic merit of these legal arguments, it may be suggested, remains unchanged as between the two Court rulings; it is simply that the Court majority's policy response to those arguments has changed dramatically in the intervening years, in the light of the general political evolution of the Court itself and of the United Nations as a whole, over the same time period.

3. Namibia (South West Africa), 1971.
The Substantive Issue: Judicial Activism Vindicated

The decision of the Court in *Namibia*, on the substantive issues, was rendered in two separate votes by 13 to 2, and by 11 to 4. [35] There are, however, in spite of the lop-sided character of the Court Votes, no less than ten separate opinions: the official Opinion of Court which, stylistically and philosophically, seems the work of at least two different authors (on the preliminary questions, and on the substantive issues, respectively); a Declaration by Judge-President Zafrullah Khan; Separate Opinions of Vice-President Ammoun, and by Judges Padilla Nervo, Petrén, Onyeama, Dillard, and De Castro; and Dissenting Opinions by Judges Fitzmaurice and Gros.

The majority Opinion of Court, for all the fettering, restricting elements inherent in any composite opinion that is the work of more than one judicial author, has a certain vivacity and confidence and freedom from self-doubt that is unusual in the jurisprudence of the International Court of Justice up to that time. It is in the spirit, perhaps, of the unqualified judicial activism of Judge Jessup's Dissenting Opinion in *South West Africa, Second Phase* in 1966; and, like Judge Jessup's opinion before it, it does not tether itself too much within the confines of past judicial precedents. The Opinion of Court is, in fact, imaginative and innovatory in its approach to international law doctrine, as if its authors were consciously trying to break away from the old and chart out a new, legislative, policy-making *rôle* for the Court for the future. This particular thesis is borne out in a number of areas where the official Opinion of Court ventures upon significant advances in existing legal doctrine.

(a) *Inter-temporal Law: the Time Dimension in Legal Interpretation*

On the major question posed to the Court by the Security Council as to the legal consequences for States of the continued presence of South Africa in Namibia, the South African Government, as the Court found, had – "covered a wide field of history, going back to the origin and functioning of the Mandate", [36] designed to demonstrate that League of Nations' Mandates of the Class "C" category, to which South West Africa belonged in 1919, were – "in their practical effect not far removed from annexation." [37] Such an interpretation, the Court said, would be –

> "tantamount to admitting that the relevant provisions of the Covenant were of a purely nominal character and that the rights they enshrined were of their very nature imperfect and unenforceable. It puts too much emphasis on the intentions of some of the parties and too little on the instrument which emerged from those negotiations." [38]

Borrowing from its own earlier Advisory Opinion of 1950 on the *International Status of South West Africa* [39], the Court reiterated that –

> "in the setting-up of the mandates system 'two principles were considered to be of paramount importance: the principle of non-annexation and the principle that the well-being and development of such peoples form "a sacred trust of civilization." ' " [40]

This was prelude to the Court's venture into a re-formulation of the notion of inter-temporal law. Inter-temporal law, on this approach, did not connote a closed body of principles, conceived and applied as at time past – in this case, the time of entry into force of the League of Nations Mandates system in 1919; but something rather more dynamic, lending itself to progressive, generic interpretation and reformulation over the years, in accord with changing societal conditions and expectations:

> " ... The Court is bound to take into account the fact that the concepts embodied in Article 22 of the (League of Nations) Covenant ... were not static, but were by definition evolutionary, as also, therefore, was the concept of the 'sacred trust'. The parties to the Covenant must consequently be deemed to have accepted them as such. That is why, viewing the institutions of 1919, the Court must take into consideration the changes which have occured in the supervening half-century, and its interpretation cannot remain unaffected by the subsequent development of law, through the Charter of the United Nations and by way of customary law. Moreover, an international instrument has to be interpreted and applied within the framework of the entire legal system prevailing at the time of the interpretation. In the domain to which the present proceedings relate, the last fifty years, as indicated above, have brought important developments. These developments leave little doubt that the ultimate objective of the sacred trust was the self-determination and independence of the peoples concerned. In this domain, as elsewhere, the *corpus iuris gentium* has been considerably enriched, and this the Court, if it is faithfully to discharge its functions, may not ignore." [41]

(b) *Constitutional Separation-of-Powers within the United Nations: Relation of the Court to the General Assembly and Security Council*

In a written statement submitted to the Court by the Government of France, and the oral arguments by the Government of South Africa before the Court, it was contended that the U.N. General Assembly in adopting Resolution 2145 (XXI) in 1966, had acted *ultra vires* [42] : Resolution 2145 was the one whereby the General Assembly declared "terminated" the South African Mandate over South West Africa. This particular legal argument is best seen, I think, in the Annex to the Dissenting Opinion of Judge Fitsmaurice:

> "When, by its Resolution 2145 of 1966, the Assembly purported to declare the termination of South Africa's mandate, on the basis of alleged fundamental breaches of it, and to declare this not merely as a matter of opinion but as an *executive* act having the intended operational effect of bringing the Mandate to an end – or registering its termination – and of rendering any further administration of the mandated territory by South Africa illegal, – it was making pronouncements of an essentially juridical character which the Assembly, not being a judicial organ, and not having previously referred the matter to any such organ, was not competent to make.
>
> There is nothing unusual in the view here expressed. On the contrary it represents the normal state of affairs, which is that the organ competent to perform an act, in the executive sense, is not the organ competent to decide whether the conditions justifying its performance are present. In all other fields a separation of functions is the rule. Thus the legislature is alone competent to enact a law, – the executive or administration alone competent to apply or enforce it, – the judiciary alone competent to interpret it and decide whether its application or enforcement is justified in the particular case ... Where the matter turns, and turns exclusively, on considerations of a legal character, a political organ, even if it is competent to take any resulting action, is not itself competent to make the necessary legal determinations on which the justification for such action must rest. This can only be done by a legal organ competent to make such determinations.
>
> "It must be added that besides being *ultra vires* under this head, the Assembly's action was arbitrary and high-handed,

inasmuch as it acted as judge in its own cause relative to charges in respect of which it was itself the complainant, and without affording to the 'defendant' any of the facilities or safeguards that are a normal part of the judicial process."[43]

The response of the Court majority, as set out in the Opinion of Court, was direct and categorical. First, on the question whether the Court could examine the validity of the General Assembly Resolution and the related Security Council Resolution, even though the Security Council's request for Advisory Opinion was not itself directed to this question, and whether the Court could, in effect, "act as a court of appeal from their decisions",[44] the Opinion of Court affirms that –

> "the Court does not possess powers of judicial review or appeal in respect of the decisions taken by the United Nations organs concerned."[45]

Examining these objections, nevertheless, – "in the exercise of its judicial function and since objections have been advanced"[46], the Opinion of Court returned to the *South West Africa, Second Phase* decision of the Court of 1966, and to the angry political reaction to that 8 to 7 majority judgment, in the General Assembly and elsewhere:

> "Without dwelling on the conclusions reached in the 1966 Judgement in the *South West Africa* contentious cases, it is worth recalling that in those cases the applicant States, which complained of material breaches of substantive provisions of the Mandate, were held not to 'possess any separate self-contained right which they could assert ... to require the due performance of the Mandate in discharge of the "sacred trust"' (I.C.J. Reports 1966, pp. 29 and 51). On the other hand, the Court declared that: '... any divergences of view concerning the conduct of a mandate were regarded as being matters that had their place in the political field, the settlement of which lay between the mandatory and the competent organs of the League.' (ibid., p. 45). To deny to a political organ of the United Nations which is a successor of the League in this respect the right to act, on the argument that it lacks competence to render what is described as a judicial decision, would not only be inconsistent but would amount to a complete denial of the remedies available against fundamental breaches of an international undertaking."[47]

The Court majority thus argues against any formal separation-of-powers approach, – such as to be found especially in classical Western-based national constitutional law doctrine – to the definition and application of the decision-making competences of the principal organs of the United Nations – Court, General Assembly, and Security Council. The Court majority's position seems to be that these are all part of a general problem-solving competence of the United Nations, the responsibility for whose exercise they share in common; so that if the problem-solving process should break down or otherwise seem to become clogged – as happened, evidently, with the Court's decision in *South West Africa, Second Phase* in 1966 – it would be quite unreasonable to stand on ceremony and insist on trying to maintain some abstract, *a priori*, watertight compartments-style division or differentiation of decision-making powers at the expense of actual problem-solving. On this view, the judicial self-restraint consciously applied by the 8 to 7 Court majority in *South West Africa, Second Phase* in 1966, towards a great political *cause célèbre* of the day, compelled, by way of compensation, some reciprocal and coordinate action by one or more of the other U.N. principal organs – General Assembly, Security Council – to fill the gap as to effective decision-making in a crisis situation.

The Court likewise rejected the contention that the General Assembly –

> "acted unilaterally as party and judge in its own cause. In the 1966 Judgement in the *South West Africa* cases ..., it was found that the function to call for the due execution of the relevant provisions of the mandate instruments appertained to the League acting as an entity through its appropriate organs. The right of the League 'in the pursuit of its collective, institutional activity, to require the due performance of the Mandate in discharge of the "sacred trust" ', was specifically recognised (ibid., p. 29). Having regard to this finding, the United Nations as a successor to the League, acting through its competent organs, must be seen above all as the supervisory institution, competent to pronounce, in that capacity, on the conduct of the mandatory with respect to its international obligations, and competent to act accordingly." [48]

(c) *Fact-Finding and the Possibilities of Judicial Notice*

The Government of South Africa had expressed doubts as to whether the Court was competent to give an opinion, or whether, for that matter, the Court should give an opinion, if, in order to do so, it should have to make findings as to extensive factual issues. [49]

In particular, South Africa argued that the consideration set forth in Resolution 2145 (XXI) relating to the failure of South Africa to fulfil its obligations in respect to the administration of the mandated territory, called for a detailed factual investigation before the General Assembly could adopt Resolution 2145 (XXI) or the Court pronounce upon its validity. [50]

The Court majority's response was to invoke the doctrine of Judicial Notice and formally take under consideration matters of general public knowledge and already within the public domain in regard to the South African administration of South West Africa, thus recalling Judge Jessup's approach to fact-finding, in his Dissenting Opinion in *South West Africa, Second Phase* in 1966, where he took judicial notice of the "accumulation of expressions of condemnation of *Apartheid*", as "proof of the pertinent contemporary international standard." [51] In the present, *Namibia* matter, the Court majority took note that –

> "The failure of South Africa to comply with the obligation to submit to supervision and to render reports, an essential part of the Mandate, cannot be disputed in the light of determinations made by this Court on more occasions than one. In relying on these, as on other findings of the Court in previous proceedings concerning South West Africa, the Court adheres to its own jurisprudence." [52]

(d) *The Notion of Illegality: A Passive or an Active Condition?*

By Resolution 2145 (XXI) of 1966, the General Assembly had voted to declare "terminated" the South African Mandate over South West Africa. As the Opinion of Court in *Namibia*, in 1971, notes, –

> "lacking the necessary powers to ensure the withdrawal of South Africa from the Territory, [the General Assembly] enlisted the cooperation of the Security Council by calling the latter's attention to the resolution, thus acting in accordance with Article 11, paragraph 2, of the Charter." [53]

The Security Council, as the Opinion of Court notes, responded to the General Assembly Resolution 2145 (XXI) in a series of Resolutions over the next several years, culminating, for present purposes, in Security Council Resolution 276 (1970) which is referred to, in terms, in Security Council Resolution 284 (1970) requesting the Court for the Advisory Opinion on the "legal consequences for States of the continued presence of South Africa in Namibia", in the first place. [54]

In its preamble, Security Council Resolution 276 (1970) had reaffirmed General Assembly Resolution 2145 (XXI). In its operative part, after condemning South African non-compliance with the various General Assembly and Security Council resolutions on Namibia, Security Council Resolution 276 (1970) had declared, (in its paragraph 2), that – "the continued presence of the South African authorities in Namibia is illegal"; and that consequently all acts taken by the Government of South Africa "on behalf of or concerning Namibia after the termination of the Mandate are illegal and invalid". Finally, Security Resolution 276 (1970) had, (in its paragraph 5), called upon –

> "all States, particularly those which have economic and other interests in Namibia, to refrain from any dealings with the Government of South Africa which are inconsistent with operative paragraph 2 of this resolution."

As to the effect to be attributed to the Security Council declaration contained in paragraph 2 of its Resolution 276 (1970), the Court majority in the *Namibia* Advisory Opinion in 1971 noted, in the Opinion of Court –

> "the qualification of a situation as illegal does not by itself put an end to it. It can only be the first, necessary step in an endeavour to bring the illegal situation to an end."[55]

The Court majority considered, in particular, that it would be –

> "an untenable interpretation to maintain that, once such a declaration had been made by the Security Council under Article 24 of the Charter, on behalf of all member States, those Members would be free to act in disregard of such illegality or even to recognize violations of law resulting from it."[56]

The Court majority also rejected the criticism that, because –

> "the relevant Security Council resolutions are couched in exhortatory rather than mandatory language ... therefore, they do not purport to impose any legal duty on any State nor to affect legally any right of any State."[57]

The Court majority went on from this to conclude that –

> "a binding determination made by a competent organ of the United Nations to the effect that a situation is illegal",

produced – "an obligation, especially upon Members of the United Nations, to bring that situation to an end."[58]

For the South African Government, this meant, the Court said, the obligation to "withdraw its administration from the Territory of Namibia."[59] For other member-States of the United Nations, the obligation was –

"to recognize the illegality and invalidity of South Africa's continued presence in Namibia; ... to refrain from lending any support or any form of assistance to South Africa with reference to its occupation of *Namibia*."[60]

While the precise determination of the acts permitted or allowed was, in the Court majority's view, a matter within the competence of the appropriate political organs of the United Nations, and especially the Security Council, the Court majority nevertheless went on to list, *in extenso*, certain categories of actions now prohibited to member-States of the United Nations – "because they may imply a recognition that South Africa's presence in Namibia is legal":[61]

– entering into treaty relations with South Africa in all cases in which the Government of South Africa purports to act on behalf of or concerning Namibia;

– with respect to existing bilateral treaties, invoking or applying those treaties or provisions of treaties concluded by South Africa on behalf of or concerning Namibia which involve active intergovernmental cooperation;

– sending diplomatic or special missions to South Africa including in their jurisdiction the Territory of Namibia, and sending consular agents to Namibia;

– entering into economic and other forms of relationship or dealings with South Africa on behalf of or concerning Namibia which may entrench its authority over the Territory.[62]

The illegality of the South African Government's continued presence in Namibia connoted then, in the Court majority's view as expressed in its formal response to the request for Advisory Opinion, not merely the abstract recognition of such illegality but also positive implementation by member-States of the United Nations in terms of –

"refrain[ing] from any acts and in particular any dealings with the Government of South Africa implying recognition of the legality of, or lending support or assistance to, such presence and administration."[63]

(e) *United Nations Law as General International Law: Applicability to Non-Member States*

While noting that Articles 24 and 25 of the U.N. Charter obligated only member-States to accept and carry out the decisions of the Security Council, the Court majority concluded, nevertheless, that non-member States were also bound in regard to Namibia:

"In the view of the Court, the termination of the Mandate and the declaration of the illegality of South Africa's presence in Namibia are opposable to all States in the sense of barring *erga omnes* the legality of a situation which is maintained in violation of international law: in particular, no State which enters into relations with South Africa concerning Namibia may expect the United Nations or its Members to recognize the validity or effects of such relationship, or of the consequences thereof. The Mandate having been terminated by decision of the international organisation in which the supervisory authority over its administration was vested, and South Africa's continued presence in Namibia having been declared illegal, it is for non-member States to act in accordance with those decisions .... All States should bear in mind that the injured entity is a people which must look to the international community for assistance in its progress towards the goals for which the sacred trust was instituted."[64]

4. The Court and Judicial Law-Making. "Academy of Jurists" or "Responsible Magistrature"?

In the Annex to his Dissenting Opinion in *Namibia*, 1971, Judge Fitzmaurice referred with approval to comments made by the one-time American judge on the old Permanent Court of International Justice, Manley Hudson,[65] on the necessity for the Court to keep – "within the limits which characterize judicial action", especially in exercise of the Court's Advisory Opinion jurisdiction; to act – "not as an 'academy of jurists' but as a responsible 'magistrature' ".[66]

In its approach to its official ruling in *Namibia*, 1971, the Court majority has, clearly, consciously sought to avoid or overcome the fettering preliminary, jurisdictional, essentially adjectival-law based considerations that so inhibited and limited its access to substantive international law issues of a high policy character, touching on the "new" International Law, in *South West Africa, Second Phase* in 1966. The angry political reaction, especially on the part of Third World countries in the U.N. General Assembly, to the narrow, 8 to 7 majority judicial decision of 1966, and the deepening sense of frustration at the apparent barring of World Community action directed towards the legal ending of *Apartheid* in Southern Africa, undoubtedly encouraged the Court majority, in *Namibia* in 1971, to liberating themselves from conceivedly unnecessary and irrelevant proceduralisms in favour of the breakthrough to substantive law-making. Did the Court majority, in its apparent anxiety to compensate politically for the 1966 decision, act too cavalierly, in its 1971 ruling, in disposing of the series of preliminary, procedural points – judicial disqualification for interest; appointment of *ad hoc* judges; the respect for what Mr. Justice Frankfurter of the United States Supreme Court called "*rôles* and missions" and the functional differentiation between the Court and the other principal organs of the United Nations? Certainly, the Dissenting Opinions in 1971 are, on these particular points, powerful and persuasive in their legal reasoning; where, by comparison, the Official Opinion of Court often seems elliptical or non-responsive to the legal arguments advanced before the Court. What is involved, at base, is a fundamental philosophic disagreement, within the ranks of the judges, as to the proper *rôle* and function of the World Court at this particular point of time in the political evolution of the United Nations and in the general development of international law. The Court majority in *Namibia*, 1971, as reflected in the official Opinion of Court, seems to have resolved finally to try to break the political impasse over Southern Africa effectively existing in all the principal U.N. organs; and this involves, for a tribunal which, throughout its history between the two World Wars in the old P.C.I.J. era, and during the post-World War II period in the current I.C.J. phase, has remained "judicial" in a European sense (both Western and Eastern Europe) and resolutely non-"American", venturing into a policy-making approach with which it has hardly had the time to become familiar or always easy and elegant in the concrete application. The Court minority, by comparison, rests with the more traditional, more strictly "judicial" conception of the Court's *rôle* as a U.N. organ separate from though coordinate with the Security Council and General Assembly; and this yields rather more satisfactory results on the narrower problem of congruence with the Court's past jurisprudence, though it may hardly answer the larger problem of the Court's constitutional responsibility, in common with the other principal organs of the United Nations, for community problem-solving on the main tension-issues of international law of our times.

Chapter III

JUDICIAL SELF-RESTRAINT: THE FRENCH NUCLEAR TESTS CASES

1. Sociological Jurisprudence and Judicial Law-making

The decision of the French Government to conduct high altitude nuclear test explosions in the South Pacific in 1973 and 1974, had, evidently, important implications for that new international environmental protection law that burgeoned so suddenly in the late 1960s and that may already have passed its apogée.[1] The World Energy crisis from the end of 1973 onwards turned national decision-makers' attention increasingly to problems of international trade and balance of payments, at the expense, if need be, of interests in ecology and the human life-style. But in another and more general way, the French Government's nuclear test explosions provided an opportunity for the attempt at contemporary definition and concretisation of that older international law of good neighbourliness or comity that, in its international relations aspects, draws heavily upon the best Civil Law and Common Law national legal traditions.[2]

The concern in the present study is not with these more general, substantive international law questions except so far as they arise interstitially to the consideration of essentially adjectival law, institutional questions, – here, the *rôle* of the World Court in the international law-making process. These adjectival law, institutional questions go to the special competence of the Court in the elaboration and refinement of new norms of international law, and to the limitations necessarily imposed on the Court by essentially the same considerations that cabin and confine judicial review when it operates in a purely internal, national, municipal law context,[3] – namely, procedural limitations inherent in the case/controversy system and even in the Advisory Opinion base to the exercise of Court jurisdiction; intellectual limitations imposed by the canons of construction and by conventional legal reasoning, both Civil Law and Common Law; limitations of expertise, stemming from highly specialised judicial training and academic legal formation, whether Civil Law or Common Law, that traditionally do not go beyond Law as strictly defined to other Social Sciences like Economics, Commerce, and Sociology, or *a fortiori* to the Natural Sciences and Engineering; political limitations resulting from the dependent character of the judicial office and the essentially indirect modes of judicial selection and the absence of anything approaching a "political mandate" that only a direct popular election can confer; and, finally, the limitations of effectiveness, stemming from the lack of any practical, institutionally-based authority to follow up Court decisions with concrete enforcement procedures against recalcitrant parties refusing to accept the Court's decisions or even to acknowledge the Court's jurisdiction in the first place.

The emphasis in the present study, then, is upon the judicial process and the creative opportunities for, and also the very real limitations upon the exercise of a judicial policy-making, legislative *rôle* in the elaboration of the "new" international law of the present era of transition and rapid change in the World Community[4]. The Legal Realist and Sociological[5] schools of Jurisprudence have demonstrated in systematic, scientific-empirical way[6], the limitations of traditional legal logic as applied to the judicial process, and the very many ambiguities inherent in the conventional legal categories[7] which open the way for what Cardozo called interstitial judicial legislation[8]. There is, of course, a necessary and proximate, almost symbiotic relation between Law and Society – between the formalised norms of statutes, court decisions and other positive law texts, as written, and the basic societal facts and conditions of the community in respect to which that positive law is to operate[9]. The societal facts necessarily operate to condition and to limit, and if not properly taken into account by the official decision-maker, to frustrate, the positive law prescriptions, as originally written. This is, of course, one of the basic truths of Sociological Jurisprudence – the all too frequent gap between the Law-in-Books and the Law-in-Action. The lesson, here, is as to the socio-ethical limitations to effective legal action[10] – constituting a counsel of prudence, directed to judicial decision-makers among others, about the dangers of trying to jump too far ahead of the society in which the decision-makers must operate, lest an overly ambitious or premature venture in community policiy-making on the part of the judges should turn out to be counter-productive and so delay or even frustrate altogether the cause of fundamental legal change[11]. Another main lesson from Sociological Jurisprudence is as to the need for recognition of what Mr. Justice Frankfurter has designated as the "*rôles* and missions" in law and the law-making processes: [12] that, at any particular time and in respect to particular social problems, some agencies of government may be more suited to community policy-making than other agencies of government; and that, as a general principle and especially for the more highly politicised problems, the courts may often be rather less effective in community problem-solving than the other, more overtly and avowedly, political organs of government. [13] A contemporary European jurist, who has demonstrated, in his own concrete judicial activities, an imaginative capacity for judicial innovation, identifies this problem, in another context, when he refers to the problem of the "political legitimacy" of judicial law-making. [14]

2. The Historical Background to the French Nuclear Test Explosions in the South Pacific

The ultimate historical foundations for the French Government's high-altitude nuclear tests in 1973 and 1974 are no doubt to be found in more than a decade of "Third Force" thinking on the subject of an independent French and European foreign policy, with the rapid approach of the Soviet-U.S. *détente* foreshadowed by the peaceful resolution of the Cuban Missile Crisis in October, 1962. In its specifically Gaullist manifestations, European "Third Force" doctrine looked to the development of a distinctively French or Continental European nuclear "force de frappe" as a deterrent to possible Soviet adventurism in Continental Europe consequent upon the Soviet–U.S. *détente* and any resultant, eventual withdrawal of the U.S. nuclear strike force from Europe. [15] Some of the more intransigent Western political opponents of the late President Charles de Gaulle have, of course, argued that the French quest for French or Continental European nuclear weapons and the concomitant French Government investment in a systematic nuclear tests programme represented no more than a stage in the development of a "politique de grandeur", involving the pursuit of symbols and national prestige unrelated to specific and immediate national foreign policy objectives. Be that as is may, the French Government did not sign the Moscow Test Ban Treaty of August, 1963, and has certainly refused, following on this non-adherence to the Treaty, to accept the *avant-garde* legal argument that the principles of the Test Ban Treaty, with the treaty's interdiction of nuclear tests in the atmosphere and in certain other specific places, have, by virtue of the near universality, though not unanimity, of national adherences to the Treaty, become part of general, customary international law binding even on non-signatories to the Treaty as a sort of international *jus cogens*.

By contrast the Australian and New Zealand Governments, during the earlier, pre-*détente* era when they were each part of the United States-created interlocking system of Western defensive military alliances around the World, had cooperated freely, and indeed most positively and enthusiastically, with the United States and British Governments in those Governments' development and testing of their own nuclear weapons in the South Pacific. The active assistance and involvement of the Australian and New Zealand Governments in these nuclear test explosions had extended, specifically, to territories and areas under the jurisdiction and control of the Australian and New Zealand Governments themselves. The political justification for the Australian and New Zealand support for, and direct participation in, nuclear test explosions in the South Pacific in that earlier historical era, had to be founded by Australian and New Zealand political leaders in the argument that the possession by the Western political-military bloc of properly-tried and tested nuclear weapons, was a crucial element in the policy of nuclear deterrence, itself part of the over-all Western policy of "Containment" in Soviet-Western relations in the period of the Cold War. The present political switch of the Australian and New Zealand Governments from their erstwhile uninhibited direct involvement in the U.S. and British nuclear testing in the South Pacific area has to find its own special political justification, if at all, in the ending of the Cold War era and in the emergence of the Soviet-U.S. *détente*: these special societal facts of the World Community from the early 1960s onwards lead on to the politically more contentious argument – contentious, since not accepted, obviously, by France or by China or by certain other lesser powers – that the achievement and concretisation of the Soviet-U.S. *détente* in the Moscow Summit accords of May, 1972, has rendered otiose and unnecessary both the Nuclear Deterrence policy in general and also, and specifically, the acquisition of new nuclear technology on the part of countries not now having their own nuclear *force de frappe*. Actually, the political switch of the Australian and New Zealand Governments over nuclear testing in the South Pacific area, after 1972, finds its explanation in rather simpler internal political considerations – the replacement, in that year, in both countries, of long-term Right-wing, conservative governments that had been committed, from the beginning of the Cold War era onwards, to a strong Western military and nuclear posture *vis-à-vis* the Soviet Union, by Socialist, Labour Party governments with long historical traditions of political neutralism and of support for general disarmament, if need be on a unilateral basis.

3. The Political Background to the French Nuclear Test Explosions in the South Pacific

As at the beginning of 1972, there had been a total of 869 nuclear test explosions of which somewhat under two-thirds had been U.S. explosions and somewhat under a third Russian; with the French contribution being 43 tests (or just under 5 per cent), and the Chinese 12 tests. [16] The tests themselves divided, over-all, almost evenly between aerial and underground explosions, with a slight preponderance in numbers in favour of underground tests. The preponderance in favour of underground tests was most marked in the case of the United States – almost two to one – though this preponderance was increasing all the time, in the case of the two superpowers, the Soviet Union and the United States, as a result of their compliance with their obligations as to the interdiction of above-the-ground nuclear test explosions in accord with the Moscow Test Ban Treaty of 1963, and as a result also of their scientific perfection of their own national systems of underground nuclear testing. In the case of France, however, the 43 nuclear test explosions up to the beginning of 1972 were broken down into 30 above-the-ground, and 13 underground explosions. All the French underground explosions were conducted in the Sahara, as were 4 atmospheric tests; while the remaining 26 atmospheric tests were conducted in the Pacific. [17]

The particular French nuclear tests which were the subject of the Australian and New Zealand complaints in 1973 and 1974 were conducted at the site of the atolls of Mururoa and Fangataufa in the Tonamotou Archipelago in French Polynesia. The reasons given by the French government for the choice of this site were that the territory concerned was French and also uninhabited and situated in a zone little frequented by maritime lines or commercial airlines. In addition, the site was very far away from inhabited regions – 1,200 kilometres from Taihiti; 990 kilometres from Pitcairn Island; between 2,500 and 2,800 kilometres from Tonga and Fiji; 6,400 kilometres from the South American coast; and, lastly, 4,000 kilometres from Auckland, New Zealand, and 6,600 kilometres from Sydney, Australia. [18]

The French tests in the South Pacific were not merely above-the-ground: the blasts were effectuated under a balloon, and not on the surface of the ground. According to the French Government, the purpose of the blasts' being made under a balloon and at a certain altitude, was to avoid all interaction between the ball of fire resulting from the explosion and the surface of the ground or water, and so to avoid an effect that normally occurs in on-the-ground explosions, namely the tearing up of important quantities of radioactive debris and earth which later, after vaporisation and cooling off, fall to earth in the form of granules supporting fissionable products. In the case of explosions under balloons at high altitudes – following this scientific thesis – the radioactive particles which form are, because of the absence of intimate contact with the surface of the ground and the water, of minimal dimensions and they elevate themselves very rapidly into the upper atmosphere or stratosphere where their radioactive quality is quickly diminished.[19]

The French Government contended that the effect of the French nuclear test explosions in the South Pacific upon the complainant states, Australia and New Zealand, (and also Fiji which eventually sought, unsuccesfully, to intervene before the World Court) were slight. It was pointed out that the prevailing winds, at all altitudes, in the South Pacific over the French test site are from West to East, – that is, in the opposite direction to the complainant states and towards an ocean zone devoid of inhabitants until the South American coast is finally reached 6,000 kilometres away to the East. Further, it was contended, the French tests represented very weak quantities of radiation in comparison to the over-all total of nuclear experiments – in fact 1.8 percent of the radiation resulting from the various U.S., Russian, Chinese, and British tests; and that the doses of radiation involved in the French nuclear tests were very much less than the total levels of natural radiation to be found in various parts of the World today, for example in Brittany, the Vosges, or the Central Massif of France itself; or in Minaes Geraes in Brazil or in Kerala in India. Again it was contended that the annual levels of artificial radiation resulting, for example, from medical tests in the industrialised countries, or even from a simple intercontinental jet aircraft flight, were very much greater than the radiation doses resulting from the French tests in the South Pacific.[20] Statistically-based arguments of this sort are, of course, always open to counterdemonstration, and the French arguments on this point were in fact immediately contested by the Australian and New Zealand Governments. Nevertheless, in the First Phase decision of the World Court on the Australian–New Zealand complaints against France, on June 22, 1973, Judge Ignacio-Pinto, in his dissenting opinion to the Court majority ruling, made telling use, against the Australian and New Zealand arguments, of a New Zealand study commissioned in 1972 by the New Zealand Institute of International Affairs, which concluded that testing of nuclear weapons up to that time would – "not present a significant health hazard to the people of New Zealand or the Pacific Territories with which it is associated"; and that the then proposed French nuclear tests in the South Pacific would – "add fractionally but not significantly to the long-lived fall-out in these areas".[21]

4. The Juridical Aspects of the French Nuclear Tests Cases

The political decision by the newly-elected Socialist governments in Australia and New Zealand to challenge the French Government's holding of above-the-ground nuclear tests in the South Pacific in 1973, involved, also, a secondary, machinery-institutional decision going to the choice of means or techniques for effectuating that challenge, namely the eschewing of conventional diplomatic negotiations and discussion in favour of juridical action before the World Court. The main lines of the Australian–New Zealand argument on the substantive issue of the legality of the French nuclear tests were easy enough to anticipate in advance of any actual pleadings – the claimed existence of general principles of international law, recognized and re-stated by the Moscow Test Ban Treaty of 1963 but not necessarily coterminous with that treaty or limited to it for purposes of their juridical force, outlawing above-the-ground nuclear tests; the claimed existence, at the international law level not less than at the national, municipal law level, of principles of good neighbourliness forbidding one state from gratuitously causing harm to the territory, or people, or property of another state and applicable to the case of fall-out from nuclear test explosions; and, finally, claimed interferences with well-recognised principles of state sovereignty caused by nuclear test explosion fall-outs and by the proclamation of security zones on the High Seas and similar control measures during the pendency of such nuclear tests. But before any such substantive law issues could be reached, with all their implications for the development of a "new" international law as to environmental protection or a new species of *jus cogens* in the area of nuclear disarmament and control of nuclear testing, a formidable adjectival law issue had to be overcome, – namely, the jurisdiction of the World Court to hear a complaint against France on the part of Australia and New Zealand. In World Court jurisprudence, not less than in internal, national jurisprudence, the preliminary, procedural question of jurisdiction must normally be decided before the substantive legal issues in a case or controversy can be canvassed by the court. Since the World Court's jurisdiction is, by definition in terms of Article 36 of the Court Statute,[22] consensual and established in the ultimate by the will of the party against whom the jurisdiction is sought to be invoked, the first enquiry had to be directed to the nature and character of the French Government's adherence to the Court's jurisdiction. At the time of the Australian–New Zealand complaint to the Court, the relevant French adherence to the Court's jurisdiction was that filed by the French Government on May 20, 1966 in which the French Government formally accepted the compulsory jurisdiction of the Court in terms of Article 36 (2) of the Court Statute, but also excluded from that acceptance of jurisdiction – "disputes concerning activities connected with national defence".[23]

In the French Government's view, the then current French nuclear tests in the South Pacific were activities connected with the French national defence and therefore *ipso facto* excluded from the World Court's jurisdiction, with the consequence that the Court would have no competence to proceed with the Australian–New Zealand complaint. On this ground, the French Government refused to recognise the existence of any valid legal dispute concerning France of which the Court could take cognisance, and refused to enter a formal appearance before the Court. The French Government, in a letter to the Court on May 16, 1973, formally invoked the "national defence" reservation to jurisdiction and submitted that the Australian-New Zealand complaint should be removed from the list. The Court itself had been advised of the Australian–New Zealand complaint on May 9, 1973, and then on May 14, 1973, of a further Australian–New Zealand request for the indication of interim measures; and the Court had advised the French Government accordingly.

The French Government, since denying any jurisdiction on the part of the Court in relation to France in the situation presented by Australia and New Zealand, therefore took no further part in the proceedings of the Court, though the French member of Court, Judge Gros, as a regularly elected judge of the Court, sat on the case and participated fully in the interim and final judgments in the case.[24] The French Government White Paper on the Nuclear Tests, published in Paris in June, 1973,[25] constitutes a succinct and well-reasoned statement of the French Government's position on the facts and the law of the then pending Court proceedings, and fills the gap constituted by the absence of a French Government presence in the actual oral pleadings before the Court. In many respects the French White Paper approaches the character of the *factum* or extended written brief, covering formal legal issues and the factual and legal argumentation advanced by any one party of his own position thereon, common in North American Supreme Court practice. In the context of World Court proceedings where a heavy – some would say, too heavy – emphasis is given to oral pleadings before the Court at the expense of written argument filed with the Court by the parties, it might be said that the French White Paper constitutes the clearest and most concise formal statement by any of the parties to the Nuclear Tests conflict as to its own position in the matter, and a very welcome extra-mural addition to the Court's records.[26]

By contrast, the Australian and New Zealand position had to be to deny that the French limited adherence to the Court's jurisdiction of May 20, 1966, concluded the matter of jurisdiction, – an obligation that the Australian and New Zealand Governments attempted to discharge by pointing to the General Act for the Pacific Settlement of International Disputes of 1928 which they claimed to be still in force and binding France to the Court's jurisdiction in terms of Article 37 of the Court Statute,[27] To this, the French Government replied that the General Act of 1928 was intimately bound up with the old League of Nations and must be regarded as having lapsed into desuetude with the collapse of the League of Nations system; and that, in any case, even if the General Act of 1928 were to be regarded as being still in force, the latest, 1966, French adherence to the Court's jurisdiction with its "national defence" reservation, must, on normal principles of construction, cut down and restrict, to the extent of any incompatibility, the earlier, not so limited French acceptance of the Court's jurisdiction based on the 1928 General Statute.[28]

Strangely, the Australian and New Zealand Governments do not appear to have stressed too strongly the issue of whether the "national defence" reservation to the 1966 French adherence to the Court's jurisdiction was not itself subject to judicial review and interpretation: either it was to be purely subjective as a test and thus self-defining from the viewpoint of the French Government; or else objective, and therefore capable of scrutiny as to whether there was in fact a real and proximate relation to national defence of the activities complained of. A much more substantial objection of the French Government, with important implications for the future of the World Court's jurisdiction, was that the affair of the nuclear tests that was now being submitted to the World Court by Australia and New Zealand was not fundamentally juridical, but a purely political problem. This French Government objection thus raised the basic issue of the boundary line between law and politics for purposes of the World Court's practical exercise of jurisdiction.[29] For the French objection focussed upon the very real question of whether the Court as, at best, a dependent policy-making organ, should not, in simple political self-defence and as a rule of elementary political prudence, apply canons of judicial self-restraint in the interest of immunising itself as far as possible from great political *causes célèbres*.

5. The World Court Order of June 22, 1973,[30] and the Grant of Interim Measures of Protection

If there were no Court jurisdiction in the first place, there would, presumably, be no Court jurisdiction to issue interim measures pending final determination: otherwise the Court would be hoisting itself by its own bootstraps into jurisdiction. On the other hand, to allow a mere denial of jurisduction by any one party to end the matter then and there would be a most intolerable situation for any Court. The simple and certainly most direct solution for the Court in the present case would have been to rule on the jurisdictional issue forthwith and then, if it found in favour of jurisdiction, to proceed to at least preliminary examination of the substantive legal issues, with the right to grant interim relief measures at any time once the issue of jurisdiction had been determined in favour of the existence of jurisdiction.

This part of the Court's Interim Order of June 22, 1973, and the supporting judicial opinions in the Nuclear Tests case are not, it must be said, completely satisfying. The jurisdictional issue did not, on its face, seem a particularly complex matter or one requiring unusual time for decision. It may be suggested that it called either for a strict application of the Court's statute with its stress on the consensual aspect of adherence by States to the Court's compulsory jurisdiction and a conclusion, presumably, against jurisdiction; or else a clear policy decision by the Court stressing why it felt it desirable to adopt a flexible approach to jurisdiction and to extend the Court's competence wherever possible – if need be against the direct wishes of the States concerned. None of the majority judicial opinions filed in support of the Court's Order of June 22, 1973, treat directly of this point. Instead, the majority opinions proceed to the issue of the need to grant interim measures, without canvassing in depth of the preliminary, procedural, adjectival law issue of whether jurisdiction exists in the first place – the necessary condition precedent to any ruling on the substantive legal issues.

The actual judicial holdings of June 22, 1973, in the Nuclear Tests case, taken in concert, constitute an enigma. We know that two of the Judges, – the President, Judge Lachs, and the American judge, Judge Dillard – were prevented by illness from participating in the case. Counting the *ad hoc* judge from Australia, Sir Garfield Barwick, this meant a bench composed of 14 judges deciding on the Interim Order. The Court, in its actual Order signed by the Vice-President, Judge Ammoun, indicates that its majority decision was rendered by 8 votes to 6.[31] Among the majority group comprising in all eight judges, four other judges – Judge Jiménez de Aréchaga,[32] Sir Humphrey Waldock,[33] Judge Nagendra Singh,[34] and *ad hoc* judge Sir Garfield Barwick,[35] filed individual, specially concurring opinions. Just who are the remaining three majority judges is not indicated in the Court's actual Order, and these remaining three majority judges are nowhere identified expressly by names. Among the minority judges, Judges Forster,[36] Gros,[37] Petrén[38] and Ignacio-Pinto[39] each filed individual dissenting opinions. But the other minority judges are nowhere identified in the Court's Order, or in the various Opinions filed in support of it.

What are we to make of the votes and opinions of the five judges unaccounted for in the Court's Order or in the various individual Opinions, both majority and minority, – Judges Bengzon, Onyeama, de Castro, Morozov, and Ruda. It is not, on the face of it, a very satisfying official explanation and rationalisation of what is, even in terms of the Interim Order, a fairly novel decision that would have benefited by some fairly substantial justification in terms of past Court jurisprudence. The logical conclusion must be that the internal differences on the Court were marked and deeply-felt, and that this accounts for an apparently deliberate decision on the part of a number of judges on the Court not to render explicit either their reasons or their actual vote on the Court Order of June 22, 1973.

6. The World Court Judgment of December 20, 1974:[40] the Issue has become Moot!

The final judgment of the Court in the *Nuclear Tests* case, rendered on December 20, 1974, throws some light on, but gives no complete explanation of, the internal politics of the Court's Interim Order of June 22, 1973. It is officially indicated, in the final judgment of the Court, that that decision is rendered by a vote of 9 to 6:[41] Judge-President Lachs and Judge Dillard had each returned from their illnesses to take part in the final judgment, President Lachs in fact signing the majority judgment, rendered against jurisdiction by the vote of 9 to 6. This time the dissentient judges are clearly identified by name, in terms of a joint dissenting opinion, signed by Judges Onyeama, Dillard, Jiménez de Aréchaga, and Sir Humphrey Waldock,[42] and in two individual dissenting opinions filed by Judge de Castro,[43] and *ad hoc* Judge Barwick,[44] respectively. The change from the Court majority of 8 for purposes of the issuance of the Interim measures of protection on June 22, 1973, to the minority of 6 dissenting from the Court's final judgment of December 20, 1974, in effect against jurisdiction, is partly accounted for by the absence from the Court rendering the final judgment of Vice-President Ammoun and by the evident defection of Judge Nagendra Singh from the erstwhile majority for the Interim Order. Since, however, Judge Dillard, returning from his sick bed to take part in the final judgment, now rallied to the erstwhile majority and new minority position in favour of jurisdiction, this would leave one Judge unaccounted for from the Interim Order majority of 8. Was it, perhaps, Judge Bengzon, who publicly adhered to a joint declarartion, signed by himself and Judges Onyeama, Dillard, Jiménez de Aréchaga and Sir Humphrey Waldock on the issue of the advance "leak" of the Court's actual vote on the final judgment of December 20, 1974, and appended to the Court's final judgment?[45] It is simply not clear from the final judgment and the individual judicial opinions filed with it. The new majority of December 20, 1974, against the exercise of jurisdiction, sees, as we have said, the official judgment of the Court written by Judge-President Lachs[46], and individual, specially concurring opinions filed by Judges Forster[47], Gros[48], Petrén[49], and Ignacio-Pinto.[50]

The final judgment of the Court of December 20, 1974, addresses itself to questions, essentially, of procedural, adjectival law. Though, in the end result, it is a decision against the exercise of jurisdiction to rule on the substantive international law questions, the Court nevertheless addresses itself to a special issue not adverted to in the earlier argument and in the earlier judgment and judicial opinions issued for purposes of the Interim Order of June 22, 1973, this special issue being one which, because of its particular factual base, could presumably not have been adverted to before. The Court majority judgment of December 20, 1974, is therefore not in formal conflict with the majority judgment of June 22, 1973, on the Interim Order, and in no way purports to over-rule that earlier judgment; though, in the end result, as we have suggested, it does effectively depart from or reject the judicial philosophy that dominated the earlier judgment. It is evident, from the crucial switch of three votes from the erstwhile majority of June 22, 1973, that judicial personalities may have been important to the final judgment of December 20, 1974, in its eventual outcome; and it may be speculated whether the Interim Order vote of June 22, 1973, might not have been different if President Lachs and Judge Dillard had not been prevented from illness from participating in the Interim Order judgment.

The Court's reasoning, for purposes of the final judgment of December 20, 1974, adopts what we may call a basically "Anglo-Saxon" juridical approach to the exercise of Court jurisdiction. It concludes, in essence, that the original dispute between Australia and New Zealand on the one hand, and France, has become moot because of supervening facts affecting France's position. Following the Court's reasoning, there is, in consequence, no longer effectively a case or controversy before the Court; and no basis, therefore, for the Court's purporting to exercise jurisdiction further in the matter. The reasoning and internal logic is impeccable; and the result is one which the late Mr. Justice Brandeis of the United States Supreme Court would certainly have approved in the insistence upon the existence of a proper jurisdictional base as a prior, adjectival law condition to the issuance of any judicial pronouncement upon substantive law questions [51]. As is noted in the Court's official opinion in support of its final judgment:

> "The Court has in the past indicated considerations which would lead it to decline to give judgment. The present case is one in which 'circumstances that have arisen render any adjudication devoid of purpose.' (*Northern Cameroons, judgment,* I.C.J. Reports, 1963, p. 38). The Court therefore sees no reason to allow the continuance of proceedings which it knows are bound to be fruitless. While judicial settlement may provide a path to international harmony in circumstances of conflict, it is none the less true that the needless

continuance of litigation is an obstacle to such harmony.

Thus the Court finds that no further pronouncement is required in the present case. It does not enter into the adjudicatory functions of the Court to deal with issues *in abstracto*, once it has reached the conclusion that the merits of the case no longer fall to be determined. The object of the claim having clearly disappeared, there is nothing on which to give judgment."[52]

Accepting the Judgment's fundamental procedural, adjectival law premise that the Court should not proceed to render substantive decisions on disputes that no longer exist, there could conceivably be argument as to the nature and quality of the facts effectively causing the disappearance of the original dispute between Australia–New Zealand and France, – in effect, the declarations by various high officials and spokesmen for the French Government indicating the termination of any further above-the-ground nuclear tests on the part of France in the South Pacific. As the Court had little difficulty in establishing, these French governmental declarations were all made at the highest level of political authority – by President Giscard d'Estaing himself, by the French Foreign Minister, and by the French Minister of Defence – and made in systematic and sustained and repeated fashion from June 8, 1974, onwards[53]. To be sure, these French Governmental declarations were not, for the most part, made in formal exchanges with the Australian and New Zealand Governments so as to give use to the more normal style of limited, *inter partes* estoppel. This part of the official opinion for the Court, however, is imaginative and innovatory in the best traditions of World Court jurisprudence and follows along lines already developed in earlier Court opinions in which it has essayed a new flexibility as to the international law-making process in general and as to the Court's duty of deference to the older juridicial notion that the sources of international law doctrine constitute a group of closed categories that jelled once and for all in some bygone era and that are incapable of creative adjustment to new societal conditions in the World Community. As the Court goes on to note in its official opinion:

"It is well recognised that declarations made by way of unilateral acts, concerning legal or factual situations, may have the effect of creating legal obligations. Declarations of this kind may be, and often are, very specific. When it is the intention of the State making the declaration that it should become bound according to its terms, that intention confers on the declaration the character of a legal undertaking, the State being thenceforth legally required to follow a course of conduct consistent with the declaration. An undertaking of this kind, if given publicly, and with an intent to be bound, even though not made within the context of international negotiations, is binding. In these circumstances, nothing in the nature of a *quid pro quo* nor any subsequent acceptance of the declaration, nor even any reply or reaction from other States, is required for the declaration to take effect, since such a requirement would be inconsistent with the strictly unilateral nature of the juridical act by which the pronouncement by the State was made.

Of course, not all unilateral acts imply obligation; but a State may choose to take up a certain position in relation to a particular matter with the intention of being bound – the intention is to be ascertained by interpretation of the act. When States make statements by which their freedom of action is to be limited, a restrictive interpretation is called for."[54]

On the issue of the relative degree of formality necessary to confer juridical force and status upon such unilateral acts by States, the Court is clear and categorical:

"With regard to the question of form, it should be observed that this is not a domain in which international law imposes any special or strict requirements. Whether a statement is made orally or in writing makes no essential difference, for such statements made in particular circumstances may create commitments in international law, which does not require that they should be couched in written form. Thus the question of form is not decisive. As the Court said in its Judgment on the preliminary objections in the case concerning the *Temple of Preah Vihear*:

Where ... as is generally the case in international law, which places the principal emphasis on the intentions of the parties, the law prescibes no particular form, parties are free to choose what form they please provided their intention clearly results from it. (ICJ. Reports 1961, p. 31).

The Court further stated in the same case: "the sole relevant question is whether the language employed in any given declaration does reveal a clear intention ..." (*ibid.*, p. 32)."[55]

In the ultimate, this part of the Court's determination, involving the creation of juridical facts rendering moot the original dispute brought before the Court, was rested upon the principle of good faith, as part of the new international law of cooperation succeeding upon the international law of friendly relations (peaceful co-existence):

> "Trust and confidence are inherent in international cooperation, in particular in an age when this cooperation in many fields is becoming increasingly essential. Just as the very rule of *pacta sunt servanda* in the law of treaties is based on good faith, so also is the binding character of an international obligation assumed by unilateral declaration. Thus interested States may take cognisance of unilateral declarations and place confidence in them, and are entitled te require that the obligation thus created be respected." [56]

7. The Specially Concurring Opinions in the World Court Judgment of December 20, 1974: there never was a justiciable dispute!

The official opinion, for the Court majority, in the final judgment of December 20, 1974, is based, as already noted, on procedural, adjectival law grounds, and in particular the premise that Courts should not proceed to render substantive law rulings once an issue becomes moot. If this may be called a ruling on a preliminary, jurisdictional question, there remains an other preliminary, jurisdictional question which, it may be argued, the Court should, as a matter of logic, decide as its first priority question, namely whether a justiciable dispute existed in the first place. This is the basis, (allowing for individual nuances of approach), of the four separate, specially concurring opinions filed in the Court's final judgment of December 20, 1974, by Judges Forster, Gros, Petrén, and Ignacio-Pinto, who rallied, nevertheless, to the official opinion of the Court to help constitute the final, 9 to 6 vote in favour of the Court's rejecting jurisdiction. The philosophical positions of the four specially concurring judicial opinions are, in fact, reasonably close to the general spirit and emphasis of the official opinion of the Court, of December 20, 1974. This official Opinion of the Court in fact bears all the evidence of a "Chief Justice's" opinion, of the sort made celebrated by the great Chief Justice Charles Evans Hughes of the United States Supreme Court. There, the presiding officer of a tribunal seeks to bring the members of his Court together by maximising the grounds of agreement and concord; and, where necessary, by basing his own opinion on deliberately modest grounds so as to rally the greatest number of wavering judicial votes possible. [57]

Confirmation of this thesis lies, perhaps, in the statistics of the two World Court decisions of June 22, 1973 and December 20, 1974, respectively: a majority of 8 judges in favour of exercising jurisdiction, at least for purposes of issuing the Interim Order, which would become 9 with the return from illness of Judge Dillard, finds itself reduced to a minority of 6 when the Court, for purposes of the final judgment, declines jurisdiction on the argument that the affair has become moot. The minority position in the June 22, 1973, Interim judgment, and the majority position in the December 20, 1974, final judgment are sufficiently similar, generically, to support the thesis that the crucial switch in votes within the Court to make up the new majority against the exercise of jurisdiction was the product of the political give-and-take and skills of compromise inherent in the exchanges in the Court conference room; and in these inter-personal dealings the *rôle* of the more senior members of the Court – especially if they combine high juridical expertise and practical political-diplomatic experience – should become intellectually persuasive for purposes of the final decision.

In his specially concurring opinion attached to the final judgment of December 20, 1974, Judge Forster recurs to the basic point made in his dissenting opinion attached to the Interim Order of June 22, 1973:

> "That the Australian claim was without object was apparent to me from the very first, and not merely subsequent to the recent French statements: in my view it lacked object *ab initio*, and radically.
>
> The recent French statements adduced in the reasoning of the Judgment do no more than supplement (to useful purpose, I admit) what I conceived to be the legal arguments for removal of the case from the Court's list." [58]

Judge Forster added, for good measure, to refute any suggestion that the original Australian–New Zealand proceedings or the Court's interim Order of June 22, 1973, might have, whatever the doubts as to their jurisdictional base, contributed to bringing about a politically acceptable result, namely cessation of the French above-the-ground nuclear tests:

> "I personally have noted nothing in the French statements which could be interpreted as an admission of any breach of positive international law; neither have I observed in them anything whatever bearing any resemblance to a concession

wrested from France by means of the judicial proceedings and implying the least abandonment of that absolute sovereignty which France, like any other State, possesses in the domain of its national defence.

As for the transition from atmospheric to underground tests, I see it simply as a technical step forward which was due to occur; that, and no more."[59]

Judge Gros, in his specially concurring opinion to the final judgment, recurs, like Judge Forster, to his own earlier, dissenting opinion attached to the Court's Interim Order of June 22, 1973, that there never was a legal dispute subject to the Court's jurisdiction. He also, however, for good measure, enters into an extended historical examination of the Australian Government's attitude *vis-à vis* French nuclear tests, demonstrating that from 1963 until the end of 1972 the Australian Government had at no time advanced the argument as to the unlawfulness of the French nuclear tests. This particular claim was in fact put forward for the first time in an Australian Note of January 3, 1973, stemming directly from a change of Government in Australia with the election of a Socialist (Labour) Government that was officially committed to opposing the "development, proliferation, possession and use of nuclear, chemical and bacteriological weapons".[60] On the other hand, from 1952 onwards the Australian Government had associated itself with various atmospheric explosions above or in the vicinity of its own territory, and by its conduct had expressed an unequivocal view in favour of the lawfulness of those tests in the Pacific, – beginning with the British atmospheric nuclear explosion effected on October 3, 1952, in the Montebello Islands near the north-west coast of Australia, and continuing through the October 15, 1953 British test at Woomera in Australia, two further series of British tests on May 16 and June 19, 1956, in the Montebello Islands, and other British tests on September 27, and October 4, 11 and 21, 1956, in South Australia. On March 3, 1962 the Australian Government had specifically and in terms approved the United States Government's decision to carry out nuclear tests in the South Pacific; and on March 16, 1962, had given permission to the United States to make use of Christmas Island for nuclear tests, more than 20 such tests being in fact carried out between April 24 and June 30, 1962, with tests at very high altitude being carried out at Johnston Island from July 9 to November 4, 1962.[61] In contrasting this Australian Government approval and active endorsement of British and U.S. nuclear tests in the South Pacific with its condemnation of Communist Chinese and French nuclear tests, Judge Gros raised the issue of political special pleading:

> "It is not unjust to conclude that, in the eyes of the Australian Government, what should be applauded in the allies who might protect it is to be frowned upon in others: *Quod licet Jovi non licet bovi...* [62]
>
> The applicant [Australia] has disqualified itself by its conduct and may not submit a claim based on a double standard of conduct and of law. What was good for Australia along with the United Kingdom and the United States cannot be unlawful for other States. The Permanent Court of International Justice applied the principle – 'allegans contraria non audiendus est' in the case of *Diversion of Water from the Meuse,* Judgment, 1937, P.C.I.J., Series A/B, No. 70, page 25". [63]

The other main theme in Judge Gros' specially concurring opinion was the notion that the French nuclear tests constituted a political dispute, involving the independence, or the vital interests, or the honour of the State, and therefore sensibly beyond the jursidiction of any Court. Citing with approval the writings of the then Professor Hersch Lauterpacht and the French Government's own draft law on its accession to the General Act of Geneva of 1928 [64], Judge Gros went on to conclude:

> "There is a certain tendency to submit essentially political conflicts to adjudication in the attempt to open a little door to judicial legislation and, if this tendency were to persist, it would result in the institution, on the international plane, of government by judges; such a notion is so opposed to the realities of the present international community that it would undermine the very foundations of jurisdiction." [65]

Judge Petrén, in his specially concurring opinion, relies upon Article 67 of the 1972 Rules of Court to conclude that the admissibility of the original Australian–New Zealand application was of an exclusively preliminary character, consideration of which could not be deferred until the examination of the merits. [66] In Judge Petrén's view, the admissibility of the application depended on the existence of a rule of customary international law prohibiting States from carrying out atmospheric tests of nuclear weapons giving rise to radio-active fall-out on the territory of other States. For these purposes, the resolutions voted in the United Nations General Assembly could not be regarded as equivalent to *legal* protests made by one State to another, but simply as indicating the existence of a strong current of opinion in favour of proscribing atmospheric nuclear tests. The Australian claim thus belonged to the *political* domain, and was situated outside the framework of international law as it existed today. It was, from the very institution of proceedings, devoid of any object on which the Court could give a decision. [67]

Judge Ignacio-Pinto, in his own specially concurring opinion, reaffirmed his earlier view, set out in his dissenting opinion to the Court's Interim Order of June 22, 1973, that in view of what he characterised as the – "all too markedly political character" of the case, the Australian request should have been rejected, from the outset, as being ill founded. [68] Though regretting that the Court had not earlier set out to regulate the questions of jurisdiction and admissibility, [69], Judge Ignacio-Pinto approved the Court's final judgment – "inasmuch as it respects the principle of sovereign equality of the member States of the United Nations. France must not be given treatment inferior to that given to all other States possessing nuclear weapons, and the Court's competence would not be well founded if it related only to the French atmospheric tests." [70]

Judge Ignacio-Pinto's most telling comment, however, is reserved for the general issue of jurisdiction, and the consensual basis on which the World Court's own jurisdiction is predicated:

> "... The Judgment [of the Court] rightly puts an end to a case one of whose consequences would, in my opinion, be disastrous – I refer to the disregard of Article 36, paragraph 2, of the Statute of the Court – and would thereby be likely to precipitate a general flight from the jurisdiction of the Court, inasmuch as it would demonstrate that the Court no longer respects the expression of the will of a State which has subordinated its acceptance of the Court's compulsory jurisdiction to express reservations." [71]

8. The Dissenting Opinions to the World Court Judgment of December 20, 1974

The dissenting judicial votes to the Court's final judgment of December 20, 1974, are represented by a joint opinion signed by Judges Onyeama, Dillard, Jiménez de Aréchaga, and Sir Humphrey Waldock, and by separate opinions on the part of Judge de Castro and of *ad hoc* Judge Barwick.

The Joint Dissenting Opinion of the four Judges does take up specifically the point that the Court's majority procedural holding that the Australian–New Zealand complaint has become moot, logically presupposes an even prior procedural holding that the Court had jurisdiction in the first place:

> "It is difficult for us to understand the basis upon which the Court could reach substantive findings of fact and law such as those imposing on France an international obligation to refrain from further nuclear tests in the Pacific, from which the Court deduces that the case 'no longer has any object', without any prior finding that the Court is properly seised of the dispute and has jurisdiction to entertain it ....
>
> The conclusion thus seems to us unavoidable that the Court, in the process of rendering the present Judgment, has exercised substantive jurisdiction without having first made a determination of its existence and the legal grounds upon which that jurisdiction rests". [72]

The main thrust of the four Judges' Joint Dissenting Opinion, involves, however, it may be suggested, a somewhat different political conception to that of the Court majority as to the basic approach to the exercise of Court jurisdiction and the extent to which the Court should feel itself constrained by traditionally respected case/controversy limitations to the exercise of a judicial law-making *rôle* at the instigation of individual parties.

Inherent in the majority opinion of the Court, signed by Judge-President Lachs, is the notion that it is for the Court to identify the object of the litigation before the Court and that it is not necessarily constrained by the subjective pleadings of the parties:

> "Thus it is the Court's duty to isolate the real issue in the case and to identify the object of the claim. It has never been contested that the Court is entitled to interpret the submissions of the parties and in fact is bound to do so; this is one of the attributes of its judicial function ... [73]
>
> In the circumstances of the present case, although the Applicant has in its Application used the traditional formula of asking the Court 'to adjudge and declare' ... the Court must ascertain the true object and purpose of the claim and in doing so it cannot confine itself to the ordinary meaning of the words used." [74]

If the official Opinion of Court thus seems to establish an objective test as to the nature of the issue before the Court and, by implication, severely to limit the ability of the individual parties to shape and control the practical exercise of the Court's discretionary law-making *rôle*, the four Judges' Joint Dissenting Opinion concedes on this point to the subjective intentions of the parties:

"Basically, the Judgment is grounded on the premise that the sole object of the claim of Australia is 'to obtain a termination of' the 'atmospheric nuclear tests conducted by France in the South Pacific region. (para. 30) ....

In our view the basic premise of the Judgment which limits the Applicant's submission to a single purpose, and narrowly circumscribes its objective in pursuing the present proceedings, is untenable. In consequence the Court's chain of reasoning leads to an erroneous conclusion. This occurs, we think, partly because the Judgment fails to take account of the purpose and utility of a request for a declaratory judgment and even more because its basic premise fails to correspond to and even changes the nature and scope of Australia's formal submissions as presented in the Application."[75]

Concerning this joinder of issue between majority and minority judges in the Court's final judgment of December 20, 1974, it can be said that the intellectual conflict cannot be resolved by considerations of traditional legal logic. The basic conflict goes to differing conceptions of the nature and scope of the judicial office and of the proper *rôle* of courts in community policy-making, and to the differing approaches to the exercise of court jurisdiction inherent in those conceptions. The appraisal of the legal merits of each of these conceptions must turn, ultimately, on political considerations such as the relative degree of common-sense and realism involved in each, having regard to the necessarily dependent *rôle* of the courts, in general, as organs of community policy-making, and to the special limitations imposed upon the World Court, in particular, in comparison to national Supreme Courts, for purposes of the elaboration and refinement and concrete application of new norms of law – the limited, term-of-years, character of the judicial office on the World Court; the essentially voluntary, consensual aspect of its jurisdiction; the absence of a firm, effective, enforcement power; the diffuse, pluralistic character of the community in respect to which it must operate.

The second main part of the four Judges' Joint Dissenting Opinion goes to the question of whether the Court had jurisdiction in relation to France in the circumstances of the present case.[76] This question had been passed over, *sub silentio* in the majority Opinion of the Court of December 20, 1974; though in the spirit of that opinion, it would be a question that was irrelevant in the light of the Court's actual holding that the issue had become moot. The four majority Judges appending individual, specially concurring

Opinions as annexes to the Judgment of the Court – Judges Forster, Gros, Petrén, and Ignacio-Pinto had, however, all firmly rejected any question of Court jurisdiction over France in the circumstances of the case, while embracing also the Opinion of the Court's ruling that the affair had become moot.

The four Judges' Joint Dissenting Opinion's affirmation of the existence of World Court jurisdiction over France in the present case,[77] is rested principally upon France's accession to the General Act of 1928 and upon the absence from such French accession of any exception as to "national defence"; upon the rejection of the argument that the General Act of 1928 had fallen into desuetude with the disappearance of the old League of Nations system;[78] and upon a conclusion of the continued binding force of the General Act as between Australia and France.[79] The four Judges also rejected the argument that the French Government's 1966 declaration of adherence to the Court's jurisdiction, with its exclusion, specifically and in terms, as to "national defence", prevailed over the French adherence under the General Act of 1928.[80]

It remains to add that Judge de Castro, in his individual dissenting opinion to the Court's final judgment,[81] put forward essentially the same arguments in favour of the existence of Court jurisdiction over France in the facts of the present case; and went on, from there, in contending for the admissibility of the Australian–New Zealand application, to argue that, on the basis of the general duty of each State not to use its territory for acts contrary to the rights of other States;[82] the Swiss federal litigation between the Cantons of Solothurn and Aargau; and finally the U.S.–Canada Trail Smelter Arbitration, Australia and New Zealand were entitled to argue the substantive law question of France's duty to put an end to the deposit of radio-active fall-out on their territory.[83]

The remaining individual dissenting opinion, that of *ad hoc* Judge Barwick, the longest opinion filed in the Court's final Judgment, does not go substantially beyond the international law arguments canvassed in the other dissenting opinions.[84]

9. An Inarticulate Major Premise to the Court's Final Judgment? The Conduct of the Parties: the Australian "leak" of the Court's Judgment on the Interim Order

The enthusiastic endorsement of or cooperation in the British and U.S. nuclear tests in the Pacific, on the part of the Australian

Government over a sustained period of years, gave rise, as we have seen above, if not to a direct estoppel against the Australian Government in its current complaint against the French nuclear tests, at least to the invocation of general equitable principles, going to equality of treatment and the notion that a State cannot apply a double standard in its international relations, reserving one treatment for its favoured allies and quite another and lesser treatment for all others.[85] The relative insensitiveness on this point, on the part of the Australian Government, is one of the more striking features of its political handling of the French nuclear tests case: the Australian Government never seemed to accept that a mere change in the internal, party political complexion of the government of a State cannot derogate from ordinary international law principles as to the continuity of State personality and the notion that actions of any government of a State are normally binding upon its successors.

Again, allowing, as the U.N. General Assembly's Committee on Friendly Relations has recognised in its final Report and accompanying Declaration of Principles,[86] that judicial settlement is only one method, and not always necessarily the best method, of international problem-solving, one may wonder why the Australian Government chose to escalate to the method of a formal complaint to the World Court without fully exhausting the more conventional and low-key diplomatic methods which the lack of substantial equities on its own part, – due to the prior Australian involvement in its own allies' nuclear tests in the Pacific – might have suggested as the wiser course. Was it the fact that the present Australian Government had chosen to make the non-proliferation of nuclear and other weapons a main plank in its successful election campaign that had unseated the long-time Conservative coalition Government of Australia[87], and that a judicial test seemed to offer more mileage from the public relations viewpoint? In the event, the World Court's final Judgment of December 20, 1974, by taking the Court out of the affair altogether removed any possibility of the Court's becoming embroiled, by indirection, in past internal, party political conflicts within a litigating State.

A bizarre episode, associated with the Court's decision on the Interim Order of June 22, 1973, tends to confirm, however, the reservations already suggested as to the political wisdom of the Australian Government's tactical approach to conflicts-resolution. On June 21, 1973, one day before the Court's decision on the Interim Order was read at a public sitting, the Prime Minister of Australia announced at a public dinner meeting in Australia that the World Court's decision would be 8 to 6 in favour of Australia,[88] thus correctly forecasting the actual announcement by the Court. In a subsequent letter of June 27, 1973, the Australian Prime Minister suggested that this forecast had been no more than speculation on his part.[89]

In a special declaration annexed to the Court's final Judgment of December 20, 1974, Judge-President Lachs commented, on behalf of the Court majority:

> "Good administration of justice and respect for the Court require that the outcome of its deliberations be kept in strict secrecy and nothing of its decision be published until it is officially rendered. It was therefore regrettable that in the present case, prior to the public reading of the Court's Order of June 22, 1973, a statement was made and press reports appeared which exceeded what is legally admissible in relation to a case *sub judice*.
>
> The Court was seriously concerned with the matter and an enquiry was ordered in the course of which all possible avenues accessible to the Court were explored.
>
> The Court concluded, by a resolution of March 21, 1974, that its investigations had not enabled it to identify any specific source of the statements and reports published.
>
> I remain satisfied that the Court had done everything possible in this respect and that it dealt with the matter with all the seriousness for which it called."[90]

Judge Gros, in his specially concurring opinion, threw some further light on the episode, in commenting upon the Court's decision, by a resolution adopted by a majority vote of 11 to 3, on March 21, 1974,[91] to close its investigations of the Australian "leak" which Judge Gros regarded as a breach of Article 54(3) of the Court Statute, requiring the deliberations of the Court to – "take place in private and remain secret".[92] In seeming to reject what he characterised as "the crystal-gazing explanation relied on by the [Australian] Prime Minister ... with the attribution of an oracular *rôle* to the Australian advisers",[93] Judge Gros declared himself convinced that –

> "a judicially conducted enquiry could have elucidated the channels followed by the multiple disclosures noted in this case, the continuity and accuracy of which suggest that the truth of the matter was not beyond the Court's reach. Such is the meaning of my refusal of the resolution of March 21, 1974, terminating an investigation which was begun with re-

luctance, conducted without persistence and concluded without reason."[94]

Judge Petrén, in his specially concurring opinion, also indicated that he had voted in the negative in the Court vote of March 21, 1974, to end its enquiry into the premature disclosure by the Australian Prime Minister of its decision and also the actual voting figures, in the Interim Order of June 22, 1973:

"I wish to state my opinion that the enquiry referred to was one of a judicial character and that its continuance on the bases already acquired should have enabled the Court to get closer to the truth. I do not agree with the decision whereby the Court excluded from publication, in the volume of *Pleadings, Oral Arguments, Documents* to be devoted to the case, certain documents which to my mind are important for the comprehension of the incident and the search for its origins."[95]

On the other hand, the four Judges taking part in the Joint Dissenting Opinion, joined this time by Judge Bengzon, issued a joint declaration, appended to the Court's official judgment, upholding the Court against criticisms that it was tardy or dilatory in its follow-up to the Australian "leak":

"The examination of the matter carried out by the Court did not enable it to identify any specific source of the information on which were based the statements and press reports to which the President Judge Lachs has referred. When the Court, by eleven votes to three, decided to conclude its examination it did so for the solid reason that to pursue its investigations and enquiries would, in its view, be very unlikely to produce further useful information."[96]

The Australian Prime Minister, for his part, immediately after the Court's final judgment of December 20, 1974, refusing the Australian application, made his symbolic trip to Canossa by going to Paris and officially calling on President Giscard d'Estaing.[97]

10. Judicial Legislation and the French Nuclear Tests Case. An Appraisal

For the student of Sociology of Law, the most interesting aspects of the French *Nuclear Tests* case are those going to the international law-making process, and to the special political-institutional *rôle* of the World Court in comparison to other organs of

World Community policy-making. On some views, the Court, in the French *Nuclear Tests* case, may have seemed to march its troops up the hill in the Interim Order of June 22, 1973, and then to march them right down again in the final judgment of December 20, 1974. Was the Court's apparent *volte face* between these two decisions the result of casual, fortuitous elements such as the unexpectedly supervening illness that prevented two key members with great experience in the shifting relations between International Law and International Politics, President Lachs and Judge Dillard, – from sitting in for the vote on the Interim Order of June 22, 1973? On a purely superficial view, there would seem to be some strong evidentiary support for such a thesis, having regard to their *rôle* in the final judgment of December 20, 1974.

The Court emerges as the proponent of judicial self-restraint in the final judgment of December 20, 1974, though, be it noted, a judicial self-restraint fully consonant with the rigorously procedurally-based approach to judicial policy-making insisted upon by well-known judicial liberals like Mr. Justice Brandeis and Mr. Justice Frankfurter of the United States Supreme Court. For Brandeis and Frankfurter, this implied that judicial legislation should only be ventured on in concrete problem-situations where the jurisdictional grounds were correct.

The tension between stability and change in any judicial approach to the international law-making process is perhaps well demonstrated in the example of the Court's President at the time of the *Nuclear Tests* decisions, Judge Lachs. As a U.N. General Assembly national delegate and as a law professor in his own right, Dr. Lachs had tried to cut through the sterile juridical formalism that would deny normative legal quality to the principle of the non-orbiting of nuclear weapons in space vehicles, simply because it did not, in its origins and prior to its concretisation in treaty form in the Space Treaty of January 27, 1967 [98], fit into the historical group of closed categories of formal sources of law. While the legal *avant-garde* might claim this particular principle as an international legal norm, prior to its rendition in treaty form, by virtue of its root in a U.N. General Assembly Resolution of October 17, 1963 [99] contemporary international legal science would, for the most part, deny law-making quality to U.N. General Assembly Resolutions, as such. Rather than provoke an interminable debate over a complex political-institutional question of contemporary international organisation, going to the arenas for international law-making, and thus delay recognition of an emergent new legal principle that is basic to international security and cooperation, why not cut through to the facts? The two key participants having the technological capacity to orbit nuclear weapons in space vehicles – the Soviet Union and the United States – had each sufficiently indicated their intention to observe the principle and to accept it as legally binding upon them; so why not accept this legal fact as creating, in itself, a congruent legal norm? [100] This is, in essence, the concept common both to North American and also Scandinavian Legal Realism, of Law as Fact! In the *North Sea Continental Shelf* cases [101] , Judge Lachs, in his Dissenting Opinion, continued a creative approach to the international law-making process in suggesting that West Germany might be bound by the principles of the Geneva Convention of 1958, even though West Germany had never ratified the Convention, since the principles of the Convention, by virtue of the near universality of their acceptance by States, had now become part of general, customary international law. [102] On that occasion, Judge Lachs also stressed the importance of governmental statements and of State reliance upon them. [103]

This line of thought is continued in the World Court's Advisory Opinion of 1971 on *South-West Africa* [104] , where the Opinion of the Court makes important advances in regard to the development of new principles of international law and, even more importantly perhaps, in regard to the giving of new content to old principles. The Court's opinion, taking a dynamic view of the concept of inter-temporal law, goes on to give a new contemporary connotation to illegality that has important implications for *Apartheid*; and the Court opinion also displays an unaccustomed flexibility as to international legal fact-finding and the *rôle* of judicial notice. The Court's opinion, finally, easily crosses the legal positivist barriers against acceptance that the general principles of international law may be binding even upon a non-member State of an international organisation. [105]

This review is prologue to the basic question of why a Court majority with a demonstrated record of imagination, innovation and leadership in the creation and refinement of new norms of law and in the international law-making process in general, should prefer the course of judicial self-restraint in the French *Nuclear Tests* case. Sociological Jurisprudence, with its attention to the wise choice of arenas and techniques for the effectuation of community policy-making can, I think, help us in understanding the Court majority's choice in the French *Nuclear Tests* case.

First, recognising that particular cases serve, in the ultimate, as the vehicles for judicial policy-making, there is obviously a certain margin of judicial descretion available as to the choice of the particular case to serve as the foundation for policy-making ventures. While the World Court's docket is certainly more limited than that of national Supreme Courts and so it cannot be quite as cavalier as those other Courts in rejecting the obviously flawed records as possible candidates for "test case" status, the fact remains that the Australian–New Zealand Application, by national Supreme Court standards, hardly seemed on adequate base for any sustained judicial policy-making ventures. This conclusion flows, I think, inevitably, from the politically compromised character of the Australian and New Zealand complaints against France, granted their past twenty years of enthusiastic support for British and U.S. nuclear test explosions in the Pacific area generally and in Australia itself. Pious protestations by newly-elected Governments could not wipe clean the slate from twenty years of practice by their predecessor Governments. The supervening Fiji intervention in the case,[106] while no doubt free from this particular vice, suffered from the fact that it arrived tardily and without, apparently, any prior record of concern or protest against nuclear tests in the Pacific, under whatever national sponsorship (British, American, French). A further fact contributing to the politically flawed character of the Australian–New Zealand Applications, and inhibiting their serving as a really satisfactory vehicle for sustained judicial policy-making was the never properly explained "leak" by the Australian Prime Minister of the Court's Interim Order and of the actual judicial vote thereon: it raised questions of the respect for the integrity of the judicial process on the part of the moving parties in what was, after all, an adversary-style proceeding. If the safeguarding of the judicial process might not necessarily suggest an automatic verdict for the respondent, in the absence of explanations from the applicants that the Court as a whole would regard as sufficient, it still would render very difficult any Court decision, on the merits, in favour of the applicants, granted the bizarre circumstances of the Australian "leak".

As a second question, on the particular facts of the Australian–New Zealand complaint, including, especially, those facts found by the complaining parties themselves and therefore, presumably, beyond the complaining parties' capacity to put in issue, it may be doubted whether the complaining parties satisfactorily discharged their burden of establishing even a *prima facie* case of damage to themselves resulting from the French nuclear tests in the South Pacific. This evident failure goes both to the substantive international law counts upon which the complainant States sought to base their application for relief against France, in which damage is a necessary element; and also to the existence even of a sufficient legal interest to give the complaining States *locus standi* in the case. This conjunction of *lacunae* in the Australian–New Zealand complaint going both to its substantive and its adjectival law base, confirms the general impression that the two States' applications hardly represented a useful occasion for judicial legislation in an important developing area of the "new" international law – namely, the international law of environmental protection, involving the duty of any one State not gratuitously to do damage to other States.

As a third, and much more fundamental question, the Court's jurisdiction rests, in the ultimate, on the voluntary consent of the parties. The consensual basis of the Court's jurisdiction, in sharp contradistinction to all those national Supreme Courts that effectively indulge in judicial legislation, means that the Court must exercise great prudence as to invoking strained or difficult legal constructions as a ground for seeking to impose its jurisdiction upon unwilling States. When so many States that are committed to expanding and strengthening the Rule of Law in the World Community either have not opted to accept the compulsory jurisdiction of the Court or else, like Canada in regard to its Arctic Waters Pollution Prevention Act of 1970, have found reasons for cutting down and limiting the jurisdiction already conferred on the Court,[107] it may be suggested that it ill behoves the Court to try to drag States to the court-room door. The political consequence is likely to be that they may not appear, or that they may withdraw or cut down whatever jurisdiction they have already conferred on the Court. The French Government's political response to the World Court's hair-line, 8 to 6, majority, of June 22, 1973, granting the Interim Order against France, was a formal advice to the United Nations on January 2, 1974, that as from January 10, 1974, France was withdrawing forthwith her acceptance of the compulsory jurisdiction of the Court.[108] This was a body-blow that the Court could hardly afford to sustain from one of its long-time champions and original Founding Fathers,[109] but one, it may be suggested, that might perhaps have been anticipated as a political consequence of the majority decision of June 22, 1973, on the Interim Order.[110] The majority decision of December 20, 1974 in the final Judgment, thus appears in retrospect more and more like a necessary, even if somewhat belated, political corrective to what Charles Evans Hughes, speaking of the Dred Scott decision of the United States Supreme Court, characterised as one of the Court's great self-inflicted wounds.[111] The over-all lesson, from the two judgments of the Court in the French *Nuclear Tests* case, would seem to be that a high political dispute that might better, in all the political circumstances of the case, have been settled by conventional diplomatic means through the give-and-take of bilateral negotiations and exchange, in conventional international political arenas, was prematurely or over-hastily brought into the international judicial arena[112] and that it just did not serve as a satisfactory vehicle for sustained judicial policy-making in a major new area of international legal concern.[113] The prompt and effective withdrawal of the Court, in terms of the final Judgment of December 20, 1974, should, on this thesis, succeed in minimising any damage to the Court caused by the premature venture in judicial policy-making in the Interim Order of June 22, 1973,[114] and it offers the extra premium of some valuable new additions to international legal doctrine, particularly as to the normative legal effect of conduct, including unilateral acts or declarations, by individual States and as to the principle of good faith as a cardinal principle of the new international law of cooperation that one hopes is succeeding to the era of the *détente*.[115]

Chapter IV

OPENING TO JUDICIAL ACTIVISM: THE WESTERN SAHARA ADVISORY OPINION

In the Advisory Opinion rendered on October 16, 1975, in the *Western Sahara* affair,[1] the Judges of the International Court of Justice are philosophically divided among themselves. But the Court, it may be suggested, demonstrates itself as an international institution in evolution, as the awareness of the opportunities for the Court as an international law-making, and not simply law-applying, institution in an era of rapid change in the World Community has become more widespread after the bitter political recriminations directed against the Court in the aftermath of its 1966 *South West Africa* decision.[2]

1. The World Court qua Court

The International Court of Justice, and its lineal predecessor the Permanent Court of International Justice, considered as Courts, are in so many respects *sui generis*. Those of the Court's current critics who would like to increase its political *rôle* and sponsor a more activist, legislative, policy-making approach on the part of the judges in their decisions and Advisory Opinions, so often cite that most political of all Courts, the United States Supreme Court, as a model. Yet when one compares basic elements of constitutional structure and internal organisation and actual decision-making practices, it is apparent that the United State Supreme Court represents a polar extreme, as a final tribunal, to the World Court, the one element of the openly political character of the nomination and election of the judges on the Court excepted. It is this "political" election of the members of the Court, it might be argued, that gives a tribunal its own affirmative mandate to fill the gaps in the law and legislate intenstitially or even avowedly – what has been identified as a Court's political legitimacy.[3] Yet in all other respects the World Court seems to differentiate itself clearly from the American Court and indeed from all other "Anglo-

Saxon" tribunals; so that purported analogies from their experience may run the risk of being inaccurate and also misleading in terms of the concrete conclusions to be drawn from their experience.

Much more, of course, the World Court resembles a classical Continental European Civil Law tribunal – something that is not surprising considering the strongly Continental European roots of the Permanent Court of International Justice above all but also of the successor International Court of Justice. In addition, as detailed examination of the record of membership of the two successive World tribunals over the years amply confirms, the overwhelming majority of the judges have been, in their professional training and specialist expertise, Continental European Civil Law jurists.[4] Even in more recent years when the Continental European component in the Court's membership has been diluted numerically as the World Community has broadened to include the Third World, the new judicial recruits from the Third World have been preponderingly drawn from European-derived Civil Law systems,[5] with the special qualities of legal reasoning and legal method and legal thought-ways generally deriving therefrom. If, however, the World Court is a Civil Law tribunal in its basic character and style, it is, after all, a Civil Law tribunal with a difference. Its judges are elected for a term of years only, without the continuity of service that fairly generally characterises Continental European tribunals; they will not always have the specialised, in-service, career judicial training imposed under the Continental European legal *régime*; and they may also be, in measure, public figures, in contrast to the conscious anonymity that normally pervades Continental European tribunals. Beyond that, in terms of Court collegiality and notions of internal self-discipline and cohesion, the World Court does break away significantly from Continental European stereotypes. While the World Court's official opinion renders service to the concept of collegiality of decision-making and opinion-writing, with its actual authorship or draftmanship being only with difficulty and under certain specialised circumstances discernible,[6] the members of the Court, even where they formally adhere to the official opinion of the Court, feel free to exercise their right to file ancillary Declarations or Separate Opinions under their own individual names;[7] and those who disagree with the Court's official opinion will usually file formal Dissenting Opinions.[8] The World Court's work thus lacks the benefits of the modest virtues that normally characterise the opinions of Continental European Civil Law tribunals: a concise, succinct statement of the Court's decision and of the basis for the Court's reasoning leading to the decision; and the elimination of "Byzantinism" and of the temptation to take purely rhetorical positions, through the essentially anonymous, consensus-based decision-making and opinion-writing that finally emerge. No doubt, some greater disposition on the part of the members of the World Court to cooperate in implementing those parts of the Rules of Court dealing with the office and functions of *rapporteur* for the Court's opinion in any case could help fill the gap between the World Court's practice and that of more classical, Continental European models. But the fact remains that half a century of the World Court's own practice the other way suggests that the Court make an affirmative virtue of the freedom its members have always claimed and exercised to file individual opinions, whether dissenting or specially concurring, under their own names with the consequent extra opportunities for developing or projecting new trends in International Law doctrine and for testing experimental hypotheses as to what International Law ought to be in any new problem-situation.

In the *Western Sahara* affair, the advantages and disadvantages of this essentially unique pattern of internal practice that the World Court's members have developed over the years – neither wholly Civil Law nor yet Common Law – are readily apparent. In the Advisory Opinion there is the official Opinion of Court, signed by the then President of the Court, Judge Lachs.[9] But, in addition, there are three separate Declarations, filed respectively by Judge Gros,[10] Ignacio-Pinto,[11] and Nagendra Singh;[12] six Separate Opinions, filed respectively by Vice-President Ammoun,[13] and Judges Forster,[14] Petrén,[15] Dillard,[16] De Castro,[17] and *ad hoc* Judge Boni;[18] and one Dissenting Opinion filed by Judge Ruda.[19] With a bench of sixteen Judges (including the *ad hoc* Judge) participating in the rendering of the Court's Advisory Opinion, ten separate Declarations or Opinions apart from the official Opinion of Court, make it difficult to speak meaningfully of any Common Law-style *ratio decidendi* and to discover for just what the Court's ruling stands as authority. Yet, the actual votes of the Judges are revealed, on the two preliminary, procedural questions of whether to render an Advisory Opinion on the two main issues involved, as having been by 13 to 3 and 14 to 2 respectively;[20] and on the two substantive issues themselves, the latter issue being in two parts, as having been 16 to 0, 14 to 2, and 15 to 1, respectively.[21] The plethora of separate judicial opinions on issues on which, when it came to the showdown, there was very little division in the actual judicial votes, is, it may be suggested, only in part a consequence ot the differences in legal traditions (Common Law, Civil Law, received Common Law, received Civil Law), among the members of the Court today. In measure, however, it reflects ideological differences among the members of the Court as to the future trends and directions of the World Community and the desired movement of International Law doctrine itself; and these differences of viewpoint, it may be suggested, can expect to be augmented, in the future, as the new political majorities in the United Nations General Assembly and Security Council become aware of the opportunities for novation or re-writing of International Law through the World Court and ultimately, therefore, through the political processes of nomination and election of the Court's judges. Finally, it may be suggested, there is an extra, casual or fortuitous element in the Court's work today, facilitated perhaps by special features of the Court's own Rules and exacerbated by the intellectual strains of the Court's members having to decide, as judges, in an era of rapid societal change in the World Community, – a tendency to indulge in what may be characterised as pejorative special opinions in which there may be a temptation to score debating points off one's judicial colleagues and even a Court majority of which one has oneself formed part. [22] Such a practice, if sustained, must certainly dissipate a good deal of the creative intellectual energies of the Court, and certainly weaken the impact of its majority opinions as to what the law is and what, beyond that, it ought to be in the future.

2. The World Court and its Choice of Jurisdiction

The *Western Sahara* question came to the World Court on an Advisory Opinion reference from the U.N. General Assembly (Resolution 3292 (XXIX) of December 13, 1974) requesting a judicial response to the two questions: [23] –

> "I. Was Western Sahara (Rio de Oro and Sakiet El Hamra) at the time of colonisation by Spain a territory belonging to no one (*terra nullius*)?
> If the answer to the first question is in the negative,
> II. What were the legal ties between this territory and the Kingdom of Morocco and the Mauritanian entity?"

The General Assembly Resolution requesting the Advisory Opinion made specific reference, in its Preamble, to Resolution 1514 (XV) of December 14, 1960 (Declaration on the Granting of Independence to Colonial Countries and Peoples), and also "reaffirmed" the right of the population of the Spanish Sahara to self-determination in accordance with Resolution 1514 (XV).[24] It also called upon Spain, as the administering Power, to postpone the referendum it then contemplated holding in Western Sahara – "until the General Assembly decides on the policy to be followed in order to accelerate the decolonisation process in the territory, in accordance with resolution 1514 (XV), in the best possible conditions, in the light of the advisory opinion to be given by the International Court of Justice."[25]

The World Court divided, as we have noted, on the preliminary, procedural issue of whether to render an Advisory Opinion at all – 13 to 3 on the first question, whether Western Sahara was *terra nullius* at the time of colonisation by Spain; and 14 to 2 on the second question, of the legal ties between Western Sahara and the Kingdom of Morocco and the Mauritanian entity. The points of contention, within the Court, may be resumed under two main heads – the nature of the Court's Advisory Opinion jurisdiction, and the importance of not confusing Advisory Opinion jurisdiction with jurisdiction as to contentious proceedings or allowing it to be used as a cover for the same; and, again, the nature of a "legal question" and the importance of not allowing the Court either to be drawn into discussion of abstract, philosophical issues remote from actual problem-solving, or else to venture upon high political issues where the Court's intervention might actually impede or delay eventual political solutions.

The first of these points of contention involved a re-examination of a leading holding of the predecessor Permanent Court of International Justice, in the matter of the *Status of Eastern Carelia*, in 1923.[26] In that matter, the Court had declined to exercise Advisory Opinion jurisdiction on the basis, apparently, of the principle that a State – there the Soviet Union – could not be compelled, without its consent, to submit its disputes with other States, – there Finland – to the Court's jurisdiction. This was the substance of Spain's argument against the Court's exercise of Advisory Opinion jurisdiction in the Western Sahara matter, namely that the moving parties, Morocco and Mauritania, were attempting to achieve indirectly, through the Advisory Opinion route, what they could not achieve directly through contentious proceedings in view of Spain's lack of consent to any such contentious jurisdiction. Was that in fact the basis of the P.C.I.J. holding in the Eastern Carelia matter, in 1923? The I.C.J., in the current, *Western Sahara* matter, proceeded, in the Opinion of Court, to distinguish and limit the *Eastern Carelia* holding on the basis that, there, one of the States concerned, the Soviet Union, was neither a party to the Statute of the Permanent Court nor, at the time, a Member of the League of Nations:

> "... lack of competence of the League to deal with a dispute involving non-member States which refused its intervention was a decisive reason for the Court's declining to give an answer. In the present case, Spain is a Member of the United Nations and has accepted the provisions of the Charter and Statute; it has thereby in general given its consent to the exercise by the Court of its advisory jurisdiction".[27]

The Court went on to cite, with approval, its own earlier ruling in the *Interpretation of Peace Treaties with Bulgaria, Hungary and Romania, First Phase*, in 1950,[28] when it had also had to consider the question of the continued relevance of the Permanent Court's holding in the *Status of Eastern Carelia*. The Court, in the *Interpretation of Peace Treaties*, had spoken of a –

> "confusion between the principles governing contentious procedure and those which are applicable to Advisory Opinions.
>
> The consent of States, parties to a dispute, is the basis of the Court's jurisdiction in contentious cases. The situation is different in regard to advisory proceedings even where the Request for an Opinion relates to a legal question actually pending between States. The Court's reply is only of an advisory character: as such, it has no binding force. It follows that no State, whether a Member of the United Nations or not, can prevent the giving of an Advisory Opinion which the United Nations considers to be desirable in order to obtain enlightenment as to the course of action it should take. The Court's opinion is given not to the States, but to the organ which is entitled to request it; the reply of the Court, itself an 'organ of the United Nations', represents its participation in the activities of the organisation, and, in principle, should not be refused".[29]

In taking this broader, more flexible view of its Advisory Opinion jurisdiction, the Court also rejected a further Spanish argument as to the relevance of Spain's own lack of consent to the proceedings, namely that the matter at issue was a territorial dispute and that – "the consent of a State to adjudication of a dispute concerning the attribution of territorial sovereignty is always necessary",[30] presumably whatever the procedural origin of the Court's jurisdiction. The Court rejected this argument on the score that the request for an opinion did not call for adjudication upon existing territorial rights or sovereignty over territory.[31]

Still another Spanish objection went to the limitations of fact-finding in Advisory Opinion-based proceedings. Although noting that this consideration had played a *rôle* in the Court's declining jurisdiction in *Status of Eastern Carelia*, the Soviet Union's refusal to participate having there created the difficulty of making an enquiry into facts concerning the main point of controversy, [32] the Court felt that the situation in the present matter was entirely different and distinguishable, Mauritania, Morocco, and Spain having furnished – "very extensive documentary evidence of the facts" [33] and also, together with Algeria and Zaire, having presented their views on these facts and on the observations of the others; while the Secretary-General of the United Nations had also furnished a dossier of documents concerning the discussion of the question of the Western Sahara in the competent U.N. organs. [34]

A more limited and technical Spanish objection to the Court's accepting jurisdiction related to the interpretation of the actual definition of the Court's Advisory Opinion jurisdiction in the U.N. Charter itself and in the Court Statute. Article 96 of the U.N. Charter authorises the giving of an Advisory Opinion – "on any legal question", [35] as does Article 65 (1) of the Court Statute. [36] The Spanish argument, here, was that the two substantive questions now referred by the General Assembly to the Court for Advisory Opinion were – "not legal, but are either factual or are questions of a purely historical or academic character". [37]

As to this, the Court responded by suggesting, on the authority of its holding in *Namibia* in 1971, [38] that – "a mixed question of law and fact is none the less a legal question" within the meaning of Article 96 of the Charter and Article 65 (1) of the Court Statute. [39] Citing its holding in *Conditions of Admission of a State to Membership in the United Nations (Article 4 of the Charter)*, [40] the Court rejected the contention that it should not deal with a "question couched in abstract terms", pointing to its *dictum* there that the Court – "may give an advisory opinion on any legal question, abstract or otherwise", [41] in order to reject the restrictive view of the scope of its Advisory jurisdiction. [42] At the same time the Court recorded, on the facts, its conclusion that the matters on which the General Assembly now sought its opinion were – "for a practical and contemporary purpose". [43] In the same vein, the Court also rejected the further Spanish contention, addressed to jurisdiction, that the proceedings were "devoid of purpose", the United Nations having already, according to this Spanish contention, affirmed the nature of the decolonisation process applicable to Western Sahara in accordance with the General

Assembly's Resolution 1514 (XV) establishing the general principles of Decolonisation: the Court, here, accepted Moroccan and Algerian arguments to the effect that the General Assembly had not finally settled the principles and techniques to be followed, being free to choose from a wide range of solutions compatible with the two basic principles of self-determination and of national unity and territorial integrity.[44] The final Spanish argument as to jurisdiction – that the questions posed by the General Assembly were "academic and legally irrelevant",[45] was rejected by the Court on the basis that while General Assembly Resolution 1514 (XV) provided the basis for the process of decolonisation since 1960, it was complemented by Resolution 1541 (XV) which opened up a choice of options for non-self-governing territories, – emergence as a sovereign independent State; free association with an independent State; or integration with an independent State;[46] and the Advisory Opinion given by the Court in the present proceedings would – "furnish the General Assembly with elements of a legal character" relevant to its further treatment of these alternative possibilities.[47]

3. The Court and International Problem-Solving: the Opinion of the Court

The first substantive question posed to the Court by the U.N. General Assembly was whether Western Sahara was, at the time of colonisation by Spain, a territory belonging to no one (*terra nullius*). The Court concluded, for these purposes, that the time of colonisation by Spain should be considered as the period beginning in 1884 when Spain proclaimed a protectorate over the Rio de Oro. While Spain had mentioned certain earlier acts of alleged display of its sovereignty in the 15th and 16th centuries, it had done so, as the Court noted, only to enlighten the Court as to the remote antecedents of the Spanish presence on the West African coast and not to prove any continuity between those acts and the Spanish proclamation of the protectorate in 1884. The period beginning in 1884 thus constituted the temporal context within which the two substantive questions addressed to the Court by the General Assembly should be answered.[48]

On this basis, the Court reasoned that the question whether or not Western Sahara was *terra nullius* at the time of colonisation by Spain was to be interpreted by reference to the law in force at that period, 1884. But a determination that Western Sahara was *terra nullius* in this case would be possible only if it were established that at that time the territory belonged to no one. On the specific facts, the Court found that at the time of colonisation Western Sahara was inhabited by peoples who, if nomadic, were socially and politically organised in tribes and under chiefs competent to represent them. Further, in colonising Western Sahara, Spain itself did not proceed on the basis that it was establishing its territory over *terra nullius*; for, even in the Royal Order of 1884, it was proclaimed that the King of Spain was taking Rio de Oro under his protection on the basis of agreements which had been entered into with the chiefs of the local tribes, the Order expressly referring to the "documents which the independent tribes of this part of the coast" had signed with Spain and also announcing that the King of Spain had confirmed the "deeds of adherence" to Spain. Likewise, as the Court noted, in negotiating with France the limits of the Spanish territory of Rio de Oro with French colonial territories to the North, Spain did not rely upon any claim to the acquisition of sovereignty over a *terra nullius*.[49] For these reasons, the Court was able very quickly to respond to Question I and to conclude that Western Sahara was not, at the time of colonisation by Spain, a "territory belonging to no one (*terra nullius*)".[50]

The second question referred to the Court by the General Assembly asked the Court to state what were the "legal ties" between Western Sahara and "the Kingdom of Morocco and the Mauritanian entity". Noting that the meaning of the term "legal ties" would also have to be decided in the temporal context of the time of colonisation by Spain – 1884, – the Court observed that that term, unlike *terra nullius* in the first question, did not have in itself a very precise meaning. Its meaning would therefore have to be found in the object and purpose of the General Assembly Resolution 3292 (XXIX) referring the request for the present Advisory Opinion to the Court.[51]

At the time of its colonisation by Spain, the Court found, Western Sahara, as an area of desert with low and spasmodic rainfall, was being exploited almost exclusively by nomads. The sparcity of the resources and the spasmodic charcter of the rainfall compelled all those nomadic tribes to traverse very wide areas of the desert, with the consequence, that the nomadic routes of none of them were confined to Western Sahara. Not infrequently, the Court noted, one tribe had ties with another, either of dependence or of alliance, which were essentially tribal rather than territorial ties or ties of allegiance or vassalage.[52]

Morocco's claims to "legal ties" with Western Sahara at the time of colonisation by Spain had been argued to the Court as a claim to ties of sovereignty on the ground of an alleged immemorial possession of the territory, this immemorial possession itself being based not on an isolated act of occupation but on the public display of sovereignty, uninterrupted and uncontested for centuries – indeed, and this in reliance on historical works, on a series of events stretching back to the Arab conquest of North Africa in the 7th Century A.D. To refute the suggestion that the "far-flung, spasmodic and often transitory character of many of these events" rendered the historical material somewhat equivocal as evidence of possession of the territory, Morocco invoked the Permanent Court's decision in the *Legal Status of Eastern Greenland* case, [53] pointing both to the geographical contiguity of Western Sahara to Morocco and the desert character of the territory as sufficient to establish Morocco's claim to a title based "upon continued display of authority". [54] But while the Court did accept that its predecessor, the Permanent Court, had recognised, in the *Eastern Greenland* case, that in the case of claims to sovereignty over areas in thinly populated or unsettled countries, "very little in the way of actual exercise of sovereign rights" might be sufficient in the absence of a competing claim, [55] the Court still felt that the present case was distinguishable from the facts of *Eastern Greenland.* Even if somewhat sparsely populated, the Western Sahara was a territory across which socially and politically organised tribes were in constant movement and where armed incidents between these tribes were frequent; and there was a paucity of evidence of actual display of authority unambiguously relating to Western Sahara. Nor was the difficulty cured by introducing the argument of geographical unity or contiguity, the argument of geographical unity also being somewhat debatable. [56]

In perhaps the most interesting and novel part of its argument on the substantive issues, Morocco asked the Court to take account of the special structure of the Sherifian State, its special character consisting in the fact that it was founded on the common religious bond of Islam existing among the peoples and on the allegiance of various tribes to the Sultan through their *caids* or sheikhs, rather than on the notion of territory. [57] Morocco also invoked certain acts claimed to point to the internal display of Moroccan authority and also certain international acts said to constitute recognition by other States of its sovereignty over the whole or part of the territory – variously, documents concerning the appointment of *caids*, the alleged imposition of Koranic and other taxes, certain "military decisions" constituting resistance to foreign penetration of the territory, visits by the Sultan of Morocco in person in 1882 and 1886. In general, the Moroccan argument was that Western Sahara has always been linked to the interior of Morocco by common ethnological, cultural and religious ties. [58]

By contrast, Spain denied any documentary evidence or other traces of a display of political authority by Morocco with respect to Western Sahara: the so-called appointments of *caids* by Morocco were, in the Spanish view, only titles of honour bestowed on existing and *de facto* independent local rulers: and Spain also challenged the evidence of the payment of taxes by tribes of Western Sahara. Even the acts of resistance in Western Sahara to foreign penetration, cited by Morocco, were said by Spain to have been nothing more than occasional raids to obtain booty or hostages for ransom and to have nothing to do with display of Moroccan authority. Spain finally questioned, on geographical and other grounds, the unity of the Saharan region with the regions of southern Morocco. [59]

The Court, for its part, concluded that the conflicting evidence did not support Morocco's claim to have exercised territorial sovereignty over Western Sahara. [60] The evidence did not, in the Court's view, shew that Morocco displayed effective and exclusive State activity in Western Sahara: it did, however, provide indications that a legal tie of allegiance had existed at the relevant period between the Sultan of Morocco and some, but only some, of the nomadic peoples of the territory. [61]

The Court then turned to various international acts invoked by Morocco as shewing that the Sultan's sovereignty was directly or indirectly recognised by foreign countries as extending to the Western Sahara: a series of Moroccan treaties, including a treaty with Spain of 1767, and treaties of 1836, 1856 and 1861, with the United States, Great Britain and Spain respectively, dealing with the rescue and safety of mariners shipwrecked on the coast of Western Sahara; a Moroccan treaty with Great Brittain of 1895; diplomatic correspondence with Spain; a Franco-German exchange of letters of 1911. [62] The treaty of 1767 between Morocco and Spain raised some interesting issues of interpretation, including an apparent conflict between the Arabic text which Morocco maintained was the only "official text", and the Spanish text which Spain contended was also an official text. [63] In the Court's view, however, the sum total of all this documentary material was not to establish international recognition by other States of Moroccan territorial sovereignty in Western Sahara at the time of the Spanish colonisation. Some of the documents, for example, the Franco-German exchange of letters in 1911, were directed rather to definition of rival European political interests.[64] On the other hand, though not meeting the tests of international recognition of territorial sovereignty on the part of Morocco, some elements, and more especially the material relating to the recovery of shipwrecked sailors, did provide international recognition, at the time of Spanish colonisation, of authority or influence of the Sultan of Morocco over some nomads in Western Sahara. If not any legal tie of territorial sovereignty between Western Sahara and the Moroccan State, at least there were indications of a legal tie of allegiance between the Sultan of Morocco, and some, though only some, of the tribes of the territory, and also of some display of the Sultan's authority or influence with respect to those tribes.[65]

The Court then turned to the question of the legal ties, if any, existing between Western Sahara at the time of its colonisation by Spain, and the Mauritanian entity.[66] It was admitted by Mauritania that, at the time of Spanish colonisation, there was no Mauritanian State in existence and that the present statehood of Mauritania "is not retroactive".[67] In the Court's view, there could therefore be no question of legal ties of State sovereignty with the Mauritanian entity, but only some other, (lesser), type of legal ties.[68] The Court noted that the "Mauritanian entity" – a term first employed in the U.N. General Assembly debates in 1974 – was, at the time of the colonisation, in the view of the present Mauritanian Government, a distinct human unit characterised by a common language, way of life and religion, and having a uniform social structure.[69] Within the entity, there were, according to the Mauritanian Government, "great confederations of tribes, or emirates whose influence, in the form sometimes of vassalage and sometimes of alliance, extended far beyond their own frontiers".[70] According to Mauritania, it was a community having its own cohesion, its own special characteristics, and a common Saharan law concerning the use of waterholes, grazing lands and agricultural lands, the regulation of inter-tribal hostilities and the settlement of disputes.[71] Mauritania also laid emphasis on the special characteristics of the Saharan area and the nomadic existence of many of the tribes, life in the arid areas requiring the continuous quest for suitable pastures and water-holes and each tribe having a well-defined migration area with established migration routes determined by the location of water-holes, burial grounds, cultivated areas and pastures.[72] As the Mauritanian Government contended,

"the colonial Powers, ... in drawing frontiers took no account of these human factors and in particular of the tribal territories and migration routes, which were, as a result, bisected and even trisected by these artificial frontiers".

The tribes continued nevertheless to make their traditional migrations, these facts of life of the region being finally recognised by France and Spain in 1934 in concluding an administrative agreement to prevent any obstacles to the nomadic existence of the tribes. The Mauritanian argument was thus that at the time of Spanish colonisation, the concepts of "nation" and of "people" explained the position of the inhabitants of the Mauritanian entity, an entity which, despite its political diversity, bore the characteristics of an independent nation, "formed of tribes, confederations and emirates jointly exercising co-sovereignty". [73]

The Spanish Government, in reply, argued that this was a mere "cultural phenomenon, limited in time and space" which could not be "identical with an alleged entity of which the significance was mainly geographical and which had wider limits"; further, that the "idea of an entity must express not only a belonging but also the idea that the component parts are homogeneous". [74] In sum, according to Spain, there was no proof of any tie of allegiance between the tribes inhabiting the territory of Western Sahara and the Mauritanian tribes, – "over and above the mere sociological facts of nomadic life". [75] Finally, the present Islamic Republic of Mauritania could not, in Spain's view, be regarded as the direct successor to the alleged historical Mauritanian entity, since the notion of Mauritania was born in 1904 at a time when the territory of Western Sahara was claimed by Spain already to have had an existence well established in fact and in law. [76]

The Court, for its part, while finding that, at the time of the Spanish colonisation, there existed many ties of a racial, linguistic, religious, cultural and economic nature between various tribes and emirates whose peoples dwelt in the Saharan region today comprised within the Territory of Western Sahara and the Islamic Republic of Mauritania, [77] nevertheless concluded that there was no "tie of sovereignty, or of allegiance of tribes, or of 'simple inclusion' in the same legal entity". [78] The Court, in looking to the existence of "legal ties" other than sovereignty, expressly took note of the fact that the migration routes of almost all the nomadic tribes of Western Sahara crossed what were to become the colonial frontiers and traversed, *inter alia*, substantial areas of what is today the territory of the Islamic Republic of Mauritania. [79] The basic elements of the nomads' way of life, the Court found, were –

"in some measure the subject of tribal rights, and their use was in general regulated by customs. Furthermore, the relations between all the tribes of the region in such matters as inter-tribal clashes and the settlement of disputes were also governed by a body of inter-tribal custom".[80]

These legal ties between the territory of Western Sahara and the "Mauritanian entity" were thus, in the Court's view, – "ties which knew no frontier between the territories and were vital to the very maintenance of life in the region."[81]

While concluding, therefore, that no tie of territorial sovereignty had been established, on the evidence presented, between the territory of Western Sahara and either Morocco or the Mauritanian entity, the Court also ruled that legal ties of allegiance did exist, at the time of Spanish colonisation, between the Sultan of Morocco and some of the tribes living in the territory of Western Sahara; and that rights existed, including some rights relating to the land, which constituted legal ties between the Mauritanian entity, as understood by the Court, and the territory of Western Sahara.[82] As the Court concluded its response to the second question posed by the U.N. General Assembly in its request for Advisory Opinion:

"Thus the Court has not found legal ties of such a nature as might affect the application of Resolution 1514 (XV) in the decolonisation of Western Sahara and, in particular, of the principle of self-determination through the free and genuine expression of the will of the peoples of the Territory".[83]

The Court had, in passing, dealt with the problem of the overlapping character of the respective legal ties claimed by both Morocco and Mauritania in respect to Western Sahara at the time of Spanish colonisation.[84] Both Morocco and Mauritania had emphasised that, in their view, the overlapping left "no geographical void" – no "no-man's-land" – between their respective ties with Western Sahara.[85] In the Court's view, the overlapping arose simply from the geographical locations of the migration routes of the nomadic tribes; nor was the complexity of the legal relations of Western Sahara with the neighbouring territories at that time fully described without mentioning that the nomadic routes of certain tribes passed also within areas of what is present-day Algeria.[86] In the Court's view, therefore, the significance of the geographical overlapping was not that it indicated a "north" and a "south" without a "no-man's-land": its significance was rather that it indicated the difficulty of disentangling the various relationships existing in the Western Sahara region at the time of colonisation by

Spain.[87] The Court had already indicated its view that the questions posed to the Court by the U.N. General Assembly with the request for Advisory Opinion did not envisage – "any form of territorial delimitation by the Court".[88] In framing its answers to the questions, the Court could not be unmindful of the purpose for which the Court's opinion was sought – "to assist the General Assembly to determine its future decolonisation policy and in particular to pronounce on the claims of Morocco and Mauritania to have had legal ties with Western Sahara involving the territorial integrity of their respective counstries".[89]

4. Divisions within the Court: the Preliminary, Jurisdictional Issue

The Court's holdings on the two substantive questions were, as we have noted, achieved in voting terms with a surprising degree of unanimity. On the first substantive question – whether Western Sahara was, at the time of colonisation by Spain, *terra nullius*, the Court's vote was 16 to 0 in favour of a negative response. On the second substantive question, the Court, though denying ties of sovereignty to exist in either case, nevertheless voted 14 to 2 that other legal ties existed between Western Sahara and Morocco at the time of Spanish colonisation; and voted 15 to 1 that other legal ties existed between Western Sahara and the "Mauritanian entity" at the time of Spanish colonisation. Granted the fact of only one formal Dissenting Opinion, how then does one explain the presence, in addition to the official Opinion of Court signed by the President of a plethora of individual judicial Declarations (three) and of individual Separate Opinions (six)?

The answer clearly lies in deeply-felt differences of opinion within the Court. These differences are certainly in a very large degree genuine intellectual differences, with the judges responding in measure to a World Community that is undergoing rapid transition and change at the present time; and they are differences of a sufficient magnitude that the ordinary skills of negotiation and compromise within a plural, multimember tribunal, have hardly been able to bridge them or cover them over, for they reflect differing attitudes to the desirable direction and degree of change in International Law itself in correspondence with the general societal change in the World Community. Yet some elements of the differences of opinion seem to be personal in character too, and are reflected perhaps in a somewhat tendentious, even pejorative note that occasionally enters into the language and styling of some of those Declarations and Separate Opinions.

Judge Gros, in his Declaration, had serious reservations as to the Court's handling of the preliminary, jurisdictional issue. From the beginning, in Judge Gros' view, it was apparent that the General Assembly was asking the Court to give an opinion on a precise legal question: was Morocco entitled to claim reintegration of the Western Sahara territory into the national territory of Morocco to which, according to Morocco, it belonged at the time of colonisation by Spain? [90] Judge Gros considered that there was no dispute between Morocco and Spain [91] – no bilateral dispute which could be detached from the general discussion of the claim of the Government of Morocco to reintegration of the Territory, [92] the two Governments, Morocco and Spain, having explicitly chosen decolonisation in the context of the United Nations. [93] The legal question thus raised by Morocco before the General Assembly, with the support of Mauritania coming only in 1974, might be analysed as a multilateral legal controversy in a debate on the future status of the territory of Western Sahara. [94]

The principal consequence of the apparent confusion, as Judge Gros saw it, in the Opinion of the Court, between the alleged bilateral dispute (Morocco *versus* Spain) and a legal question falling within the Advisory competence of the Court, was an erroneous decision taken as to the composition of the Court – *semble*, the appointment of the *ad hoc* Judge, Judge Boni; and further, the fact that the presentation of the Advisory Opinion amounted to a precise transposition of what was customary in contentious proceedings. [95] On the other hand, Judge Gros also criticised the Court majority for "allow[ing] one of its Members to sit although he had in the United Nations committed himself on one element in the discussion". [96]

Treating the matter in the form in which it had originated – as an Advisory Opinion proceeding – Judge Gros indicated his doubts as to the propriety of the Court's replying at all to the first question referred to it by the General Assembly, (the *terra nullius* question), on the score that the – "question was not a legal one, that it was purely academic and served no useful purpose", [97] and here he also accepted Judge Dillard's view that the question was a "loaded" one. [98]

On the second question, (as to the "legal ties"), Judge Gros insisted that not legal ties, but ethnic, religious or cultural ties were involved. [99] The Opinion of Court was – "an idyllic vision of what was a harsh reality". [100] You could not speak of a legal tie of allegiance, since this was – "a concept of feudal law in an extremely hierarchical society". [101]

As Judge Gros concluded:

> "The Court cannot attribute a legal nature to facts which do not intrinsically possess it: a court does not create the law, it establishes it. If there is no rule of law making it possible for it to assert the existence of the alleged legal ties, the Court oversteps its *rôle* as a judicial organ by describing them as legal, and its finding is not a legal finding .... Economics, sociology and human geography are not law ...". [102]

All this, in Judge Gros' view, confirmed the –

> "current trend in the Court to reply to problems which it raises itself rather than to that which is submitted to it". [103]

Judge Petrén, who had been closely associated with Judge Gros in the Court's decisions in the French *Nuclear Tests* cases, [104] also joined him in the present case, in his Separate Opinion, in adopting much of the reasoning and argument in Judge Gros' Declaration. He had doubts as to the Court's decision to appoint an *ad hoc* judge, querying whether the "legal question actually pending between two or more States" – in the present context, between Morocco and Spain – might not actually have ceased to exist at the time when the Court made its decision on that point: Judge Petrén also considered that the most salient characteristic of the questions referred by the General Assembly to the Court was that they concerned the – "legal categorisation of situations which belong to a time now long past". [105] For purposes of the stipulation in Article 65 (1) of the Court Statute that the Court may give Advisory Opinions on "legal questions", could the Court have submitted to it – "questions concerning the legal assessment of situations which have ceased to exist"? [106] Answering his own question in the negative, Judge Petrén declared that the Court –

> "is not an historical research institute. There are numerous problems of the history of law to which no definitive answer has yet been given. Yet no one would think of submitting to the Court the question, for example, of the authenticity of the will of the Emperor Trajan, or whether the invasion of Britain by William the Conqueror was justified". [107]

In turning to the present case, Judge Petrén denied that any legal question was pending between Morocco and Spain; since Morocco did not dispute the present sovereignty of Spain over the territory, and both Morocco and Spain accepted, for its decolonisation, the application of the resolutions of the General Assembly. [108] While the decolonisation of a territory might raise the question of the "balance to be struck between the right of its population to self-determination and the territorial integrity of one or even of several States", in Judge Petrén's view – "questions of this kind are not yet considered ripe for submission to the Court". [109]

Judge Dillard joined forces, this time, with Judges Gros and Petrén from whom he had differed on the actual vote though not, seemingly, the main thrust of the reasoning, in the French *Nuclear Tests* case Final Judgment. Judge Dillard queried, from the outset of his Separate Opinion, "both the existence and relevance of any legal question", [110] the necessary base of any exercise of the Court's Advisory Opinion jurisdiction. As Judge Dillard suggested, – "it was immediately apparent that the two questions were exclusively confined to an historical period and ... invited an enquiry which, while no doubt historically fascinating, was far removed from any contemporary problem whatever"; and here Judge Dillard dropped a footnote specifically referring to Judge Petrén's Separate Opinion. [111]

As Judge Dillard continued, –

> "the notion that a legal question is simply one that invites an answer 'based on law' appears to be question-begging and it derives no added authority by virtue of being frequently repeated. Nor is it apparent that an exclusively historical question could be automatically converted into a legal one merely because of the use of a legal term such as *terra nullius* or because the question itself baptised the term 'ties' with a legal label by referring to them as 'legal ties' a device which also appeared to be question-begging. More important, it seemed difficult to discern any contemporary *legal* relevance to any answer the Court might give if it were confined to the status of a territory some 90 years ago the title to which was not in dispute then or now.
>
> "Finally it did not appear to me sufficient to say that the questions would be rendered legally relevant on the mere assumption that the answers would tend to enlighten the General Assembly in the exercise of its political functions. Absent from this assumption was the notion of contemporary *legal* relevance". [112]

The balance of Judge Dillard's Separate Opinion is a sustained critique of the reasoning in the official Opinion of Court, and particularly that part of the reasoning relating to the existence or otherwise of "legal ties" between the territory of Western Sahara and Morocco and Mauritania. In Judge Dillard's view:

"... A concept of law and hence of 'legal' ties is misconceived if patterned on the kind of sense of obligation which now prevails in post-Reformation western oriented societies. In these societies, ever since the Reformation, the sense of obligation to the sovereign has been sharply focussed on his secular authority which is not only paramount but permits a dissociation between obligations owed to the State and those owed to religious authority.

Concepts of this kind are not applicable to a society, such as prevailed in the Sahara, in which a distinction between *modes* of authority are not sharply delineated and are not part of the consciousness of people. It is artificial, therefore, to say that a tie is not 'legal' merely because it fails to qualify as one in which a sense of obligation is owed vertically to the secular power of someone with authority".[113]

5. Divisions within the Court: the Substantive Issue and the "New" International Law

In contrast to these three specially concurring opinions that offer elements, it may be suggested, of veiled dissents directed to the logical analysis and reasoning of the Court majority, are three other specially concurring opinions, coming this time from Third World judges. These latter three opinions, it may also be suggested, come rather close to being veiled dissents from the official Opinion of Court; but the grounds of criticism of the official Opinion of Court go, now, not to procedural, but to substantive law questions, setting in opposition classical International Law doctrine and the so-called "new" International Law.

The strongest and most sustained of these opinions is that of Vice-President Ammoun, who draws very strongly, for his own views, on the arguments advanced in the oral hearings before the Court by the legal representatives of the Republic of Zaire and of the Republic of Algeria who had intervened in the case.

The Senior President of the Supreme Court of Zaire, Bayona-Ba-Meya, Judge Ammoun noted, had, in his pleadings before the Court, gone on to –

"dismiss the materialistic concept of *terra nullius*, which led to this dismemberment of Africa following the Berlin Conference of 1885. Mr. Bayona-Ba-Meya substitutes for this a spiritual notion: the ancestral tie between the land, or 'mother nature', and the man who was born therefrom, remains attached thereto, and must one day return thither to be united with his ancestors. This link is the basis of the ownership of the soil, or better, of sovereignty. This amounts to a denial of the very concept of *terra nullius* in the sense of a land which is capable of being appropriated by someone who is not born therefrom. It is a condemnation of the modern concept, as defined by Pasquale Fiore, which regards as *terra nullius* territories inhabited by populations whose civilasation, in the sense of the public law of Europe, is backward and whose political organisation is not conceived according to Western norms .... This is the reply which may be given to the participants in the Berlin Conference of 1885 ...". [114]

Judge Ammoun then adopted with approval the reasoning of Ambassador Mohammed Bedjaoui of Algeria who, in his pleadings before the Court, identified three distinct epochs in the evolution of the International Law as to acquisition of title to territory:

(1) Roman antiquity, when any territory which was not Roman was *nullius*.

(2) The epoch of the great discoveries of the sixteenth and seventeenth centuries, during which any territory not belonging to a Christian sovereign was *nullius*.

(3) The nineteenth century, during which any territory which did not belong to a so-called civilised State was *nullius*. [115]

In short, Judge Ammoun concluded, –

"the concept of *terra nullius*, employed at all periods to the brink of the twentieth century, to justify conquest and colonisation, stands condemned. It is well known that in the sixteenth century Francisco de Vittoria protested against the application to the American Indians, in order to deprive them of their lands, of the concept of *res nullius*". [116]

In the context of the present case, Judge Ammoun then turned to the principle of self-determination and specifically to what he described as "the legitimate struggle for liberation from foreign domination", the legitimacy of which he saw as affirmed by the General Assembly "in at least four resolutions ... which taken together already constitute a custom". [117]

Nothing, in Judge Ammoun's view, more clearly shewed the will for emancipation than that struggle for liberation – "... more decisive than a referendum, being absolutely sincere and authentic". [118] On this basis, Judge Ammoun rejected the Spanish Government's plea for a referendum to determine the future status of Western Sahara, Judge Ammoun accepting here certain statements by the Spanish Foreign Ministry which indicated, in his view, that the Spanish campaign for a referendum was linked to the – "recognition in favour of Spain, ... of special privileges as well as the grant of a right preferential to that of other countries with regard to the economic development and joint exploitation of the said territory". [119]

Judge Ammoun was joined, in his discussion of the spatially and temporally limited, "Western" or "classical" International Law character of the concept of *terra nullius*, by Judge Forster who, in his Separate Opinion, indicated his disagreement with the majority Opinion of Court so far as the Opinion of Court concluded that the materials and information presented to it did not establish any ties of territorial soverneignty between Western Sahara and the Kingdom of Morocco and the Mauritanian entity. The Opinion of Court, in Judge Forster's opinion, went too far in –

> "minimising the exceptional importance of the geographical, social and temporal contexts of the problem .... It is Africa of former times which is in question, as to which it cannot arbitrarily be required that its institutions should be a carbon copy of European institutions, for on that basis almost the entire African continent would have to be declared *terra nullius*". [120]

This was a theme recurred to by *ad hoc* Judge Boni, who, in his Separate Opinion, also reproached the majority Opinion of Court for not having –

> "taken sufficient account of the local context. As regards Morocco, insufficient emphasis has been placed on the religious ties linking the Sultan [of Morocco] and certain tribes of the Sakiet El Hamra. For these tribes, the Sultan was Commander of the Faithful, that is to say, the Steward of God on earth for all matters, whether religious or not. He was thus regarded not only as religious leader but as director of their temporal affairs. The legal ties between them were thus not only religious – which no one denies – but also political, and had the character of territorial sovereignty. [121]
>
> The solution which I advocate, and which confers a character of territorial sovereignty on the ties that existed between Morocco and Western Sahara, leads to the same conclusion: obligatory consultation of the inhabitants of Western Sahara on their future, in pursuance of General Assembly Resolution 1514 (XV)." [122]

6. Divisions within the Court: Mixed Procedural and Substantive Conflicts

The remaining special Declarations and Separate Opinions appended to the Opinion of Court and also the lone Dissenting Opinion, do not present the same clear-cut joinders of issue with the official majority position as do, on the one hand, those opinions, in the positivistic, "classical" International Law stream that fault the majority for its handling of the procedural, adjectival law, jurisdictional issue; and, on the other hand, those opinions that would go well beyond the official majority position on the substantive issues in seeking an express rejection of the "classical" International Law doctrine as to territorial sovereignty and its modes of acquisition and an affirmative proclamation of a "new" International Law position in keeping with contemporary World Community expectations.

Thus, Judge Ignacio–Pinto, in a brief, one-page Declaration, rallied to Judge Petrén's position in characterising the substantive questions posed by the General Assembly to the Court as being –

> "loaded questions, leading in any case to the answer awaited in this particular instance, namely the recognition of rights of sovereignty of Morocco on the one hand and of Mauritania on the other over some part or other of Western Sahara".[123]

Judge Nagendra Singh, for his part, devoted his short Declaration to issues, variously, of fact-finding – for example, the lack of evidence, at the time of Spanish colonisation, of the existence of one single State, comprising the territory of Western Sahara and either Morocco or Mauritania, which would have been dismembered by the coloniser and thus justify reunion on decolonisation.[124] Judge Nagendra Singh also discussed the relations of the Court to the General Assembly, suggesting that even if the procedures for decolonisation lie within the exclusive province of the General Assembly, the Court does not trespass on the prerogatives of the General Assembly in pointing out the – "relationship between the existence of the legal ties and the decolonisation process".[125] He finally turned to the principle of self-determination, with the comment that – "the consultation of the people of the territory awaiting decolonisation is an inescapable imperative whether the method followed on decolonisation is integration or association or independence".[126]

Judge Ruda, the lone Judge to file a formal Dissenting Opinion, expressly denied the existence, at the time of Spanish colonisation, of "legal ties" between the Kingdom of Morocco and the territory of Western Sahara. In his view, those legal ties of allegiance and authority described in the Opinion of Court were not legal ties, but "merely personal ties";[127] and he was not convinced that the various letters and documents mentioned in the Opinion of Court or any other information submitted to the Court afforded – "clear indication of permanent, real and manifested acceptance either of allegiance or of the Sultan's political authority over tribes in Western Sahara".[128] On the other hand, Judge Ruda indicated, he voted in favour of the existence of legal ties between the Mauritanian entity, as understood by the Court, and the territory of Western Sahara because the ties here were, – "in my view, legal ties of a territorial character".[129] Judge Ruda's Dissenting Opinion is a short (two-page) opinion and, as the lone formal Dissenting Opinion, it constrasts sharply with some of the key concurring opinions – both special Declarations and Separate Opinions – in respecting the principle of comity and deference, on the part of a judicial minority, to the official majority judicial position as expressed in the Opinion of Court.

Finally, Judge De Castro, as a permanent member of the Court but one also cast in the *rôle*, as the national of one of the interested parties, Spain, of balancing the *ad hoc* Judge, Judge Boni, filed a Separate Opinion, – in this case much the longest opinion – 46 pages, – of any opinion apart from the Opinion of Court. The range of Judge De Castro's Opinion is very wide: he notes, for example, "the existence of 'new aspects to the problem of the Sahara' – economic aspects (the Bu Craa deposit) and political aspects (Morocco's relations with Mauritania and Algeria)".[130]

On the preliminary, jurisdictional question, Judge De Castro noted that the Court's Advisory Opinion jurisdiction is predicated upon the existence of a "legal question";[131] and he quoted with approval Charles De Visscher's definition that a legal question is "any question capable of receiving an answer based on law", and that the Court would refrain from replying to a question which "depended upon considerations extraneous to the law".[132] Judge De Castro concluded that the question of the existence of ties at the time of the colonisation by Spain could not be capable of receiving an answer based on law, since – "the answer would have to be based on *the proof* of historical facts", and this notwithstanding that – "the old Court was not afraid of studying historic rights, even going back to the year 900."[133]

On the question of the ties existing at the time of the colonisation of the territory of Western Sahara by Spain and their legal efficacy, Judge De Castro had some interesting comments: did these ties –

> "have the validity of acquired rights, unaltered by the passage of time, or of contingent rights which could still be exercised, or were they subject to the rules of intertemporal law? The question is not a new one; it is a question of the validity of historic rights." [134]

As Judge De Castro noted, the Court had already had to consider the validity of legal ties in accordance with intertemporal law, and he cited the *Minquiers and Ecrehos* case [135] as authority for the proposition that the Court does not find it necessary to "deal with pointless historic controversies", and that an – "original title ceases to be valid if there are new facts to be considered on the basis of new law." [136]

In the present context, Judge De Castro felt,

> "changes of facts and changes in the law to be applied cannot be ignored. Just before colonisation by Spain, the territory had a status which was governed by the law in force at that time. But that status had not crystallised and was not fixed *ad aeternum*. It was subject to changes in the times.
>
> First of all, there was colonisation. Colonisation is now condemned to die out; but the colonial fact was a new fact with sociological and legal implications". [137]

Judge De Castro's conclusion was that the legal ties, such as they were, that Morocco or Mauritania might have had with the territory of Western Sahara at the time of colonisation by Spain were subject to the rules of intertemporal law; and this, in his view, meant that those ties "cannot stand in the way of the application of the principle of self-determination", [138] a proposition that he had interpreted as connoting the – "principle that the peoples of non-self-governing territories have the right to decide upon their own destiny and to decide freely, and by democratic means, either to become independent or to become integrated with an independent State". [139] In the special context of the Spanish Government's announced policy on decolonisation of the territory of the Western Sahara, at the time of the Court's hearings and the Court's decision, this implied the Spanish Government's holding of a referendum within the territory. [140]

7. Conclusions

(a) *Internal Court Organisation*

The most immediately noticeable element in the Court's work in the *Western Sahara* Opinion is the lack of unity and of internal cohesiveness and cooperation on the part of the individual Judges, a condition that is not merely not covered over by the apparent near unanimity of the final judicial votes but that seems actually accentuated by the antinomy between the voting consensus and the opinion-writing dissonance. By Anglo-Saxon, Common Law Court standards, the Opinion of Court cannot be said to represent a reasonable balance or compromise between the majority judges – a lowest common denominator, at least, of agreement between them as to substantive conclusions and as to the reasoning in support thereof.[141] It may well be a tribute to the powers of intellectual leadership and influence of the then President of the Court that he should have been able to marshall such a decisive judicial vote in favour of the Court's final conclusions;[142] but factors in the Court's internal organisation and practice as well as genuine philosophical differences or personality conflicts, seem to have contributed to the judicial votes' not being accompanied – more properly, perhaps, preceded – by an equivalent policy or doctrinal consensus.

It is almost impossible to extract what Common Lawyers call a *ratio decidendi* or common principle of decision from the Opinion of Court and the accompanying majority Declarations and Separate Opinions. Tested by Common Law judicial standards these Declarations and Separate Opinions seem to miss the point of a judicial special concurrence. For they read rather like a collection of judicial essays, with the individual judicial authors feeling free, on occasion, to make a personal *tour de force* or to take debating points against the official Opinion of Court, instead of applying the canons of judicial self-restraint of municipal tribunals and limiting themselves to a brief statement of what they accept in the official Opinion and where and for what legal reasons they would regard themselves as unable to accept that official Opinion.[143] Some of these special Declarations and Separate Opinions might possibly better have been deposed as Dissenting Opinions,[144] with the individual authors accepting, then, the concomitant obligation of precisely defining and limiting their intellectual legal disagreements with the official Opinion of Court. By way of comparison, Judge Ruda's lone formal Dissenting Opinion might, perhaps, be taken as a model of how to express – succinctly and appositely, – individual judicial grounds of disagreement with an official majority Opinion of Court.

Criticisms of this character tend, of course, to reflect Common Law judicial standards and tests as they are generally recognised and accepted in the Common Law world. Looking to the Court as it now exists, however, several factors in its distinctive internal organisation and practice may fairly readily be identified as contributing factors in the weaknesses manifested in the *Western Sahara* Opinion. The President of the Court is elected for a term of three years, [145] and though he is legally eligible for re-election, [146] by convention and practice within the Court he never is, and the office rotates within the Court. [147] The convention as to rotation of the Presidency on the World Court, perhaps inevitable politically with a multi-national tribunal, might, under ideal circumstances, encourage and assist collegiality and a sense of collective responsibility on the part of the Court as a whole; but it weakens the possibilities of long-term leadership and direction which, in the case of a multi-national international tribunal, would seem to be far more necessary than with a relatively more homogeneous and predictable national court. Again, the factors normally making for collegiality in a national tribunal which could compensate for any lack of intellectual authority and influence in the Chief Justiceship where that office either changes frequently through death and retirement or else where it may happen to have a weak incumbent – namely, continuity of service and experience on the part of a number of senior Justices – are hardly present with a tribunal like the World Court whose members are elected for a term of years, nine years, only, [148] and who, though eligible for re-election, [149] may not, for reasons of their normally fairly advanced age, choose to run again, or else may not, in fact, because of the operation of political factors in the system of elections to the Court, [150] be re-elected. Thus the authors of two of the more interesting opinions in the *Western Sahara* case – Judge Petrén, with his important contribution to an emergent, analytical positivist strain of interpretation on the Court, and Vice-President Ammoun, with his innovatory opening towards the "new" International Law, – are no longer members of the Court, Judge Petrén having been defeated in his candidacy for re-election at the regular, triennial elections to the Court in the Autumn of 1975, and Vice-President Ammoun not having presented his candidature at that time. By way of comparison, the Indian Supreme Court and the Canadian Supreme Court, which have usually had quite short terms for their presiding officers through a fairly general tradition of promoting the most senior Associate Justice in length of service when the Chief Justiceship falls vacant, have been able effectively to counter-balance any incidental weaknesses in their presidency by an acceptance of collegial responsibility on the part of the senior Associate Justices who, once appointed, hold office until retirement on reaching a fixed age limit.[151] The West German Federal Constitutional Court which, perhaps more nearly than other national tribunals, serves as an analogue to the World Court in regard to judicial selection in that its judges are also elected for a term of years only, has been able to obtain substantial continuity in its membership through the operation of the party political system in the appointment and re-appointment of judges through the system of indirect, Parliamentary elections enjoined by West German constitutional law for the Associate Justiceships and also the Presidency and Vice-Presidency of that Court.[152] The World Court is, as we have remarked, sufficiently distinctive in its internal organisation and practice, – neither strictly Common Law nor strictly Civil Law – to be labelled as *sui generis*; yet it would seem, by the same token, to have the major strengths and advantages of neither one system nor the other.

(b) *Court Jurisdiction. The Advisory Opinion Jurisdiction*

One of the two strong elements of disagreement, within the Court majority in the Western Sahara Opinion, related, as we have noted, to the Court's jurisdiction to grant an Advisory Opinion and to whether, in particular, there was a "legal question" present for purposes of Article 96 of the U.N. Charter and Article 65 of the Court Statute. The Court, for these purposes, characterised the Permanent Court's holding in the *Status of Eastern Carelia*,[153] as having "no parallel" and being "entirely different" – a distinction that the Court related to the facts, first, that Spain, unlike the Soviet Union in *Eastern Carelia*, was both a party to the Statute of the Court and also a Member, at the time, of the relevant World organisation;[154] and, second, that Spain, unlike the Soviet Union in *Eastern Carelia*, had actively participated in the Advisory Opinion proceedings before the Court and "furnished very extensive documentary evidence of the facts", so that there was no issue of "inadequacy of the evidence", as in *Eastern Carelia*, operating, "for reasons of judicial propriety", to prevent the Court from giving an opinion.[155]

That being so, it might still have been better for the Court, if it could not, in Common Law terms, "overrule" *Eastern Carelia*, at least to have indicated more substantial reasons for "distinguishing" it in the present case – perhaps, a "political questions"-style limitation, that the World Court, no more than national courts, does not like to act in vain and must recognise the limitations of *effectiveness* [156] where it seeks to operate adversely to a Great Power in the absence of that Great Power's full and genuine consent to jurisdiction on the part of the Court. Such a policy consideration, it may be suggested, operated as an inarticulate major premise to the Court majority's holding in the Final Judgment in the French *Nuclear Tests* case in 1974, [157] and it would seem to make good sense now also in the contemporary re-interpretation and application of the *Eastern Carelia* holding of 1923.

Looking, however, to the apparent *ratio* of *Eastern Carelia* and comparing it to the facts of the instant case, it seems difficult to avoid the conclusion that in the instant case an actual dispute *inter partes* was decided, or at least ruled upon tangentially, in the interstices of an Advisory Opinion proceeding. It was, of course, a dispute *inter partes* the participants in which, and also their degree of mutual opposition and common interest, may be said to have changed signigicantly during the pendency of the proceedings before the Court and certainly after the Court's holding [as to which, see *infra*]; but that would not change the character of the proceedings in *Western Sahara* as inherently adversary, though reaching the Court in the guise of an Advisory Opinion proceeding. It might, of course, be submitted that granted the limitations to the number of States adhering to the Court's compulsory jurisdiction and the very serious reservations that so many of those States would apply to their own acceptance of that jurisdiction, it is reasonable for a tribunal that is starved as to number and range of matters coming before it, to welcome the opportunity for filling the gaps in its calendar through liberal, expansive interpretation of its Advisory Opinion jurisdiction. The risk of over-ready recourse to that Advisory Opinion jurisdiction is, of course, subject to control in that that jurisdiction may only be invoked by the U.N. General Assembly or Security Council, or by other U.N. organs and specialised agencies when expressly so authorised by the General Assembly. [158] Insofar as the General Assembly is a body of coordinate authority to itself, the Court owes it a certain duty of deference under ordinary principles of intra-governmental comity. Such a judicial policy seems implicit in the Court's deriving, with approval, from its holdings in *Interpretation of Peace Treaties with Bulgaria, Hungary and Romania, First Phase*, [159] and from *Nami-*

bia[160] the proposition that – "only 'compelling reasons', should lead it to refuse to give a requested advisory opinion";[161] and from its express invocation from *Peace Treaties* of the broader, more facultative view of its Advisory Opinion jurisdiction:

> "The consent of States, parties to a dispute, is the basis of the Court's jurisdiction in contentious cases. The situation is different in regard to advisory proceedings even where the Request for an Opinion relates to a legal question actually pending between States. The Court's reply is only of an advisory character: as such, it has no binding force. It follows that no State, whether a Member of the United Nations or not, can prevent the giving of an Advisory Opinion which the United Nations considers to be desirable in order to obtain enlightenment as to the course of action it should take. The Court's Opinion is given not to the States, but to the organ which is entitled to request it: the reply of the Court, itself an 'organ of the United Nations', represents its participation in the activities of the organisation, and, in principle, should not be refused."[162]

(c) *Philosophic Differences within the Court*

More slowly, perhaps, than might have been anticipated after the Court's much-criticised decision in the *South West Africa* cases in 1966 and the resultant increasing politicisation of the processes of election of Members of the Court as the new Third World majority became aware of its voting strength in the General Assembly, philosophic differences are appearing within the Court that mirror, in measure, the gap between "classical" international law doctrine and the so-called "new" international law. These philosophic differences were manifested, in *Western Sahara*, in the conflict as to the legal status of the territory of Western Sahara at the time of Spanish colonisation on the stipulated date of 1884, and as to the spatial-temporal rules to be applied to determine that legal status. What was involved, in terms of legal doctrine, was a contemporary and quite comprehensive re-examination of the doctrinal notion of Intertemporal Law. For those Members of the Court, in *Western Sahara*, who might fairly to be said to represent the more "classical" International Law approach, the application of Intertemporal Law seemed to call for judging the legal significance today of actions and attitudes in the territory of Western Sahara in 1884 in terms of international law doctrine and its special categories as to territorial sovereignty and acquisition of title thereto, in the condition in which that doctrine actually existed as at 1884. Intertemporal Law, on this view, required for purposes of present-day analysis and classification, a jelling of international law doctrine in point of time, 1884; and, insofar as international law doctrine was in fact, in 1884, essentially derived from Western State practice over the 250 years of the development of "modern" International Law founded on societies on the rise of commerce, a jelling of international law in point of space also – the predominantly Western-based classical international law.

On the other hand, those Members of the Court reflecting more directly and immediately the trends away from classical international law doctrine towards the "new" international law seemed to be arguing, essentially, that in interpreting the legal significance today of historical events in the territory of Western Sahara in 1884, the relevant legal criteria were not simply those that might have been applied to the dispute if it had actually arisen and been decided in 1884, but the classical international law categories as to territorial sovereignty as informed by contemporary awareness of their special space-time origins and limitations. For, in effect, the Zaire and Algerian arguments, as adopted expressly by Vice-President Ammoun and also in essence by Judge Forster and *ad hoc* Judge Boni, involved the proposition that where classical international law doctrine, as at 1884, – based as it was on strictly Western-type society and strictly Western political relationships, – would, if applied, deny the existence of ties of legal sovereignty between the territory of Western Sahara on the one hand and Morocco and Mauritania, a more flexible and imaginative interpretation of the classical international doctrine so as to take account also of non-Western patterns of society and social organisation would yield a quite different answer. Such a result might be beyond the logical possibilities inherent in Intertemporal Law as it has, so far, tended, – somewhat conservatively perhaps, – to be defined and applied in international law doctrine;[163] but it would not appear to be beyond the intellectual capacities of either of the two main classical legal strains from which International Law doctrine derives – the Common Law, under the rubric of progressive, generic interpretation; and the Civil Law, in terms of Gény's notion, as applied to the *Code Napoléon*, of *la libre recherche scientifique*[164] and of teleological or purposive interpretation generally. International Law today thus presents not merely an intertemporal but also an inter-cultural aspect,[165] and its specialised techniques and reasoning should be as capable of responding, flexibly, to the one as to the other.

(d) *The Court and International Problem-solving*

The Western Sahara affair, at the time it reached the Court, involved a dispute between Spain on the one hand and Morocco and Mauritania on the other, with Zaire and Algeria intervening, so to speak, as "friends of court" and presenting arguments denying an effective Spanish acquisition of sovereignty at the time of Spanish colonization in 1884. [166] The Court's majority ruling, in the Advisory Opinion, that "legal ties", even if not ties of formal sovereignty, existed between the territory of Western Sahara on the one hand and the Kingdom of Morocco and also the Mauritanian entity, undoubtedly encouraged Morocco in the political pursuit of its objective of unification or integration of a decolonised Western Sahara with Morocco. The Court's Advisory Opinion ruling was rendered on October 16, 1975. On the same day, King Hassan of Morocco announced his "green march", – stated to be a peaceful movement of 350,000 volunteer civilians, ten percent of whom were to be women, – to recover the territory. [167] While Spain, and also Algeria, threatened force to keep Morocco out of the Western Sahara territory, [168] and U.N. Secretary-General, Kurt Waldheim, proposed mediation between the parties – now defined as being Spain, Morocco, Mauritania, and Algeria – and a temporary United Nations administration of the territory pending a referendum to determine the wishes of the population which would be held within six months, King Hassan, on November 9, 1975, suddenly called off the "green march" and ordered the Moroccan "volunteers" to return home. [169] It was then reported that on November 14, 1975, Spain, Morocco, and Mauritania had made a tripartite agreement for a Spanish withdrawal from the Western Sahara territory, to take place on February 28, 1976, leaving the territory to a provisional administration formed by Morocco and Mauritania. The agreement apparently involved an understanding that Spain would be reimbursed for its investments in the Saharan phosphates and that Spain and Morocco would continue jointly to exploit the phosphate deposits and also that Spanish fishing vessels would continue to fish in Saharan waters. [170] Morocco and Mauritania had earlier apparently reached an accord to partition the territory between them, with Morocco taking the phosphates-rich Northern half. [171] There was, however, no agreement with Algeria which, at this time, was backing a local self-determination movement, *Polisario*, claiming to represent the 70,000 indigenous inhabitants; [172] and Algeria therefore announced that it would treat the tripartite declaration on the future of the territory as null and void.[173] Moroccan troops proceeded to occupy the territory on the withdrawal of Spanish troops, and the Algerian-backed *Polisario Front* thereupon proclaimed, on February 27, 1976, the formation of a Democratic Saharan Arab Republic, and commenced guerrilla operations against the Moroccan forces.[174] Morocco and Mauritania responded, on March 7, 1976, by breaking off diplomatic relations with Algeria.[175] The situation has not, at the time of writing, been resolved definitively, but open hostilities between the three Maghreb countries have at least been avoided to date,[176] even though the Algerian-backed Western Sahara national liberation group, *Polisario*, now maintains continuing guerrilla activities against the Moroccan and Mauritanian military occupation forces in the Western Sahara territory.[177]

The World Court ruling undoubtedly facilitated the Spanish decision to withdraw from the Western Sahara territory as quickly and gracefully as possible under the circumstances; for the Spanish politic of sponsoring a referendum among the local inhabitants, which would presumably have rendered a decision in favour of an independent and autonomous, and no doubt Spanish-leaning Saharan State, foundered once and for all when it received no affirmative backing from the Court ruling. If the Spanish aims, after all, were economic ones, directed to maintenance of some at least of their phosphates-development interests, and only secondarily political,[178] these were achieved by the subsequent, non-belligerent, tripartite accord between Spain and Morocco and Mauritania.

Only Algeria was left out. The Algerian Government, even though it chose to intervene and present argument before the Court in the Advisory Opinion hearing, may well have felt disposed to quarrel, after the event, with an ultimately Court-derived solution to the Western Sahara territorial conflict. For that Court-derived solution, through its operation within the interstices of the Advisory Opinion procedures and its avoidance, therefore, of the precise and full identification of all the parties and of the range and limits of their respective interests enjoined by contentious proceedings, may be argued as having substantially overlooked one of the main protagonists and, perhaps also, as having done less than justice to its special claims and interests. In this sense, some of the objections of the specially concurring Judges, going to the limitations of the Advisory Opinion jurisdiction as a vehicle for bringing disputes before the Court, may seem warranted. As Mr. Justice Frankfurter once observed, – "Only fragments of a social problem are seen through the narrow windows of a litigation".[179]

Those main parties who were more or less informally identified as such by the Court majority – namely Morocco and Mauritania – were clearly confirmed in a feeling of self-righteousness as a result of a Court ruling that may have been overly restrictive in its conception of the total problem and the total range of parties, without full regard, for example, for the views of the local, indigenous, Western Sahara, population whose views were hardly adequately represented by the Spanish proposal for a referendum. The political colourability of the Spanish referendum proposal was, after all, soon to be demonstrated by the ease and swiftness with which Spain abandoned it in return for the *quid pro quo* of economic concessions from the successor Moroccan and Mauritanian governments. By the same token, the Court Opinion essentially passes over the claim of that other, future party, Algeria, which had intervened to plead so eloquently and effectively the case against any original Spanish acquisition of territorial sovereignty through the late-19th century act of colonisation of the Western Sahara territory. A somewhat more comprehensive, inclusive, approach by the Court, not limiting itself to the narrow boundaries of the questions as originally formulated by the General Assembly but defining the ambit of the interested parties broadly so as to embrace – in addition to Morocco, Mauritania and Spain – both Algeria and also the local, indigenous Western Sahara population, would have seemed to be within the full spirit of the Court majority's newer, more facultative approach to interpretation of the Court's Advisory Opinion jurisdiction; and might also, as it turned out, have been a more fruitful judicial approach to international legal problem-solving in the instant case. [180]

Chapter V

JUDICIAL SELF-RESTRAINT AGAIN: THE AEGEAN SEA CONTINENTAL SHELF CASE

The World Court, in an Order issued on September 11th, 1976[1], refused to grant a Greek request for the indication of Interim Measures of Protection in the continuing, and as yet unresolved, political-legal dispute between Greece and Turkey over the ownership and exploitation of the Aegean Sea Continental Shelf. The Court Order was made by a vote of 12 to 1, only the *ad hoc* Greek Judge, Judge Stassinopoulos, dissenting. Yet, in a thirteen-member Court (including the *ad hoc* Judge) for purposes of the disposition of the case, there were ten judicial opinions filed – the official Opinion of Court signed by the President, Judge Jiménez de Aréchaga[2], eight individual Separate Opinions filed, respectively, by Judges Jiménez de Aréchaga[3], Nagendra Singh[4], Lachs[5], Morozov[6], Ruda[7], Mosler[8], Elias[9], and Tarazi[10]; and the lone Dissenting Opinion already noted[11]. The key issues in *Aegean Sea Continental Shelf* – procedural, adjectival law questions pre-conditioning any Court rulings on substantive law questions – are sufficiently close to similar issues considered in the several most recent rulings of the Court – in *French Nuclear Tests, Interim Order*[12], and *Final Judgment*[13], and in *Western Sahara*[14], – and the present membership of the Court is sufficiently coterminous with the earlier benches that made those earlier rulings (in spite of the renewal of a third of the Court's membership at the periodic elections of 1975), to make some comparative analysis and evaluation of these decisions and holdings most valuable in terms of the historical unfolding or elaboration of the Court's jurisprudence for the future.

Aegean Sea Continental Shelf arose from the competitive Greek and Turkish pressing of claims to the supposedly oil-rich submarine areas of the Aegean Sea between their two countries. The conflict was a mixed political and legal one, the political elements being accentuated by the recent near-armed conflict situation between the two countries arising from Cyprus; and the legal elements being complicated by the failure of the Geneva Convention on the Continental Shelf or International Customary Law as a whole to make any explicit and unequivocal ruling on the status of a Continental Shelf between two territorially close neighbours, the sea area between whom is broken by scattered islands belonging to one of them. Turkey, according to the Greek complaint to the Court, had in 1973 granted permits to the Turkish State Petroleum Company (TPAO) for exploration for petroleum in the Aegean Sea in areas claimed by Greece as encroaching upon the Continental Shelf appertaining to certain Greek islands in the Aegean; and on August 6th, 7th, and 8th 1976, the Turkish seismic research vessel, *MTA SISMIK I*, had engaged in seismic exploration of such areas. On August 10th, 1976, the Greek Government both filed an Application and request for Interim Measures of Protection before the Court, and also requested the President of the Security Council to call an urgent meeting of the Council to discuss what it alleged were Turkey's violations of the sovereign rights of Greece in the Continental Shelf in the Aegean.

1. Court Jurisdiction to Grant Interim Measures of Protection

The Turkish reply to the Greek Application to the Court and request for Interim Measures of Protection was, first of all, to deny the Court's jurisdiction and then to suggest that, even if there were jurisdiction, the interim measures sought were not required for the protection of the rights claimed by Greece. Turkey, pursuant to its general denial of Court Jurisdiction, declined, unlike Greece, to exercise the right conferred by Article 31 (3) of the Court's Statute to choose an *ad hoc* judge; and Turkey was also not represented at the subsequent Court hearings, its response to the Greek Application, – on the model of the French response to the Australian-New Zealand complaints in *French Nuclear Tests;*[15] – being confined to a written memorandum addressed to the Court by letter on August 26th, 1976, under the title "Observations of the Turkish Government on the request of the Government of Greece for provisional measures, dated 10th August 1976."[16]

The Turkish position on jurisdiction was, briefly, (and again echoing arguments presented by France in its written memorandum filed in *French Nuclear Tests*), to deny that the General Act for the Pacific Settlement of International Disputes of 1928, which had principally been replied upon by Greece as the basis of its claim of Court jurisdiction in the present Aegean Sea Conflict, was any longer a treaty in force between Greece and Turkey. [17] A lesser, secondary Turkish argument as to lack of Court jurisdiction in regard to the present conflict was that, even if the General Act of 1928 were to be regarded as still in force and applicable, the matters now submitted to the Court by Greece fell within the terms of reservation (b) to Greece's instrument of accession to the Act, dated September 14th, 1931, which specifically excluded from the procedures descibed in the General Act – "disputes concerning questions which by international law are solely within the domestic jurisdiction of States, and in particular disputes relating to the territorial status of Greece, including disputes relating to its rights of sovereignty over its ports and lines of communication." [18]

The official Opinion of Court in *Aegean Sea*, which, as we have noted, is adhered to by all twelve judges making up the Court majority deciding the case, dealt with the Greek arguments on the general issue of Court Jurisdiction and the Turkish reply thereto, elliptically – one might almost say by indirection:

> "... it is not necessary for the Court to reach a final conclusion at this stage of the proceedings on the questions thus raised concerning the application of the 1928 Act as between Greece and Turkey, and it will therefore examine the request for the indication of interim measures only in the context of Article 41 of the Statute." [19]

Putting to one side the general issue of Court jurisdiction on the merits, without in any way attempting to decide it, the official Opinion of Court escalates immediately to the issue of the Court's power to grant interim measures, pending a final decision on the merits, and in fact disposes of the Greek application on that basis.

Does the power to grant interim measures in any case presuppose that the Court has jurisdiction, anyway, upon the merits of the case? Should the exercise of any power to grant interim measures be predicated upon a prior Court finding of jurisdiction on the merits? Three of the judges making up the Court majority in *Aegean Sea*, – Judges Morozov, Mosler and Tarazi, – thought so, and each denies categorically, in individual Separate Opinions filed with the official Opinion of Court, that Article 41 of the Court Statute, as to the Court power to indicate provisional measures, [20] can constitute in itself an independent source of jurisdiction separate and distinct from the Court's general jurisdiction as established under Articles 36 and 37 of the Court Statute. If we add to these three judges Judge Ruda who, in his Separate Opinion, also denied any Court power to consider interim measures without having first decided its own basic competence on the merits, at least *prima facie*; and Judge Lachs who stresses, in his Separate Opinion, the obligation of the Court to consider the general jurisdictional issue and to make clear its provisional views; and, finally, two judges among the majority who did not file Separate Opinions in *Aegean Sea* to this effect but who *did* take a similar position, clearly and unequivocally, in *French Nuclear Tests*, Judges Forster[21] and Gros,[22] we would be left with a majority of seven judges out of the twelve adhering to the official Opinion of Court who cannot be in agreement with the Opinion of Court's basic approach of escalating to the question of jurisdiction to grant interim measures without a prior finding, at least *prima facie*, of jurisdiction on the merits. What does that do to tidy analytical jurisprudence notions, so dear to Common Lawyers at least, of the need to have a common principle of decision, or *ratio decidendi*, for any plural-opinion, majority decision rendered by a multimember tribunal? The mystery is deepened if we consider that two more among the majority judges filing individual Separate Opinions, also seem to rally to the need for demonstration of at least *prima facie* jurisdiction on the merits before any Court exercise of interim measures: President Jiménez de Aréchaga who regards it as "devoid of sense",[23] to act otherwise, even though he believes Article 41 of the Court Statute constitutes an autonomous grant of jurisdiction; and Judge Nagendra Singh who insists on a higher degree of satisfaction than the positive but cursory test of *prima facie* jurisdiction and sees as the acid test that judgment should be within clear prospect. Even Judge Elias who, alone among the eight majority judges filing Separate Opinions, seems not to be troubled by any necessity to decide the question of jurisdiction on the merits before going on to rule under Article 41, still declares that the preliminary jurisdictional issue requires urgent and serious re-thinking.

One might have thought that this particular issue was lost, once and for all, after the gallant but losing fight by the four judges who each filed individual Dissenting Opinions, directed to this argument, in *French Nuclear Tests, Interim Order*; and who rallied –, reluctantly in terms of the ultimate *ratio* of that Opinion, – to the official Opinion of Court in *French Nuclear Tests, Final Judgment* which decided that case on other grounds – Judges Forster, Gros, Petrén and Ignacio-Pinto. The mixed opinion-writing of the majority judges in *Aegean Sea*, annexed to the official Opinion of Court in that case, suggests that the strict-jurisdictional-tests quartet (now broken up, of course) from *French Nuclear Tests* may have, with time, won over a majority of their colleagues, and that doctrinally the issue is still open to argument before the Court.

2. Interim Measures. The Nature of the Damages Required as a Condition of Court Intervention

The Opinion of Court, as we have noted, putting to one side the issue of jurisdiction on the merits, proceeds elliptically to consider whether Greece had demonstrated damage of such a nature as to require affirmative Court intervention, and in fact decides the case, on that basis. The test of the measure of damage required, for purposes of any Court intervention under Article 41 of its Statute, must, so the Opinion of Court says, be "irreparable prejudice ... to rights which are the subject of dispute in judicial proceedings and that the Court's judgment should not be anticipated by reason of any initiative regarding the matters in issue before the Court." [24] Applying such a test, the Opinion of Court concludes, quite easily, that neither the Turkish concessions nor the Turkish exploration activity could be creative of new rights or deprive Greece of any right to which in law it may be entitled; and that the activities of the Turkish vessel in question involved no "risk of physical damage to the seabed or subsoil or to their natural resources." [25] Further, even if it were established that there was a breach by Turkey of the "exclusivity" of a right claimed by Greece, such a breach "might be capable of reparation by appropriate means." [26]

If there is a point where substantial accord exists between the official Opinion of Court and the eight judges who, belonging to the majority of twelve, still felt it necessary to file individual Separate Opinions, it is surely here. In many respects it is an attractive point for consensus, for it involves deciding the case modestly, in keeping with well-accepted canons of judicial self-restraint in municipal law which argue the merits of deciding constitutional cases on lesser rather than on more substantial grounds, and of avoiding the (larger) constitutional issue as a ground of decision wherever possible. In *Aegean Sea*, we seem thus to be left with an essentially fact-oriented ground of majority decision, that is readily capable of being distinguished and limited, on the facts, in any future case. There is an avoidance, in consequence, of sounding *judicial* proclamations on general jurisdictional competence that could be potentially embarrassing or damaging in future cases.

The only qualifications for the seemingly remarkable degree of judicial consensus on this point are made by Judge Mosler and by Judge Elias. Judge Mosler, in a thoughtful Separate Opinion, raises the intellectually troubling point whether the military measures taken by both sides, Turkey and Greece, for the purposes, respectively, of the protection or supervision of the Turkish exploration vessel, and which involved a risk of armed conflict, did not constitute an aggravating circumstance additional to the basic element of continued exploration and thus perhaps begin to approach the test of "irreparable prejudice" as the condition of grant of interim measures of protection.[27] Judge Elias, for his part, in an interesting excursus into what may be called, without reproach, the *new* international law, challenged the validity of – "the apparent acceptance by the majority of the Court that, once any damage resulting from the exploration and/or exploitation by Turkey is capable of being compensated for in cash or kind, Greece cannot be said to have suffered irreparable damage."[28]

Such a test meant, in Judge Elias' view, that – "the State which has the ability to pay can under this principle commit wrongs against another State with impunity, since it discounts the fact that the injury by itself might be sufficient to cause irreparable harm to the national susceptibilities of the offended State. The rightness or wrongness of the action itself does not seem to matter. This is a principle upon which contemporary international law should frown: might should no longer be right in today's inter-State relations."[29]

3. The Legal Effects of Unilateral Declarations of State Intention

The binding effects of unilateral declarations of State intention had been the key legal element in the official Opinion of Court in *French Nuclear Tests. Final Judgment*,[30] in which the Court, by a 9 to 6 vote, had resolved not to venture upon the substantive international legal issues raised by Australia and New Zealand against France, thereby, in effect, reversing the preliminary decision in that case, when the Court, by an 8 to 6 vote, had resolved to issue an Interim Protection Order against France.[31] The majority of 9 judges for purposes of *French Nuclear Tests, Final Judgment* included four judges (Judges Forster, Gros, Petrén, and Ignacio-Pinto) who had disagreed with the grant of the Interim Protection Order, to the point of filing individual dissenting opinions; and who, for purposes of the *Final Judgment*, filed fresh individual concurring opinions denying that there ever had been a justiciable dispute able to base Court jurisdiction. The official Opinion of Court in *French Nuclear Tests. Final Judgment* chose not to rule at all on this procedural point – what, in logical terms, might be called the *prior* legal question; but instead to decide the case on another adjectival law point, namely that the whole affair had now become moot in view of various official declarations on the part of the French Government indicating their intention not to conduct any further above-the-ground nuclear tests in the South Pacific. [32]

In *Aegean Sea Continental Shelf*, the official Opinion of Court takes affirmative note of the indication by the Turkish Government in its letter to the Court, under date August 25th, 1976, that "Turkey has no intention of taking the initiative in the use of force" against Greece; [33] further, of a statement to Radio Ankara on July 24th, 1976, by the Turkish Foreign Minister to the effect that seismic research of the nature then being carried out by the Turkish vessel, *MTA SISMIK I*, "cannot establish rights in the areas where this research is carried out" [34] and, finally, of the averment in the Turkish letter to the Court under date August 25th, 1976, that "sovereign rights over the continental shelf (including the exclusive right to exploration) that may exist are not taken away or diminished by exploration.' " [35]

The flexible initiative by the Court majority in *French Nuclear Tests. Final Judgment*, eschewing, as it did, any overly positivistic insistence upon special procedures or a particular degree of formality in order to confer judicial force and status upon unilateral acts by States, [36] seems thus to be continued and extended in the official Opinion of Court in *Aegean Sea Continental Shelf*. It is not, moreover, a necessary point to the Court majority holding in *Aegean Sea Continental Shelf*, being simply an added evidentiary support for the Court finding, on the facts of the case, of no irreparable damages to Greece, – the pre-requisite, in the Court's view, to any judicial intervention in the case.

4. A Constitutional Separation of Powers? The Court and the Security Council

The official Opinion of Court in *Aegean Sea Continental Shelf* takes "cognisance of that fact that, simultaneously with the proceedings before it in respect of the request for interim measures of protection, the United Nations Security Council also has been seized of the dispute between Greece and Turkey ..." [37]; that the Security Council discussed the question at meetings held on August 12th, 13th, and 25th, 1976, *with the participation of the representatives of Greece and Turkey*;[38] and that the Security Council, on August 25th, 1976, had adopted, by consensus, Resolution 395 (1976), urging the Greek and Turkish Governments "to do everything in their power to reduce the present tensions in the area ...", "to resume direct negotiations over their differences", and "to do everything within their power to ensure that this results in mutually acceptable solutions." [39] The official Opinion of Court goes on to note that "both Greece and Turkey, as Members of the United Nations, have expressly recognised the responsibility of the Security Council for the maintenance of international peace and security; ... it is not to be presumed that either State will fail to heed its obligations under the Charter of the United Nations or fail to heed the recommendations of the Security Council addressed to them with respect to their present dispute." [40]

The official basis for invocation, by the Opinion of Court, of the parallel *political* action before the Security Council, simultaneously with the *judicial* action before the Court, was the Greek request to the Court, during the public sittings, to indicate interim measures of protection "in order to prevent the aggravation or extension of the dispute." [41] As a logical matter, the Court noted, it would, before such a request could be entertained, have to determine whether, under Article 41 of the Court Statute, the Court had such an independent power to indicate interim measures having that object. [42] In the light of its own *résumé* of the course of the parallel action before the Security Council, the Court concluded that it was not necessary to examine this point. [43]

The issue of the relation between the Court and the Security Council, – between action, simultaneously, at the judicial level and the political level – and the proper degree of deference that one major organ of United Nations policy-making should accord to another, co-ordinate institution, is, of course, a troubling one. It is much discussed in internal Municipal, Constitutional law where the precedents are many. It has been much more rarely touched on in United Nations jurisprudence.

It is adverted to by Judge Lachs in his Separate Opinion. Greece having applied simultaneously to the Court and the Security Council, "thus seeking both legal and political relief", [44] the Court, as Judge Lachs observed, was called upon to pronounce after a period of negotiations and after a resolution in which the Security Council has urged Greece and Turkey to resume direct negotiations over their differences. This, in Judge Lachs' view – "lends the case a specific and most unusual character. The time of seisin of the Court is never of its own choice, but lies in the hands of the applicants. It sometimes falls in a twilight zone as regards the situations either of fact or of law." [45]

Did the fact of the parallel, political proceedings before a main political organ of the United Nations, constitutionally inhibit the Court from pronouncing upon it? Judge Lachs thought not, adopting here several instances of the practice of the old Court (P.C.I.J.):

> "The Court does not, to my way of thinking, arrogate any powers excluded by its Statute when, otherwise than by adjudication, it assists, facilitates or contributes to the peaceful settlement of disputes between States, if offered the occasion at any stage of the proceedings .... *A fortiori* the present Court, whose Statute is much more intimately bound up with the United Nations Charter than that of its predecessor with the Covenant of the League, should the more readily seize the opportunity of reminding the member States concerned in a dispute referred to it of certain obligations deriving from general international law or flowing from the Charter .... There was in my view no statutory bar to its spelling out the legal consequences of the Security Council's resolution and the official statements of the representatives of the two States. The pronouncements of the Council did not dispense the Court, an independent judicial organ, from expressing its own view on the serious situation in the disputed area .... In going further than it has, the Court, with all the weight of its judicial office, could have made its own constructive, albeit indirect, contribution, helping to pave the way to the friendly resolution of a dangerous dispute." [46]

This beneficial, expansive view of the Court's powers without accepting any negative implication flowing from the simultaneous presence of the same problem-situation before other U.N. organs was also taken up by Judge Tarazi in his Separate Opinion. Judge

Tarazi did not view the question as one of the simultaneous use of two parallel remedies:

> "... the Security Council, unlike the Court, is a political organ. The rule *electa una via* did not have to be applied." [47]

Recognising that the Security Council Resolution of August 25th, 1976, created – "a new element requiring to be taken into consideration in the formulation of the Court's order," [48] Judge Tarazi noted that the I.C.J., unlike its predecessor the P.C.I.J., is expressly stipulated by the Charter, Article 7, as being one of the "principal organs of the United Nations"; while Article 92 of the Charter indicates that the Court's Statute is annexed to and "forms an integral part of" the Charter. [49] It flowed from this that if, by virtue of the Charter, – "the Security Council bears an essential responsibility for the maintenance of peace and security", nevertheless "the Court, if the circumstances so require, ought to collaborate in the accomplishment of this fundamental mission". [50] While considering that the Court had indeed applied itself to this task in the present case, Judge Tarazi felt that the Opinion of Court should have mentioned the Security Council Resolution in the operative part. [51]

The only other direct reference to this point is in Judge Mosler's Separate Opinion, where Judge Mosler felt that the Court had an "overall responsibility to consider the [military] situation as a whole, quite apart from its assessment of the Security Council's resolution and the reaction thereto of Greece and Turkey." [52]

5. The Court as Collegial Body. Decision-making, and Opinion-writing

The Court Order, in *Aegean Sea Continental Shelf*, as we have noted, was made by a 12 to 1 vote, with only the *ad hoc*, Greek judge dissenting. Yet, in the thirteen-member Court (including the *ad hoc* judge), there were ten judicial Opinions filed – the official Opinion of Court and eight individual Separate Opinions, plus the Dissenting Opinion of the *ad hoc* judge.

It is, as we have already noted, difficult to extract a common principle of decision – *ratio decidendi* – from the official Opinion of Court and the eight individual majority Opinions taken together, on the key jurisdictional issue of whether the Court power to grant interim measures is not predicated upon a prior Court finding of jurisdiction upon the merits of the case. According to the analysis, *supra*, the intriguing possibility remains that the official Opinion of Court's disposition of this particular issue – the *prior* issue, according to most Common Law and Civil Law conceptions – does not command the support of a clear majority of the judges deciding the case.

There is, of course, absolutely nothing in the Court's Statute requiring the official Opinion of Court to attempt a tidy reconciliation of the diverging judicial attitudes within a Court majority in any case; or to try to identify, in any formalised way, the points of individual agreement and disagreement or even the key points, in the majority's view, on which the case is decided. Article 56 (1) of the Court's statute states only that the judgment shall – "state the reasons on which it is based".[53] Arguments in favour of the attempt, in the Opinion of Court, to establish or delimit a clear *ratio decidendi*, go rather to the logical symmetry of the Court's disposition of the case and the official reasoning in support thereof. Such arguments reflect, essentially, basic Common Law conceptions of the proper functions of a multi-member tribunal; and they are not, in any case, a reflex of Civil Law attitudes where the practice of individual judicial opinion-writing, whether on the part of majority or dissenting judges, is not so very generally accepted. There is absolutely no reason why the Court, as a tribunal *sui generis*, should not maintain its own unique practice. If that may sometimes, as with some recent Court decisions, present problems in finding the actual grounds of decision, one can always, as Chief Justice Charles Evans Hughes said in justifying occasional cloudiness in Opinion-writing in the official Opinion of Court of the United States Supreme Court, leave it to the Law Journals and to history to find out what the Court has actually decided. The President of the World Court, like the Chief Justice of the United States Supreme Court, may well conclude that his prime responsibility is to facilitate political compromise within the Court and thus to build a firm majority in any case – if need be, at the expense of literary elegance in the official Opinion of Court or of logical consistency and coherence, at all times, as between all the majority Opinions.

The risks of "Byzantinism" among the Court majority in any case and among the members of the Court as a whole – perhaps present, in measure, in some earlier decisions of the present Court – do seem to be sufficiently controlled in *Aegean Sea Continental Shelf*. All eight Separate Opinions are succinct and apposite: the two longest, by Judges Elias and Tarazi respectively, are just over three pages in length, while the other six are one or two pages each, and the dissenting Opinion of the *ad hoc* Judge, (in comparison to opinion-writing in *French Nuclear Tests. Final Judgment*)[54] is just over five pages.[55] The Separate Opinions tend to focus upon specific points where the individual judicial author would want to go beyond the bounds of classical International Law or else test out or confirm some hypothesis for the future.

Among these, the procedural jurisdictional issue – whether or not to exercise jurisdiction to grant interim measures without a prior firm finding of jurisdiction on the merits – would seem to be decided, as in *French Nuclear Tests*, in favour of a facultative, liberal or expansionist view of Court jurisdiction, complemented by a conservative or restrictionist judicial view as to actually ruling on major *substantive* issues in advance of any political necessity for so doing.

On the issue of the nature of irreparable damages as a precondition to a Court intervention to decree interim measures of protection, it is now signalled to the Court majority, for the future, that perhaps such damages should not be conceived of solely as tangible and pecuniary in character, and that they might sensibly include moral damage.

There are thoughtful judicial views on the proper relationship between the Court and other coordinate organs of United Nations policy-making, and on the degree of mutual deference or forbearance that such organs should exercise in their relations *inter se*; with the strong suggestion that the Court, for the future, should reject Municipal law-based conceptions of a classical constitutional separation of powers which would be, correspondingly, limiting as to the possibilities of judicial activism.

Finally, the judicial eschewing of juridical formalism, reflected in the weight given, in *French Nuclear Tests. Final Judgment*, to the legal effect of unilateral State declarations of intention, is confirmed and strengthened, for the future, by the individual judicial *obiter dicta*, on this point in *Aegean Sea, Continental Shelf.*

Chapter VI

ALTERNATIVE LAW-MAKING MODES. THE INTERNATIONAL CODIFYING CONFERENCE: ATTRITION OF THE LAW OF THE SEA

The third United Nations Conference on the Law of the Sea, launched by a U.N. General Assembly Resolution of December, 1970, may, at various times during its long drawn-out history, have seemed to resemble the mythical Labours of Sisyphus. Four years of preparatory work in committee stage culminated in a marathon series of conference sessions in Caracas in mid-1974, extending over 10 weeks and attended by some 5,000 delegates and observers drawn from 148 States. When the Caracas sessions ended, as, indeed, has been anticipated from the outset, without producing a formal agreement, the conference was then adjourned to Geneva in the Spring of 1975; and this time a further eight-week series of conference sessions ended without an agreement. The conference was then further adjourned to New York for the Spring of 1976, for a resumed, eight-week session. The Spring, 1976, New York session was succeeded by a seven-week session in New York in August and September of 1976; to be followed, once more, by an eight-week session in New York from May to July of 1977, this latest round of negotiations ending with the promise of a still further conference in 1978. These labyrinthine proceedings brought visible dissatisfaction on the part of several major countries at least, and the hint by the head of the U.S. delegation, Ambassador Elliot Richardson, that the United States might consider withdrawing altogether from the U.N.'s Law of the Sea deliberations.[1] The conference, as envisaged, resumed again, on March 28, 1978, in Geneva, for a further eight-week session, with United Nations Secretary-General Kurt Waldheim predicting, at the half-way point, that this resumed session would end as a "limited success", with a further session inevitable in 1979.[1a]

It is perhaps not surprising that the protracted proceedings of the Third United Nations Conference on the Law of the Sea should have invited occasional humorous comment in the Press as to the professional expertise of many of its official delegates and observers or as to their degree of serious commitment to the postulated scientific objective of codifying the Law of the Sea. One very well-established North American daily newspaper, normally noted for the sobriety of its political assessments and appraisals, was even moved to compare the Conference, which it described as "float(ing) from spa to shining spa", to that "oldest established permanent floating crap game in New York",[2] historically memorialised in the well-known Broadway musical comedy, "Guys and Dolls",

Public criticisms such as these may, of course, be unfair in that they misunderstand the basic *rôle* and purpose of the Third U.N. Conference, by placing too high a trust for salvation in the Conference organisers, executive, and delegates, in attributing to them a general legislative mandate that might more properly have been exercised by, or at least shared with, other official international law-making agencies, in other official international law-making arenas, through other specialised law-making techniques and processes.

For the dispassionate scientific-legal observer, the really interesting legal questions, in this particular context, must be as to the extent to which the patent, continuing difficulties of the Third U.N. Conference have gone to issues of a relatively temporary or casual nature, involving discernible, avoidable faults in the conference planning and preparations and organisation; and as to the extent to which, by contrast, these difficulties have gone to philosophical or policy conflicts inherent in the subject matter of the Third U.N. Conference and going to the burden of balancing and reconciling the conflicting national interests involved.

1. Procedural (Adjectival) Law Problems of the Third U.N. Conference

On the first point, the planning and preparation and organisation of the Third Law of the Sea Conference, comparison with earlier international codifying efforts in the same general field is instructive. The First U.N. Conference on the Law of the Sea, meeting in Geneva in 1958, gave rise to four separate though inter-related multilateral conventions, all of which received the stipulated number of ratifications and so became law within eight years of the completion of the 1958 Geneva sessions. The second U.N. Conference on the Law of the Sea, held at Geneva in 1960, was concerned, in essence, to settle important unfinished business from the 1958 Conference, mainly the breadth of the territorial sea and fishery limits. The 1960 Conference did in fact secure majority votes for two proposals; but these votes failed to become law, the more important proposal, seeking to establish the breadth of the territorial sea, falling short by only one vote of the required two-thirds majority.

One important procedural or organisational difference between the First U.N. Conference in 1958, and the Second Conference in 1960, a difference which applies also, but in far greater degree, to the unfinished Third Conference in its 1974 and 1975 sessions at least, is that the 1958 Conference followed the by that time long-established, "classical" route to legal codification of beginning the formal conference with an agreed, basic text of draft articles formulated by some expert committee or commission capable of claiming authoritative status in its own right, this agreed, basic text forming the principal agenda of debate and discussion at the conference itself. The 1958 Conference was able to begin, in this way, with a set of 73 draft articles resulting from seven years of detailed work in the International Law Commission; and the influence of the scientific-legal expertise of the I.L.C., resulting from the high intellectual prestige and quite evident consummate technical drafting skills of its members, is all too apparent in the final texts of the four Conventions adopted by the 1958 Conference.[3] By contrast, in the interim period between the 1958 Conference and the 1960 Conference, the advice of the I.L.C. was not availed of – perhaps could not be, in view of the time factor. In the event, the I.L.C. had no specific proposals on the several major questions carried over to the resumed discussions. There was therefore no basic, expert text before the 1960 Conference, but only different proposals submitted by different governments.

In the case of the Third Conference in its 1974 and 1975 sessions even though the range of subjects to be canvassed was essentially as broad or broader as in 1958, there was no basic text but only a mass of disparate materials prepared by various working groups and delegations, these materials being highlighted by a six-volume report from a U.N. Committee – the Committee on the Peaceful Uses of the Sea-Bed and the Ocean Floor beyond the Limits of National Jurisdiction. This latter collection, so far from adhering to the I.L.C. and general "classical" drafting formula of presenting a single draft text as a basis for debate and discussion, adopted the novel drafting variant of attempting to overcome the major disagreements that patently existed on so many points by presenting the alternative, often conflicting proposals side by side, – hundreds of these in all. The problem was compounded not merely by having a profusion of different texts on the same subject, but also by the sheer quantity of materials involved, this condition being itself a product, in some part, of the marked increase in the numbers of governments participating in the Third Conference in comparison to the First Conference in 1958 – an arithmetic progression, in the case of the number of participating countries, from 86 to 148, with the added handicap that the new arrivals were not always the best prepared nor the most succinct and relevant in their contributions to the Conference debates.

There were, then, very evident problems in the operational procedures of the Third U.N. Conference on the Law of Sea in the 1974 and 1975 sessions: the failure to begin with one agreed expert text; the failure, all the more remarkable because of this omission, to make sure that the drafting committee actually appointed by the Conference would be fully representative of all the major states, and politically and intellectually authoritative in terms of its membership, and armed with effective powers to guide and develop Conference thinking;[4] and the failure, also, to achieve general satisfaction as to voting principles, going beyond the Gentleman's Agreement as to the need to exhaust the "consensus" process in the first instance,[5] which could ensure that a conference charged with developing a codifying treaty as its end product really would produce new rules capable of achieving general acceptance and not simply another exercise in a "soft law".[6] These were, of course, self-inflicted wounds which undoubtedly rendered more difficult the tasks of the Third U.N. Conference and contributed, in measure, to its eventual inability to produce agreement at either its 1974 or 1974 extended sessions.

2. International Legal Codification *versus* International Law-making

It is impossible to avoid the conclusion, however, that even with the best of procedural rules, profiting from the years of accumulated technical experience of the old League of Nations and of the United Nations itself with legal codifying conferences, the Third U.N. Conference on the Law of the Sea would still have had enormous political difficulties in overcoming the important substantive differences among the 148 participating countries that were inherent in the subject matter forming the official Agenda of the Conference. This raises, then, the further fundamental question whether the term Conference on the Law of the Sea was not in itself a misnomer, – no doubt an uninternational one but having, still, important practical consequences for the arriving at agreed new international rules to govern the *régime* of the Seas, the Sea-Bed, and marine resources generally. For legal codification, however much we recognise that it is no mere mechanical collecting and restating of pre-existing legal rules, but that it involves a creative element in which new legal principles are formulated and interpolated in the interstices of the old, is still a limited, technical operation involving certain canons of personal self-restraint on the part of the drafters involved. A mandate for legal codification is certainly not a licence, in itself, for a general exercise in law-making that acknowledges no political constraints in terms of past legal doctrine. The general, law-making conference that is not limited, in terms, to legal codification but that has a positive mandate to construct and elaborate new law, has its place, of course. But its *rôles* and missions are fundamentally different from those of the legal codifying conference, as such; otherwise the term legal codification would no longer have a precise connotation.[7]

What we are saying is that once the limits of the four multilateral Conventions produced by the 1958 U.N. Conference on the Law of the Sea are transcended, we are into issues of sheer political choice, and not the codification or restatement, however creatively, of existing legal doctrine. By this token, the 1960 Conference on the Law of the Sea could certainly, as a technical matter, have codified the existing international law as to the width of the territorial sea. As a technical, scientific-legal matter, that would have been easy indeed to do in 1960. The delegates to the 1960 Conference, however, – or at least a minority among them sufficient to impede the achievement of a two-thirds majority, simply did not like the existing customary international law rule and chose to block or impede all attempts to codify that rule in permanent statutory (treaty) form. The problem, then, in 1960, was a political one, and not a legal one. It is impossible to avoid the conclusion that the problem in the 1970s, once again, is not in finding and concretising the existing rules of the Law of the Sea, but in mobilising a sufficiency of political support and political enthusiasm behind those already existing rules of the Law of the Sea. In the absence of a legally effective consensus as to new international law rules in place of the old, the old rules, on normal principles of legal interpretation, remain in force and subject, as such, to progressive, generic extension through individual initiatives on the part of individual States or through bilateral or limited, "regional" treaties, in ways not in themselves incompatible with existing general international law.

Instead of Law of the Sea, then, as the official Agenda for the Third Conference, one might have spoken, more properly, of *régime* of the Sea or something similar,[8] thus taking away any claimed vicarious legal prestige otherwise attaching to an avowedly political act of attempting to remake the old law altogether in the image of a new political majority in the World Community.

3. The Substantive Dilemmas of the Third U.N. Conference: the "Old" Law of the Sea

Let us examine, now, the main conflicting interests present in that recently renewed political exercise entrusted to the Third U.N. Conference on the Law of the Sea.

The existing (or old) Law of the Sea is the product essentially of long-observed practice and user of States, concretised over more than three centuries into the rules of customary international law[9] and codified, in quite substantial measure, in the four Geneva Conventions of 1958. The existing Law of the Sea undoubtedly reflects, so far as it is, in itself, customary international law or at least a codification of that customary law, the interests and aspirations of the politically dominant States throughout that same time period. These were the States formed on the rise of commerce and thriving on the development of international trade and intercourse without unnecessary fetters and restrictions stemming from archaic rules and prescriptions. In contrast to the *mare clausum* of the earlier period of Papally-sanctioned Spanish-Portuguese imperial maritime hegemony, the Grotius-derived *mare liberum* of the post-Treaty of Westphalia emergent Nation-States was moved by no narrow spirit of national particularism or accompanying selfish desires to lock up the sea and its resources into a series of closed national compartments. Instead, the "modern" (post-Treaty of Westphalia) World of the emergent Nation-State developed, to an extent that, in the retrospective glance of history, can only be described as surprising, a sense of mutuality and reciprocity of interest on the part of all the then active participants in the World Community, involving the maximising of the interests of all States and the necessary cutting down, in consequence, of overly particularistic, special claims and assertions of individual States. In the full spirit of the phrase used, in a quite contemporary context, by the U.N. General Assembly as the postulated objective of a new *régime* of the Seas, the Sea-Bed, and marine resources generally, the post-Westphalia new Nation-States, in opting so resolutely for a *mare liberum*, accepted the Seas and marine resources generally as being, indeed, the "common heritage of all Mankind".

4. Contemporary Challenges to *Mare Liberum*

The phenomenon of our own times is that, after some more than three centuries of *mare liberum*, we are now seeing the emergence of a new species of *mare clausum*, not merely through uninhibited national claims as put forward in international arenas like the U.N. Law of the Sea Conferences, but also through concrete State practice as asserted through unilateral State actions trenching upon the classical freedom of the Seas and the free availability of its resources to all comers [10] – such unilateral State actions being either ineffectively protested by other States or else protested not at all since those other States are looking, in their turn, to their own possibilities as to unilateral State actions are directed to what, *quo*. Sometimes these unilateral action in a sort of general *quid pro* on objective examination, would seem to be protection of genuinely comprehensive World Community interests – to protection of the natural environment or of increasingly scarce natural resources against abuses of the classical freedoms of the Sea on the part of one or more other Nation-States whose own activities would certainly qualify, under internal, municipal law principles, as examples or case studies in *abus de droit* and so be subject to social control through law. Examples of this category of national self-help might be individual, Nation-State action of a preventive or control nature, in default of effective international or multi-State action, against marine pollution or damage to the shore-line and environment of the littoral State; or individual Nation-State action directed to protection of recognised national fishing grounds, outside national territorial waters as classically defined, against depletion or exhaustion by reckless over-fishing on the part of other States.

A further category of unilateral State action might prove, on examination, to be mixed in character: partly in furtherance of genuinely comprehensive World Community interests in default of effective World Community action, and partly designed to advance national special interests. A final category of unilateral State actions, going beyond the ambit of classical international law rules and principles, – and, regrettably, this latter category seems all too prevalent today – would be the pursuit of narrow national interests, usually of an economic character, at the expense of all other members of the World Community, and this under the guise of protection and furtherance of World Community interests: proclamation of vast so-called pollution control zones in the High Seas, going well beyond the necessities of any immediately foreseeable cases; declaration of extensive fishing monopoly zones, again extending far out into the High Seas as classically defined; the attempt to control innocent passage through traditionally recognised international straits and waterways, through the devices of extending the national territorial sea or of development of novel theories – the so-called Archipelago doctrine, for example – that by no stretch of the imagination can be regarded as analogical extensions of existing, classical International Law doctrine, and therefore as being legitimate exercises in international law-making in the absence of firm international treaties that can achieve general acceptance.

5. The Non-*rôle* of the Super-powers in Developing a new *Régime* of the Sea

Part of the blame for the anarchy of individual national claims and pretensions, trenching upon classical International Law-based doctrines of *mare liberum*, must lie, perhaps, with the super-powers. Recognizing the constructive leadership supplied by the Soviet Union and the United States, – acting jointly and cooperatively, in the era of Coexistence and of the *détente* that that subsequently gave way to, – in leading the way to the achievement and concretisation of new norms and rules of International Law in such areas as the banning of atmospheric nuclear tests, the control of nuclear proliferation, the demilitarisation of the Moon and of Outer Space generally and its safeguarding against claims of national sovereignty,[11] one is entitled to ask nevertheless why the two bloc leaders of yesterday, granted the existence of so many evident points of agreement and harmony between them as to present and future development of the Law of the Sea, the Sea-Bed, and marine resources generally, could not have devised between them a model treaty or treaties in this area, proceeding on the same principles of mutuality and reciprocity of interest that had characterised their long and patient negotiations in the area of Disarmament, and then have opened up such model treaty or treaties to general signature and ratification by other, lesser or secondary powers, just as they had done so successfully in the case of the general disarmament treaties. The answer must be that two super-powers perhaps gave too much priority to their own special (bipolar) peace-keeping interests, forgetting that with the achievement of Coexistence and of big-power *détente* generally, any treaties in this area would tend to be largely historical legal footnotes to substantive accords already reached in other, political (non-legal) arenas. When the two super-powers finally turned around to the *régime* of the Seas, it was, one might suggest, already too late. The demands of the economically underprivileged and technologically still under-developed countries for acceptance of their claims for a special national economic zone beyond the limits of the territorial sea as customarily defined and established to date, were greeted perhaps too diffidently, and certainly too dilatorily, by the super-powers. All these claims for a special national economic zone have now been happily absorbed by the Chinese Communist Government and integrated, with wit and also some literary elegance, into its campaign against the two super-powers' more traditionally-based positions on the Law of the Sea. What the Chinese now call the "Soviet Revisionist principle of the Freedom of the Seas" is linked by the Chinese to what they style as a joint Soviet-U.S. claim to a "super-powers' Maritime Hegemonism." The lesson of the Sibylline books is to accept the possible when it is still timely – a lesson which Sir Gerald Fitzmaurice drives home in regard to the ultimate failure of the 1958 Law of the Sea Conference to stabilize the breadth of the territorial sea where relatively modest limits, not incompatible with or going significantly beyond the classical International Law rules, were still capable of being successfully maintained and concretised in permanent, multilateral treaty form. [12]

6. The Main Political Conflicts of the Third U.N. Conference

(a) *The Four Geneva Conventions of 1958*

The starting point for identification and analysis of the main areas of political conflict at the Third U.N. Conference of the Law of the Sea must lie in a consideration of the four multilateral Conventions adopted at the First U.N. Conference held in Geneva in 1958:

- the Convention of the Territorial Sea and the Contiguous Zone (in force, September 10, 1964);
- the Convention on the High Seas (in force, September 30, 1962);
- the Convention on Fishing and Conservation of the Living Resources of the High Seas (in force, March 20, 1966);
- the Convention on the Continental Shelf (in force, June 10, 1964).

While the principle of the freedom of the High Seas, defined, by way of extensity, in the 1958 Convention on the High Seas, (Article 2), to comprise:
- freedom of navigation;
- freedom of fishing;
- freedom to lay submarine cables and pipelines;
- freedom to fly over the High Seas;

is basic to the concept of *mare liberum*, it has historically always included a special exception in favour of the Territorial Sea which, up to the time of the 1958, First U.N. Conference, was always considered to be, (with only some minor, historically-sanctioned variations in favour of individual Nation-States), three marine miles from the low-water line along the coast. The chance, at the 1958 Geneva Conference, formally to codify the *three*-mile limit to the Territorial Sea in Treaty form, was missed for political reasons; and the resultant opportunity to compromise politically on a *six*-mile or even a *twelve*-mile limit as a still reasonable balance between the traditional, *mare liberum* position, and the emerging, economic particularism-based claims of various Nation-States, was also lost, though lost by the narrowest of margins. The 1958 Convention on the Territorial Sea and the Contiguous Zone reflects, in terms, this political impasse for, while predicated upon the existence of the principle of a Territorial Sea, it nowhere defines the limits of that Sea. The issue of defining the width of the Territorial Sea remained, therefore, one of the prime responsibilities of the Third U.N. Conference on the Law of the Sea, and the special charge of its Committee II which was concerned with the limits of national jurisdiction.

(b) *The Territorial Sea and its Limits, and the "Patrimonial Sea"*

The difference between the political climate of the First and Second U.N. Conferences on the Law of the Sea on the one hand, and of the Third Conference, was that by the mid-1970s modest political compromises related more or less to the traditional *three*-mile limit were hardly possible any longer, in view of the plethora of special national claims, trenching upon the erstwhile freedoms of the High Seas, that had developed over the intervening decade and a half. By far the more important of these infringements on the classical freedoms of the High Seas related to the development and expansion of the concept of the Contiguous Zone, which, as late as the 1920s, was no more than a limited, embryonic notion of a special area, immediately beyond the *three*-mile Territorial Sea, in which police and customs-revenue control measures could be applied by the littoral State. In the 1958 Convention on the Territorial Sea and Contiguous Zone, it is expressly stipulated (Article 24(2)) that the Contiguous Zone may not extend beyond twelve miles from the baseline from which the breadth of the Territorial Sea is measured (that is, the low-water line along the coast). By the late 1970s, a considerable number of States, and especially those combining the twin elements of having extensive fishing and marine resources located close to their coast-lines and of having, usually, few or else very limited other natural resources, had already asserted extensive claims to national sovereignty over coastal waters and their marine resources, going well beyond the traditional *three*-mile Territorial Sea or even a *six*-mile or *twelve*-mile Sea and often extending as far out as 200 miles from the low-water line along the coast. Though some support for such unilateral extensions of sovereignty, in the case, especially, of "one-crop" countries, could perhaps be derived from international institutions as respectable and presumably (at that time) as politically detached as the World Court, [13] these newer claims obviously ran into direct conflict with the interests of the great maritime trading States having or using merchant shipping fleets; with those of the two super-powers (the Soviet Union and the United States) with their large naval fleets; and, indeed, with those of the few, unfortunate states having no identifiable marine of related resources located close to their coasts and therefore having nothing much to trade off or bargain against any carving up of the coastal waters and their resources. These latter States, for the most part, leaned firmly to the traditional rules of a *three*-mile or at least limited Territorial Sea, with, at the most, restricted police control authority extending immediately beyond the Territorial Sea. Where any, even modest extension of the Territorial Sea would result in straits that once were clearly international straits, and subject, as such, to the right of innocent passage by ships of all countries, falling under national jurisdiction, the great maritime states also pressed firmly for the maintenance and preservation of the historically "international" character of such waterways; and, equally, they resisted the claimed Archipelago doctrine under which all the waters between island groupings forming part of one national territory are national in character and fall under national sovereignty and control, (Indonesia, the Philippines, for example). It is suggested that, with respect to straits and archipelagos, a new political compromise that would guarantee the right of innocent passage or freedom of navigation through designated sea-lanes, might eventually reconcile the conflicting interests in this area; just as the idea of a *twelve*-mile Territorial Sea plus a 200-mile "economic" zone (the so-called *patrimonial sea*) [14] in which the coastal state would have exclusive fishing rights, is being advanced as a reasonable basis for contemporary novation or re-writing of the classical International Law-based *three*-mile Territorial Sea concept.

Quite obviously, the palatability and political acceptability of postulated compromise proposals such as these to established states, and particularly to the two super-powers, who tend to find that the existing, classical International Law rules correspond very well to their own national self-interest and to the political accommodations inevitably made within their own national political community to produce the external consensus reflected in their own national foreign policy at any time – for example, the practical compromise evidently made within both the Soviet Union and the United States' internal politics between national fishing interests and national defence interests – will be augmented by the political trade-offs that the contemporary extreme nationalist proponents of *mare clausum* are able to offer in other, cognate areas – the Continental Shelf, for example, and the development of the economic resources of the Sea-Bed and the Ocean Floor.

(c) *The Continental Shelf, the Sea-Bed and the Ocean-Floor, and their Resources*

The 1958 Convention on the Continental Shelf, responding to the rapid development of assertedly customary international law-based claims to an exclusive national right to exploit the mineral resources of the Continental Shelf beyond the national Territorial Sea, stemming from President Truman's Proclamation of 1945, [15] formally recorded and codified the sovereign rights of the coastal state to explore and exploit the natural resources of the Continental Shelf. The Continental Shelf itself was defined in the 1958 Convention, disjunctively, as referring:

to the sea-bed and subsoil of the submarine areas adjacent to the coast but outside the area of the territorial sea, to a depth of 200 metres or,

beyond that limit, to where the depth of the superjacent waters admits of the exploitation of the natural resources of the said areas.

The first part of the 1958 definition clearly provides firm and objectively verifiable criteria for legally limiting the political assertion of national claims. The second part of the definition, however, while it may have seemed to establish finite limits when first established in 1958, based on mining engineering knowledge of the time, has clearly been outstripped by rapidly developing science and technology which has made of its *exploitability* criterion a constantly and progressively expanding standard licensing an ever-expanding national development and utilisation of the economic and mineral resources of the Sea-Bed. While, of course, the connotation of the term Continental Shelf does not include the Ocean Floor beyond the Continental Shelf itself, no part of the Continental Shelf would be potentially excluded from national exploitation: the technological capacity of the state outside whose Territorial Sea the Continental Shelf extends alone defines and determines the spatial limits to the exercise of its sovereign rights over the Continental Shelf.[16] This is clear, as a matter of legal logic, on the strict interpretation of the terms of the 1958 Convention, and so no question can arise of any political barter or exchange of those rights as payment for a recognition of current nationalist pretensions – for, legally, that is what they are, unless and until they receive general recognition in Treaty or other form – to the patrimonial sea.

On the other hand, the legal situation of the Ocean Floor, beyond the limits of the Continental Shelf, is not so clear. It is not dealt with, in terms, in the 1958 Convention on the Continental Shelf; and it may be argued, on this basis, that since that Convention concedes to the coastal state sovereign rights of exploitation over the natural resources of the Continental Shelf, it must, by implication, deny any rights beyond the Continental Shelf's limits. On the other hand, the more normal interpretation would seem to be that, in the absence of a Treaty rule, the pre-existing customary international law rules govern, and so the Ocean Floor is open to all comers, on an equal basis, in terms of legal capacity to explore it and to develop and exploit its natural resources. It would be, of course, a formal, juridical equality only, since, quite obviously, only a handful of technologically most advanced, post-industrial States are in any position, in the foreseeable future, to take up an option to explore and usefully develop the Ocean Floor beyond the limits of the Continental Shelf.

It is this fact, perhaps more than any other, which both explains the political intransigence of certain Third World countries and especially the leaders of the so-called Group of 77, and also gives a certain air of unreality to their contributions to the debates in the Committee in the Third U.N. Conference on the Law of the Sea specially charged with examining the status of the Sea-Bed beyond national jurisdiction. Certainly U.N. General Assembly Resolution 2749 (XXV), adopted in December, 1970, – the Declaration of Principles Governing the Sea-Bed and the Ocean Floor, and the Subsoil Thereof, Beyond the Limits of National Jurisdiction – postulates that the resources of these areas are the "common heritage of mankind"; and U.N. General Assembly Resolution 2574 (XXIV), adopted in the previous year – the so-called Moratorium Resolution – purports to put these areas and their resources beyond the pale of national jurisdiction – "pending the establishment of an international *régime* in the area". These are brave assertions, of course, but they suffer from the political limitation inherent in all U.N. General Assembly Resolutions, especially since the marked increase in U.N. membership with the accession of Third World countries: they are not generally or certainly universally accepted as authoritative, binding sources of International Law except so far as they may have been affirmatively and independently accepted by all main states or all main legal systems. [17] In the absence of any authoritative new rule in this area, the major post-industrial States, which alone have the technological capacity to develop and exploit the resources of the Ocean Floor in the foreseeable future, will no doubt see fit to exercise their existing legal right, as they see it, of going ahead in accord with the capabilities and also the demands of their national technologies. When the Group of 77 contend, therefore, for an International Sea-Bed Authority that alone shall have plenary powers to control and direct Sea-Bed and Ocean-Floor activities, there is a certain element of "baying at the moon" involved in the argumentation: the proposed International Sea-Bed Authority will need the active aid and encouragement of the technologically-advanced States if it is ever to become effective, and it can obviously have no sanctions, in and of itself, to inhibit and restrain those technologically-developed countries from going ahead of their own accord with their own national plans for exploitation of the Ocean-Floor's resources. The obvious political compromise solution is one that preserves the principle of an international authority; but that would make its function a regulatory one, rather than seeking to impose direct administration and control. The basis for political give-and-take is there, of course, assuming only a certain degree of rationality and common-sense: the technologically-developed States, for example, after their own experiences with the Energy crisis and the raise in Oil prices of recent years, can see merits in the coordination of even their own plans for development of the Ocean Floor resources, in terms of the economic implications of Sea-Bed mineral production upon production from land-based mineral sources and upon the World pricing system generally. By and large, however, the technologically-advanced States would seem to have much to gain by conceding, quite readily, the principle of an international control authority in return for a more conscious modesty, on the part of the less developed countries, in their pretensions as to nationalist extensions of the Territorial Sea and the so-called patrimonial sea.

(d) *Preservation of the Marine Environment*

A third Committee of the Third U.N. Conference has been concerned with issues of the preservation of the marine environment and related questions of scientific research. While the arguments for a broad control authority (including preventive or anticipatory control) on the part of the coastal State, in zones adjacent to its coast,[18] are clear, it must be recognised that the balance of the conflicting World Community interests in this area which, not so long ago, largely favoured ecological interests has tilted a little in the other direction under the impact of the recent World Energy crisis. Yet as to no other aspect of the Third U.N. Conference's official Agenda does the congruence of the interests of the different nation-State participants seem more clear; so that here, at least, the problems seem secondary problems of an essentially lower-level, technical character that can safely be left to the professional negotiators without the need for the same dramatic political interventions directed towards effectuating ultimate political compromises that we can see, for example, in regard to the issues of the limits of the Territorial Sea, the existence of the so-called patrimonial sea, and the utilisation of the resources of the Sea-Bed and Ocean-Floor beyond national jurisdiction. The common interest of mankind in the protection of the natural environment is at least far more self-evident than the postulated common interests in other areas; and so consensus on new principles of International Law here, or even on the imaginative restatement (codification) of the "old" principles should not be too difficult, and need not necessarily wait upon political agreement upon new principles to govern the other areas to which we have referred.

7. Aftermath to the Caracas, 1974, and Geneva, 1975, Sessions of the Third U.N. Conference on the Law of the Sea

In the absence of firm new international Treaty rules that can achieve at least fairly general, if not universal, acceptance by States, the older, classical, customary International Law rules remain, as we have said, in force; and, as such, these older, classical, customary International Law rules are also capable of progressive, generic extension, in ways not incompatible with general International Law, so as to meet new problem-situations – for example, the radical new possibilities thrown up by rapidly developing science and technology.[19] In a World Community where the smaller states or the developing countries, if they are resolute and remain united, may block achievement of new codifying Treaties that will preserve the essence of *mare liberum* against too many intransigent national demands for *mare clausum*, it may be a salutary reminder to consider that, on the basis of existing, classical International Law rules and their analogical extension on traditional law-making bases, the technologically-advanced States, whether Western or Soviet (Communist), can probably lay claim to sufficient legal authority to go ahead of their own accord with plans for the development and utilisation of the economic resources of the Continental Shelf and the Sea-Bed and Ocean-Floor; and they might also be able to claim sufficient legal authority to resist any closing off of erstwhile international straits and other international waterways to the innocent passage of vessels of their own and other States. To say this is not, of course, to predict that the technologically-advanced States would ever opt politically so to act, eschewing the patient skills of compromise normally applied to the attempt to achieve any major international law-making, multilateral convention. But so far as it can be said that for some, at least, of the States participating in the Third U.N. Law of the Sea Conference, their objectives transcend the limits of legal codification as that term is normally strictly understood, it should be recognised frankly and openly that the sessions held in 1974, 1975, 1976, 1977, and 1978 – first at Caracas, then at Geneva, then at New York, and finally in Geneva once more –

amount to a high political exercise in the making of "new" international law, that is at best only secondarily a venture in legal codification; and that the international lawyer's specialised drafting talents are necessarily ancillary, in such an exercise, to the more overtly political skills of diplomatic negotiation, barter and exchange. For the international lawyer, on this view, great open-ended international gatherings like the Third U.N. Law of the Sea Conference, call for the exercise of a certain degree of intellectual modesty and prudent professional self-restraint, and also for a recognition of the limitations of one's own highly specialised legal training and legal expertise in coming up with political panaceas that are far better achieved, if they are to be achieved at all, by more overtly and avowedly political methods; and very often achieved by, – in Max Weber's phrase, – political *honoratiores* (professional Foreign Office diplomats and the like) rather than by jurists as such.

The original, 117-page, so-called "Informal Single Negotiating Text", with its many separate sections relating to fisheries, navigation, sovereignty, pollution, and off-shore resources, which was produced by the 1975, Geneva session of the Third Law of the Sea Conference[20], certainly by no stretch of the imagination corresponded to that agreed, basic legal text and draft legal articles which were supplied by the expert International Law Commission to the 1958 Geneva Law of the Sea Conference and which so facilitated a successful conclusion to the 1958 Conference. But this "Informal Single Negotiating Text", which was expressly stipulated by the President of the Conference as being "informal in character ... not prejudic[ing] the position of any delegation ... serv[ing] as a procedural device and only provid[ing] a basis for negotiation"[21], and the subsequent "Informal Composite Negotiating Text"[22], did constitute something of a political reprieve for the Third Law of the Sea Conference, giving its delegates now an extension of mandate so as to try to develop a genuinely inclusive *régime* of the Sea that will deny or restrict current excessively particularistic national claims, whether on the part of the two super-powers or of the developing countries, and at the same time open up the Sea and its resources to the new international Science and Technology on a basis that will provide the widest possible World Community participation in and sharing of its riches.

8. Conclusions. Codifying the Law of the Sea, or Making the New International Economic Development Law?

Plus ça change, plus c'est la même chose! The problems caused by the number of participating countries – hardly avoidable in a conference held under U.N. auspices where the invitations must necessarily be extended to all U.N. member countries – were compounded, at the Third Law of the Sea Conference, once again, by the sheer size of national delegations and observer groups and by the frequent absence of a sense of self-restraint or of a feeling of economy in other people's time, on the part of national orators mounting the conference platform. One may wonder again whether the original definition or popular conception of the Conference's sphere of responsibility as being the codification of the Law of the Sea, with the correlative emphasis that that necessarily brought upon legal codification techniques and legal codification processes and specialist legal codification expertise as the solvent for the international problems involved, was not misplaced. For the problems at the Third Law of the Sea Conference, over the years, have not been legal codification problems *stricto sensu*, but political ones. There have never been any particular difficulties in defining the existing positive law rules, such as they are, and even establishing the limits of analogical extension of these rules possible under the ordinary rules of construction accepted by most legal systems. The difficulty has been that while some countries have a vested interest in the maintenance of the legal *status quo* in this area, very many other countries have every reason in the World for concluding, politically, that they should reject the existing positive law as unfair or inimical to their own national self-interest, as they themselves would choose to define that. The Third Law of the Sea Conference, in fact, has not been able, – any more than other major international arenas, U.N. or other, – to escape the general pressures of the World Revolution of our times, – political-ideological and technological.[23] The process of political Decolonisation, in its original connotation of the break-up of the old European colonial Empires overseas and the entry of the old colonial territories into self-government and independence, may be now essentially consummated; but the post-Colonial, succession States are insisting on applying the principle of Decolonisation to achieve new economic objectives, including, here, the rewriting of the classical *régime* of the Sea which they see as the product, essentially, of a narrow political consensus of those dominant Western societies that were founded upon the rise of Commerce, and as reflecting the special economic interests of those Western societies.

The Third Law of the Sea Conference, on this view, so far from being a conventional exercise in legal codification or legal restatement – in this case, restatement of the classical, positive law of the Law of the Sea, – has been transformed for very many, if not most of its participants into an exercise in law-making and in the creation of economic law – of the new economic development law.

For some purposes, therefore, the Third Law of the Sea Conference has involved, over its eight years of still unfulfilled or unachieved labours, two different groups of states operating in two different universes of legal discourse. Would it have been better – in the sense of allowing for franker discussion right from the outset and of facilitating the political give-and-take and those realistic, non-moralistic compromises necessary to achieve final agreement, – if the polite fiction of a conventional exercise in legal codification had been eschewed altogether and national delegations widened accordingly so as to give prime emphasis to economists, engineers, marine biologists, and, not least, professional, non-legal, Foreign Ministry negotiators?

The threat of unilateral action based on one's own national self-interest alone, – particularly on the part of technologically advanced countries in a position to match their words with their actions, – hung over the 1978 resumed, Geneva, session, in the absence of any new, comprehensive and general, international consensus in place of the old. The statement by the Representative of the United States, on July 20, 1977, at the close of the then resumed New York sessions of the Third Law of the Sea Conference, while conceding that the latest "Informal Composite Negotiating Text" evidenced – "real progress on vital issues relating to international security and freedom of navigation", nevertheless charged that that Text – "substantially set back prospects for agreement on an international *régime* for the conduct of seabed mining." The U.S. Representative concluded that the substance of the Text on this latter issue, and also the – "lack of fair and open processes in its final preparation require me to recommend that the United States undertake a most serious and searching review of both the substance and procedures of the Conference." [24]

This U.S. Statement, it may be suggested, highlights the central problem of the whole Third Law of the Sea Conference exercise, without however offering any real solution for it, short of the implied suggestion of a U.S. [25] or general Big Power walk-out and subsequent unilateral or bilateral-style follow-up action. On the other hand, time-honoured legal stratagems for veiling over aborted attempts at legal codification – namely, the copious recourse to diplomatic vagueness or vacuousness and to purely open-ended definitions, in any general text that might be agreed upon; or else the abandonment of the search for one general text in favour of a series of little agreements on disparate subjects[26] seem only with difficulty available as a mode of diplomatic bridge-building, granted the wide divergence of basic national interests on so many fundamental issues,[27] and also the incapacity of the two super-powers to impose their own special Big Power consensus as to the *régime* of the Sea and its appropriate ordering upon other states,[28] even assuming, of course that the two Big Powers' interests were coterminous as to all points.[29]

Chapter VII

ALTERNATIVE LAW-MAKING MODES. THE GENERAL ASSEMBLY RESOLUTION: DECLARATORY, PROGRAMMATIC LAW AND THE NEW INTERNATIONAL ECONOMIC ORDER

1. Political Origins of the "New" International Law

The claims advanced in behalf of a New International Economic Order and for the corresponding changes in the basic structure of International Law that such a postulated new Order is thought to imply, have been declared, in programmatic form, in two Resolutions adopted, without vote, by the United Nations General Assembly, at its Sixth Special Session, on May 1, 1974 – the *Declaration on the Establishment of a New International Economic Order,*[1] and the so-called *Programme of Action on the establishment of a New International Economic Order*[2] ; and in the further, *Charter of Economic Rights and Duties of States,*[3] adopted by the General Assembly, at its 29th regular Session, on December 12, 1974, this time by a recorded vote of 120 to 6, with 10 abstentions.[4]

The emergence of the campaign for a New International Economic Order,[5] and the quest for its legitimation, in verbal form, in the various General Assembly Resolutions referred to, are the consequence of the widespread though often quite disparate changes occuring in the World Community in recent years. First of these great shifts in the World Community is the decline of the old bipolar system of World Public Order, based upon the balance or equilibrium of political and military forces as between the two old political-military blocs – Soviet and Western[6] – that had dominated the World Community since the end of World War II. To be sure, the signs of decay and disintegration of the old monolithic solidarity within each of the blocs had been apparent for some time before, increasing in measure as the *détente* between the two bloc leaders, the Soviet Union and the United States, was progressively attained and inter-bloc tensions correspondingly relieved. At its moment of greatest strength or *apogée*, indeed, symbolised by the Nixon-Brezhnev Summit Meeting and Summit accords in Moscow in 1972, the Bipolar model of World Public Order, posited as its continuance was upon maintenance of external compatibility of the two blocs' interests and upon internal identity or cohesion of interests of each bloc as a condition of that, began to be challenged and threatened by the fissiparous tendencies within each bloc. These had heretofore been able to be kept in check by the imperatives of maintaining a common political front during the era of Cold War conflicts. Though certain alternative models or constructs for World Public Order had been developed by Western leaders in anticipation of the demise of Bipolarity and the emergence of a more pluralistic order system in the post-Cold War era – President Kennedy's own favoured Northern Hemispheric Trading Community and a more recent pentagonal power elaboration based on the United States, the European Communities, Japan, the Soviet Union and Communist China – none of these had succeeded in becoming operational. For the necessary network of political and economic inter-relations and reciprocal interdependence from the military-strategic viewpoint had just not been created.

At the same time that East-West *détente* was being officially recorded and proclaimed at the 1972 Summit Meetings, the two bloc leaders seemed to arrive at accommodation and understanding as to the remaining unsettled issues between them, and here, specifically, the still unsettled Middle Eastern situation for which the Big Power formula appeared now very clearly to be jelling of the political-military *status quo* in a more or less permanent "no Peace-no War" situation. The Arab states, seeing no positive help emerging from their erstwhile Soviet friend and sponsor and conceiving the United States as being too firmly committed to Israeli state interests concluded that they should settle Palestinian self-determination claims and their own frontier rectification demands by their own direct action, and resolved thereupon to use the oil weapon both to impel American concessions by way of pressure on the Israeli Government and also to enforce European and Japanese neutrality in the resultant tug-of-war.

The specially-favoured position of the oil producing and exporting countries, among which the Arab countries were dominant, and as cartelised now in OPEC, enabled the Arab countries to maximise their pressures for political solutions in the Middle East. But at the same time the World Energy crisis gave a dominant *rôle* to the OPEC countries in their more general, economic personality, and enabled them to move boldly to assert their own new political-economic power in relation to the two old political-military blocs that had effectively controlled international relations in the post-War era. They suggested a new *economic* base for World Public Order for the future in place of the older military-strategic base that had characterised several decades dominated by the threat of nuclear war between the Soviet Union and the United States.

The imminent end of political decolonisation on a World-wide scale, with the pending departure of Portugal from Africa and Spain from the Western Sahara, and the to-be-expected succeeding collapse of White minority government in Rhodesia and withdrawal of White minority rule of South-West Africa (Namibia), brought a shift of emphasis from political colonialism to economic colonialism, and a new stress on giving newly independent, decolonised countries national control of their own primary products and natural resources and a unilateral licence to dispense themselves from deemed irksome legal obligations as to economic resources that had been worked out in earlier years with foreign governments or foreign or multilateral corporations.

The progressive transformation of the United Nations organisation, beginning with the 1955 "package deal" admission of a flood of new member-countries, from a Western-dominated to a more neutral (in Cold War terms) and finally to a Third World-dominated arena, as the mass numbers of the newly independent, decolonised countries were brought to bear in the General Assembly, created a new political majority coalition in the World Community with a keen awareness of the possibilities of using the General Assembly as a positive instrument for re-writing the "old" or classical International Law and substituting a "new", postulated more progressive, Third World-oriented, International Law in its place.[7]

2. The Political Composition of the New Third World Majority

The Third World is sometimes thought to be, in the United Nations, a wholly monolithic bloc. It is, in fact, a politically diverse, pluralistic association of a number of different groups of states that originated for different historical reasons and whose members came together for certain temporary, specific purposes which have, however, ripened into some more continuing alliance as much through the errors of judgment of their adversaries as for any lasting identity of interest for all problems. The political diversity of the Third World extends not merely to issues of race, religion, language, and culture, and the relative antiquity or newness of the civilisation concerned, but also to basic questions of wealth and geographical dimension, and political and economic ideology. Some Third World states have democratic governments, some have authoritarian governments. Some apply free enterprise and some collectivist or socialist principles of economic organisation. The key historically-based distinction within the current Third World majority is that between the so-called Non-Aligned Countries which originally developed as an Afro-Asian neutralist group trying to establish political disengagement from the two contending, Soviet and Western, Big Power-dominated blocs of the Cold War era;[8] and the so-called Group of 77, which developed later, in point of time, and which had a strong Latin American component and was always concerned with economic questions, and in particular with re-negotiating original economic ties and contracts with the Western industrial countries involving the development and exploitation of primary products and raw materials. The key to the concerted action in the United Nations in 1974 in behalf of the New International Economic Order is the fusion, for that specific purpose, of the main drives of the former Non-Aligned group and the Group of 77, now expanded to over a hundred member-countries. Indeed, it can be said that the successful organisation of the Third World in support of the New International Economic Order involves an extension of the influence of the Arab-Asian central core of the Non-Aligned countries' group to the Group of 77, to the point where they are now competing effectively with the Latin Americans for leadership of the Group of 77. The coalition that produced the Declaration, the Programme of Action, and the Charter of Economic Rights and Duties of States throught successive Resolutions of the U.N. General Assembly in 1974, comprises these two, overlapping groupings, plus the OPEC countries,[9] Communist China, and the Soviet Union and Soviet bloc. But it is important to remember that it is a political unity limited, even so far as its own Third World original core membership is concerned, to the political issues of colonialism and the Middle East. The splits among the Third World Countries, even at the 29th General Assembly that adopted the Charter of Economic Rights and Duties of States, upon such issues as Cyprus, Korea, and Cambodia, were marked; and raised the question of whether further fissiparous tendencies, of much greater magnitude, might not be anticipated once the process of political decolonisation in the World Community should finally be completed or once the Middle Eastern crisis should be resolved to the satisfaction of the main Arab member-countries of OPEC.

3. Operational Methodology of the New Third World Majority

When one looks at the tactical development of the Third World campaign in behalf of the New International Economic Order, one is thrown back a decade and a half to the early Khrushchev-led Soviet campaign in behalf of Peaceful Coexistence. The Soviet campaign of the early 1960's for a codification of the Law of Peaceful Coexistence looked to the postulation in one general, comprehensive law-making act, of a set of abstract, *a priori* principles. The Soviet tactics were resisted by Western legal spokesmen, partly because it was thought at the time (wrongly, it would now seem), to be an essentially propaganda exercise on the part of Soviet leaders without any serious Soviet intention of negotiating concrete agreements or compromises in actual problem-situations; and partly because of a basic disagreement as to the methodology of international law-making in an era of ideological conflict or pluralism. Instead of the abstract Code or Charter, Western leaders pressed for a pragmatic, empirical, problem-oriented, step-by-step approach that would concentrate on major tension-issues of East-West relations and on developing operational solutions in particular cases by balancing or compromising the competing East-West interests involved therein. Instead of the Sermon on the Mount, – a postulated ideal Code, – any general principles of East-West relations would be derived inductively from specific problem-situations in East-West relations and their equally specific solutions. In the end, this rigorously empirical, Western-favoured approach was essentially adopted by Soviet leaders, leading on to a whole series of low-level East-West accords and understandings in such areas as general and nuclear disarmement, space exploration, settlement of frontier and territorial questions and the like, paving the way logically and inevitably for that more general and comprehensive East-West *détente* of which the Moscow Summit Accords of May, 1972, were no more than the final confirmation. But the important thing was that the Moscow Summit Accords of May, 1972, were the final step in the process, and not the beginning of the road.

By contrast, the Third World leaders, in mounting their campaign in behalf of the New International Economic Order, might seem to have learnt nothing and forgotten nothing from the long Coexistence debate of the decade of the 1960's. There was, to be sure, a sort of formal act of Codification of Peaceful Coexistence (Friendly Relations); but it came only in October, 1970, [10] and then as a more or less polite afterthought, with the Soviet leaders seeming long since to have lost interest and to have abandoned the formal codification step to other participants with their own special interests to pursue – the Indians and the Yugoslavs for example. By insisting on the politic of one big step as opposed to a series of little steps – that is to say, one highly general and abstract list of *a priori* principles rather than a series of smaller and more limited, but actually operational accords, the Third World majority may have effectively lost not merely the possibility of obtaining unanimity in the General Assembly but, more importantly, the positive support of the major Western industrial countries that would be necessary to make the redressing of the balance of North-South economic relations implicit in any New International Economic Order, really operational. For the major Western countries who would in practice be called upon to implement the cardinal principles of the postulated New Order all either voted No or else abstained in the General Assembly Resolution adopting the Charter of Economic Rights and Duties of States. [11]

Beyond that, certain other clear and obvious errors of approved Conference method or gamesmanship seem to have been made by the Third World majority. It is perhaps not the Third World's fault that the 1974 Sixth Special Session of the U.N. General Assembly could not have been preceded by an authoritative International Law Commission-based expert report, as happened, for example, with the 1958 Law of the Sea Conference; but not, significantly, with the abortive 1960 Law of the Sea Conference. [12] The confusion over the consensus rule at the Sixth Special Session of the U.N. General Assembly in May, 1974, was, however, a much more serious defect. [13] While, on the one hand, the Third World majority, annoyed with the United States and the Western European countries' express reservations to the 1974 Declaration and Programme of Action, [14] were not disposed to compromise in regard to the December, 1974, Charter, the advanced industrial countries, seeing what they considered to be a Third World intransigence as to their reservations to the Programme of Action, decided to vote No or to abstain on the Charter vote.

The Charter, itself, though perhaps not atypical of U.N. General Assembly ventures into law-making, would still appear to leave a great deal to be desired from the viewpoint of conception and styling. On the one hand, it follows what we may call the *cornucopia* approach to legal drafting: when in doubt, throw everything in and leave it to subsequent historians to try to work out why. [15] It also embraces what has historically been characterised as the Weimar Constitution drafting principle: if faced with latent or even patent contradictions in demands pressed in the drafting stage, one should put them all in and hope that the passage of time will resolve the conflict by disposing of one or the other.[16] Thus it is that while proclaiming State sovereignty in its most exaggerated form in its opening Articles,[17] the Charter goes on to apply stern injunctions against any one state's attempting to limit or influence another state by economic measures.[18] Some parts of the Charter are general, rhetorical proclamations, as with the pronouncement on the elimination of *Apartheid;*[19] and other parts are the new "Socialist" International Law of the late 1950's and early 1960's with the postulation of a duty of the advanced industrial states to make restitution and compensation to other states.[20] There are specific articles on the Law of the Sea[21] and on environmental policy.[22] The range and coverage is so wide and diffuse, without, at the same time, evidencing an ability on the part of the dominant U.N. majority to compromise with the advanced industrial states, that one is left, at the end, with the unfortunate impression that the December, 1974, Charter, remains largely hortatory. It is nominal and not normative![23] And so the question arises, what is to make the Charter operational in terms of concrete relations between the developed and the developing countries for the future? In the economic domain, is there any reason to assume that the Charter establishes, effectively, a monopoly of conceptions of an economically-based World Public Order model? Why not a plurality of such systems, including the contemporary dominant, politico-juridical model?[24]

4. Economic Issues and Conflicts within the New Third World Majority

The pressures successfully applied by the OPEC cartel, after October, 1973, for massive increases in the World market prices for crude oil demonstrated the first real solidarity among Third World countries as to the use of the economic weapon of their control of raw materials, and may also have given developing countries a real sense of political power in the World Community and its processes, for the first time. Yet the paradox remains that the oil price increases escalated differences between Third World countries on account of those countries' extremely divergent growth rates. No such moves could occur without there being innocent victims, and the victims – those most affected by the oil price increases, – were very poor already. The Western industrial countries may have provided some help, – for instance through the Oil Facility of the I.M.F., – but they clearly preferred to favour their own affected group within the O.E.C.D. The OPEC countries, for their part, also opted to come to the aid of the poorer countries; but they applied their own system of grading according to special cultural links with themselves, and seem to have accorded highest priority to assistance to Arab countries, and thereafter to Muslim countries, and only latterly to all others. What the crisis over Oil price increases served to demonstrate, in fact, was the degree and depth of the current split within the Third World itself. For there is, by now, a "new" Third World, comprising all those Third World countries possessing important raw materials, or having a fully competitive industrial sector, or else (most fortunate of all) having both raw materials and a competitive industrial sector. These Third World countries – mainly East Asian, Middle Eastern, and Latin American, and only a few African countries, – amount by now to the World's "middle class"; and most of these countries have achieved high growth rates while the Western industrialised countries have gone through a period of severe economic recession. By contrast, there is, within the Third World bloc, a group of the really poor nations of the World – most Southern Asian countries, most African countries, and the smaller Latin American states – who can be called now the "Fourth" World. The enormous increases in grain, crude oil, and fertiliser prices, and the repercussions of the recession in the West have thrown these "Fourth" World countries into a crisis situation threatening to undermine all international and regional development aid projects. The very divergence of interests and the disparity of basic economic resources within the Third World bloc as a whole, raise, in fact, quite as many prospects for disintegration of the Third World bloc in the future as for the maintenance of that internal unity and cohesion and solidarity against the industrialised countries that was demonstrated so strikingly during the international oil prices crisis. Provided, of course, the "new" Third World is prepared to exercise generosity towards the Fourth World, the united front on economic issues should remain unbroken. The Fourth World has strongly attacked the "economic strangulation" of the poorer countries through higher oil prices, but this pressure seems to have been intended to put pressure on the oil-producing countries within the Third World bloc as a whole to help the non-oil-producers in their ranks through special oil prices and massive investment.

5. An Alternative, Economic, World Public Order Model?

Decolonisation, in its classical post-war political manifestation, is now clearly approaching its final consummation with the imminent ending of white minority rule in Rhodesia and South-West Africa (Namibia), and with some sort of multi-racial solution for the present Union of South Africa to be envisaged.[25] The so-called, second, *economic* phase of the World Revolution of our times – what is called, in the special language of the times, the struggle against "neo-colonialism" in the sense of a system of foreign economic exploitation, – is now being entered upon. The dominant goals of the New International Economic Order – reversing the "terms of trade" in World trade and reversing the terms of foreign investment, by seeking to give the developing countries unlimited sovereignty over their own economic resources, – have been sought to be achieved, tactically, primarily through raw material power with formation of producers' cartels for each basic raw material. The oil cartel, OPEC, has certainly been spectacularly succesful in gaining its objectives, though with some quite unfortunate, and presumably unintended, side effects within the Third World bloc, as we have already seen. Similar successes, if not quite on the same scale, have been achieved also with phosphates and bauxite; but the attempts to organise cartels for other raw materials have not always yielded positive results. Raw material prices have, of course, fallen as a result of the massive recession in the industrial countries; and so the success of cartels, as an economic weapon of the Third World bloc, is not clear. Indeed, the two basic demands made by the Third World – raw materials cartels, and immunity of foreign investments from the protections of classical international law, seem hardly sufficient, in themselves, as the basis of a viable world economic order. The indirect effects of massive increases in raw material prices, as a result of monopolistic cartel controls, have been to aggravate inflation and recession in the industrial countries. This has meant correspondingly fewer exports of raw materials from Third World countries to industrial countries, and higher prices for fertilisers and capital goods exported from industrial countries to the Third World, and so, in the end, less development aid from Western countries to the Third World because of the West's own financial difficulties. Hence, the end result has been a loss of growth for the developing countries.

The Third World bloc, so long as it retains its cohesion and solidarity, can certainly effectively defeat projects for Resolutions of the United Nations General Assembly aimed at achieving such current Western objectives as the introduction of a new international currency system; or such current Western and Soviet objectives as the exploitation of the mineral resources of the sea; or more general, post-industrial society desires to combat international terrorism or to control international drug smuggling. The Third World bloc can also, if it stays united, try to trade off the offer of its needed cooperation in environmental protection and population control against a far more serious commitment on the part of the industrialised countries, both Western and Soviet, to international economic development aid. But the threat of a negative vote in the United Nations General Assembly cannot, of itself, provide a recipe for positive action on the part of the World Community as a whole. On the Law of the Sea, for example, the Third World bloc has encountered, to its evident surprise, a considerable degree of Soviet bloc and Western solidarity on substantive issues. Beyond that, the Soviet Union has appeared even more committed than the West to resisting the Third World bloc's attempts to amend the United Nations Charter so as to reduce Big Power influence and political control and generally to "democratise" the United Nations and to make its main arenas more responsive to majority will.[26] Third World ventures in international law-making, it is true, have sought their main outlet through multilateral, as distinct from bilateral, action; and this implies a return to the United Nations,[27] with specialist U.N. Committees thus being transformed increasingly from technical or expert gatherings to still further arenas for the formulation and development of more general foreign policy objectives – decolonisation, elimination of neo-colonialism, national self-determination, and achievement of a New International Economic Order. But the new Third World initiatives in the main U.N. arenas are hardly likely in themselves to overcome the Big Power penchant for trying to settle their differences through bilateral negotiation and "quiet diplomacy" at Big Power Summit Meetings; and may, indeed, even accentuate past Big Power preferences for this particular type of mutual interaction.

6. Options for the West in Response to the Third World Bloc's Current Initiatives

Is there, after all, any reason to assume that this postulated new *economic* system of World public order will replace, in the near future, other, more traditional, politico-juridical models? In responding to current Third World drives for a New International Economic Order, the West would seem to have a number of different options open to it.

The first such option would be to concentrate on one's own self-interest as narrowly conceived, and to try to introduce one's own new economic order in the economic triangle formed by the United States, Western Europe, and Japan, with Western-based international economic development aid presumably being kept close to present levels.

A second clear option would be to concentrate on the key nations of the Third World, by attempting to reach a compromise or understanding with OPEC and the oil-producing nations and with a few other of the major raw material producers. Such a strategy, if successful, would certainly separate and isolate the "new" Third World from the Fourth World, and would mean forgetting altogether the New International Economic Order, except so far as that might be caught up in any deal with OPEC and other major raw material producer cartels.

The third and certainly the most positive option would be to move to set up a new and more inclusive, genuinely global economic order that would incorporate all the nations of the World; and at the same time to attempt to settle not only strictly economic problems, but also the new problems arising from interdependence such as environmental deterioration, the World population explosion and the food scarcity.

If we examine the political possibilities of adoption of any one of these alternative options, by the West, it may be instructive to look to the historical development, in the World Community, after World War II, of the movement for Decolonisation and National Self-Determination. This movement was originally spear-headed in the U.N. General Assembly by the Third World countries and did not finally become consummated until the middle 1970's but by this time it had the widespread and fairly general support and acquiescence of the Big Powers. This Third World-inspired movement inaugurated the dominant trend in International Law immediately after World War II, and all countries were eventually caught up in the making of this "new" International Law.

It now seems likely that the main Western countries, in reaction, in part, to frequent Third World tactical errors or oratorical excesses, may move cautiously in regard to the current Third World-inspired movement for a New International Economic Order. This may induce major Western countries to seek to make special bilateral deals or trade-offs with the more important, raw material producing countries among the Third World majority. Nevertheless, it is important to understand the new spirit in the World Community; and enlightened self-interest on the part of the West, not less than the West's often proclaimed public commitment to building a genuine International Law of Human Dignity, counsel acceptance of the fact that the current drive for a New International Economic Order should prove as significant, in the dialectical development of International Law for the future, as all the determined pressures for Decolonisation, Independence and National Self-Determination were before it.[28]

Chapter VIII

ALTERNATIVE LAW-MAKING MODES. PARLIAMENTARY "GLOSSES" ON THE CHARTER: THE GENERAL ASSEMBLY AND POLITICAL REPRESENTATION IN SOUTHERN AFRICA

1. From the Court to other (Parliamentary) Arenas for International Problem-solving for Southern Africa

Up to recent times the main thrust of the Third World countries in the United Nations towards political and legal effectuation in Southern Africa, and especially South West Africa, of the International Law principle of Self-Determination of Peoples has been directed to the World Court, producing a sense of political frustration throughout the decade of the 1960s as a result of the Court majority's essentially procedural, adjectival law approach and refusal, in consequence, to rule upon the substantive issue. The Third World dissatisfaction with the Court-based route to international legal problem-solving was only partly relieved by the World Court's *Namibia (South West Africa)* Advisory Opinion ruling of 1971 which was seen by many critics to have come a little too late.

In reaction to the apparant blockage of possibilities of effective action in the World Court to compel the relinquishment of the South African Mandate over South West Africa, Third World countries began to look, instead, to other arenas for international law-making. An obvious first choice among these was the General Assembly where, by the end of the decade of the 1960s, the Third World could normally expect to be able to maximise its voting majority. Non-compliance by South Africa with the term of various General Assembly and Security Council resolutions on South West Africa adopted after 1966, and with the World Court's Advisory Opinion of 1971 on the same subject suggested, logically, the application of follow-up, punitive measures or other forms of legal sanctions against South Africa, including the ultimate sanction envisaged by the Charter for persistent violation of the principles of the Charter, namely expulsion from the U.N. organisation.

The attention of Third World leaders thus turned, inevitably, to Chapter II, Membership, (Articles 3 to 6) of the U.N. Charter. But the relevant Articles of the Charter, for these purposes – Article 5 on suspension from the exercise of the rights and privileges of membership, and Article 6 on expulsion – are legally predicated, so far as any General Assembly action may be concerned, upon a prior recommendation of the Security Council to which the Big Power Veto under Article 27 (3) of the Charter would apply.

The political realities of present Big Power attitudes towards concrete, U.N.-based measures directed against South Africa, have produced a search by some Third World countries for alternative U.N. control measures to which the Big Power Veto could not constitutionally be applied. The solution seems to be action based upon Chapter IV, The General Assembly (Articles 9 to 22) of the Charter, and the argument of the inherent power of the General Assembly, as confirmed in particular in Article 21, to adopt its own procedures, and specifically those concerning the determination of the Credentials of its members. Included in this by necessary implication, it is argued, must be the power to scrutinise credentials actually presented to the General Assembly by the various State representatives and delegations; and, if need be, the power also to reject those credentials in appropriate cases – in particular, cases where the State delegation concerned does not accord with International Law principles as to representativeness or with Charter principles generally. In conventional International Law analogies, the shift is thus from a Recognition of *States* cluster of principles to a Recognition of *Governments* cluster, with the emphasis upon the right, and in some cases perhaps the duty, of the party making the decision as to the Recognition, to exercise its own independent discretion and judgment on the facts: it is the *constitutive*, and not the *declaratory*, theory of Recognition that is involved.

Applied in the case of the Union of South Africa, the decision on the legal claims of the present South African Government to seating of its official delegation to the General Assembly, may not seem to present too many moral difficulties for too many U.N. Members, – a political fact which the South African Government itself perhaps quietly conceded in not pressing its own official Delegation's Credentials for purposes of the Thirtieth Session of the U.N. General Assembly in the Autumn of 1975, and thereafter. But once adopted in the case of the Union of South Africa, a Credentials-based United Nations' scrutiny of the claims to "representativeness" of any particular State delegation or of that

State's implementation of the principle of Self-determination of Peoples, could not stop there but would have, logically, to be applied to other conflict-situations and to other conflict-regions, both "colonial" and non-"colonial". On one view, a Pandora's Box of problems would be opened – problems which the conventional declaratory theory of Recognition always sought to avoid by limiting the enquiry of the recognizing authority to a few quite precise, objective criteria like effective control of the government concerned over territory and peoples, without any particular recourse to moral standards or value judgments. On the other view, all the pressures for a "new" International Law in place of an erstwhile Western European-based "old" International Law would find their reflection and outlet in a new and more genuinely inclusive United Nations organization progressively established as a result of an on-the-merits scrutiny of the representative claims and status of all State delegations seeking accreditation at future sessions of the General Assembly.

2. The General Assembly and the South Africa Credentials Issue

General Assembly Resolution 3206 (XXIX) of September 30, 1974, approved, by a vote of 98 to 23, with 14 abstentions, the first report of the Credentials Committee excluding the representatives of the Government of South Africa. This action was followed up, immediately, by General Assembly Resolution 3207 (XXIX) of September 30, 1974, adopting, by a vote of 125 to 1, with 9 abstentions, a request to the Security Council to review the relationship between the United Nations and South Africa in the light of what the Resolution styled as South Africa's constant violation of the principles of the Charter and of the Universal Declaration of Human Rights.

The response of the Security Council, in its turn, to this General Assembly request was the Security Council vote of October 30, 1974, in which a resolution presented by Kenya, Mauritania, Iraq, and the Cameroons, recommending South Africa's expulsion from the United Nations because of its racial policies, its refusal to yield Namibia, and its violation of the United Nations' boycott of Southern Rhodesia, was not adopted, and this although there were 10 votes in favour and 3 against, with 2 abstentions. What happened in the Security Council was that three Permanent Members of the Security Council (France, Great Britain, and the United

States) voted against the resolution and so, in accordance with Article 27 (3) of the United Nations Charter, vetoed its adoption.

General Assembly Resolution 3207 (XXIX), already referred to, with its request to the Security Council, addressed itself to Chapter II (Membership – Articles 3 to 6) of the United Nations Charter. Chapters 3 and 4 establish the categories of Membership in the United Nations, in terms either (Article 3) of states which had participated in the San Francisco Conference or which had previously signed the Declaration by United Nations of January 1, 1942, and which then sign the U.N. Charter and ratify it in accord with Article 110 of the Charter (Chapter XIX – Ratification and Signature); or else (Article 4) of – "all other peace-loving states which accept the obligations contained in the ... Charter and, in the judgment of the Organization, are able and willing to carry out these obligations", and whose admission is effected by a decision of the General Assembly upon the recommendation of the Security Council. Article 5 provides for the suspension from the "exercise of the rights and privileges of membership", in the case of Members "against which preventive or enforcement action has been taken by the Security Council", by a vote of the General Assembly "upon the recommendation of the Security Council". Article 6 provides for the expulsion from the United Nations, in the case of Members which have "persistently violated the Principles contained in the ... Charter", by vote of the General Assembly "upon the recommendation of the Security Council".

3. Parliamentary History of the Membership Sections of the Charter

These Membership Articles of the Charter have been the subject of considerable juridical debate and discussion within the United Nations, from the earliest days of the Organization, – both in the General Assembly and its specialized Committees, and also in the Security Council. The Membership Articles have also been the subject of two important Advisory Opinions of the International Court of Justice, rendered in 1948[1] and in 1950[2] following upon official requests rendered by the General Assembly to the Court in terms of Article 96 of the Charter.

It was recognized, very early in the history of the United Nations, that in spite of the seemingly objective legal criteria established in Chapter II to govern Membership questions, the application of Articles 3 to 6 might give rise to serious political conflicts in concrete cases, granted the *rôle* envisaged for the Security Council in Chapter II, in the application of those criteria and the always-present possibility of the application of the Veto of a Permanent Member of the Security Council to any Membership question coming before the Security Council. The ensuing years of Big Power tug-of war, especially during the Cold War era, over the admission of new Members brought a search for ingenious political and legal methods for breaking the stalemate, involving very often a recourse to what the distinguished Danish jurist, Alf Ross, calls legal "casuistry",[3] or what the Common Law jurisprudence has traditionally called pious perjury. In the debates in the *Ad Hoc* Political Committee of the General Assembly as early as November, 1948, in an attempt to circumvent the Big Power veto in the Security Council which was then blocking action on admission of new States to the United Nations, the delegate of Argentina pointed out that while Article 4 speaks of a "recommendation" by the Security Council as a condition precedent to General Assembly action, it nowhere states that this must be a *favourable* recommendation. According to argument, it would be competent for the General Assembly to act to admit a new applicant State as a Member of the Organization even though the Security Council had not given a favourable recommendation; and the General Assembly should therefore proceed to act upon the International Court of Justice's Advisory Opinion of May 28, 1948, on Conditions of Admission of a State to Membership in the United Nations, and admit Italy, Austria, Finland, Transjordan, Portugal, and Eire, to Membership, ignoring the negative attitude of the Security Council which was based on the exercise of the Veto by a single Permanent Member.[4]

4. The Court and the Membership Issue

In its Advisory Opinion of March 3, 1950, on the Competence of the General Assembly for the admission of a State to the United Nations,[5] the International Court of Justice, in its ruling rendered by a vote of 12 to 2, necessarily rejected this argument when it declared that Article 4 (2) – "envisages a favourable recommendation of the Security Council and that only". On the other hand, the very strong dissenting opinion of the distinguished Latin American jurist, Judge Alvarez, who dissented, together with Judge Azevedo, from the Court majority ruling, appeals strongly for a break from the – "precepts of traditional or classic international law, which were established on an individualistic basis and have hitherto prevailed", and for decision on the basis of the "new international law, which is now emerging". With a political prescience that may seem surprising in an opinion rendered as long ago as 1950, Judge Alvarez, who qualifies, through his sciencific writings as well as his judicial opinions, as one of the founders of the "new International Law",[6] asserts the right of the General Assembly to appraise the actual user of the Veto in the Security Council, where a State seeking Membership in the United Nations obtains the requisite number of votes in the Security Council but would fail for admission nevertheless because of the negative vote of a Permanent Member in the Security Council. Judge Alvarez suggests that the right of Veto is not an unqualified one; but must be interpreted and applied within "proper limits", defined as matters concerning the maintenance of international peace and security in which, of course, in terms of Article 24 (1) of the Charter, the Security Council has "primary responsibility". Judge Alvarez concludes that the right of Veto may be abused; and that it is open to the General Assembly to determine this and, if the answer is in the affirmative that the Veto has been abused, to proceed with the admission to Membership without any recommandation by the Security Council.

In his emphasis upon a Continental European Civil Law-derived teleological interpretation of the Charter, directed towards what he saw as the then emerging new international "*régime* of interdependence", Judge Alvarez parallels, in remarkable measure, contemporary North American, Legal Realist, instrumental or "policy-oriented" approaches to interpretations of the Charter, first developed to by-pass or circumvent the Big Power Veto in the Security Council which might otherwise legally inhibit the United Nations from acting in a concrete problem-situation[7] – in the most notable North American-sponsored examples, the Security Council Resolutions of 1950 on the Korean question, adopted during the absence of the Soviet Union, and also the Uniting for Peace Resolution passed by the General Assembly. While clearly it would, as Judge Alvarez himself noted, be an "absurdity" if any United Nations action under Article 4 as to admission of new Members, and *a fortiori* any action under Article 5 as to suspension from the exercise of the rights and privileges of Membership, or under Article 6 as to expulsion from the United Nations, could be frustrated altogether by a Big Power veto, any political corrective action against such a situation would seem to call for the prior political support and authority of a further World Court Opinion, addressed to the same general issues as contained in the Court's Advisory Opinion of March 3, 1950, but this time directed particularly to Articles 5 and 6 of the Charter (suspension of rights and privileges of membership; expulsion).

5. Characterisation of the Problem: from "Membership" to "Credentials"

The foregoing discussion relates to the issue of Membership in the United Nations – Membership of a *State* in the United Nations. It would be relevant to, and also controlling, for any attempt to expel the State of South Africa from the United Nations, or to suspend some or all of the State of South Africa's rights and privileges of Membership, on the score of the State of South Africa's alleged violation of General Assembly Resolutions, World Court rulings, or Charter principles generally; but it does not go beyond that. There remains, however, a very considerable scope for possible United Nations action in regard to South Africa that is not related to the Membership question in general or to the Membership sections (Chapter II – Articles 2 to 6) of the Charter in particular, and that is not dependent upon a Security Council interposition with all the political risks of a frustrating Big Power Veto that any such Security Council interposition might involve.

The route through Chapter IV of the Charter (The General Assembly – Articles 9 to 22) leads to the issue, separate and distinct from the issue of the claims of a *State* as to Membership in the United Nations, of the actual representation of that State in the United Nations and its main organs. This distinction is well enough recognized in general International Law, in the Recognition cluster of legal principles, in the distinction between Recognition of States and Recognition of Governments. In the constitutional law of the United Nations, the issue of the actual political representation of a State that has already been admitted to the United Nations has been accepted, right from the outset, as something to be determined by the appropriate United Nations organ or special agency concerned. As early as the San Francisco Conference of 1945, the issue of Polish representation arose, Poland being one of the States automatically entitled to Membership in the United Nations through having signed the Declaration by United Nations of January 1, 1942: the host powers at San Francisco simply could not agree on which of the two then competing governments of Poland, – the so-called London Government or the so-called Lublin Government – should be recognized as representing Poland, and it was not until the announcement of the composition of the new Polish Government on June 28, 1945 – too late for the San Francisco Conference itself – that this question could be resolved.

The issue of Chinese *representation* – China being of course both an original member of the United Nations and also a Permanent Member of the Security Council, was raised with the United Nations as early as November 18, 1949, when the Chinese Communist Government requested the United Nations immediately to deprive the Chinese Nationalist Government of "all rights to further represent the Chinese people in the United Nations".[8] On January 10, 1950, The Soviet Union submitted to the Security Council a Resolution that the Security Council not recognize the Credentials of the Chinese Nationalist Government representative and exclude that representative from the Council. The Soviet Government raised the issue as a *Credentials* issue, and it was debated as such, the question of a Chinese State *Membership* in the United Nations hardly being open to question.[9] It was after the rejection of the Soviet Union proposal that the Soviet representative made the celebrated walk-out from the Security Council, – not to return until August 1, 1950. After the Soviet Union's delegate returned, on August 1, 1950, to take up the Soviet Union's right, on normal rotation practices, to the Security Council Presidency, the Soviet delegate, Mr. Malik, as President of the Security Council, then ruled that the Chinese Nationalist representative did not represent China and could not, therefore, take part in the Security Council debates: this ruling was challenged and over-ruled by a vote of 8 to 3.[10] The issue of Chinese representation in the Security Council and in the General Assembly remained as a prime political issue for each successive General Assembly up to the final seating of the Chinese Communist delegation in place of the Chinese Nationalist delegation in 1971, and it was each time treated as a Credentials question, separate and distinct from any issue of Chinese State *Membership* in the United Nations, – albeit, and (especially as the actual United Nations' voting on the issue became closer) treated as an "important question" requiring a two-thirds majority vote in terms of Article 18 of the Charter. (See General Assembly Resolution 1668 (XVI), December 15, 1961). The actual decision of the General Assembly, of October 25, 1971, to seat the Chinese Communist delegation was embodied in a Resolution adopted by a vote of 76 to 35, with 17 abstentions, which declares that the representatives of the

Government of the People's Republic of China are the "only lawful representatives of China to the United Nations". The General Assembly Resolution proceeds to – "restore all its rights to the People's Republic of China ... and to expel forthwith the representatives of Chiang Kai-shek from the place which they unlawfully occupy at the United Nations and in all the organizations related to it".[11] A 22-State sponsored draft Resolution which would have treated any proposal to deprive the Chinese Nationalist Government of representation in the United Nations as an "important question" in terms of Article 18 (2) of the Charter and thereby requiring a two-thirds majority, was defeated by a vote of 59 to 55, with 15 abstentions.

Treated as a *Membership* question under Chapter II (Articles 3 to 6), of the Charter, the seating of the People's Republic of China delegation in the General Assembly and the expulsion of the Chinese Nationalist Government delegation from the General Assembly would each have required prior Security Council "recommendations" as a condition precedent to any General Assembly action. Treated as a *representation* question, going to the issue of which of two competing delegations could legitimately claim to exercise the credentials of the State of China, both these matters were disposed of by the General Assembly acting of its own solo initiative. The conclusions from this contemporary United Nations Constitutional practice are clear: either the *Membership* (Articles 3 to 6) Articles of the Charter have been so transformed through developing United Nations internal Constitutional Custom and Convention that the requirement of prior Security Council "recommendation" has atrophied away and thus effectively lapsed into constitutional desuetude so that the General Assembly can now constitutionally act alone, without the Security Council; or else the actual political composition of the delegation of an existing Member-State of the United Nations is not a *Membership* question at all, but something else, for which General Assembly action alone is legally sufficient. In looking to the General Assembly's pragmatic interpretation of the Charter in its Resolution of October 25, 1971, on the "Chinese" question one is reminded of Chief Justice John Marshall's celebrated dictum, in *McCulloch v. Maryland*, that – "we must never forget, that it is a constitution we are expounding";[12] or else of Lord Sankey's scarcely less well-known truth, uttered in the Privy Council in relation to the British North America Act of 1867, that one had – "planted in Canada a living tree capable of growth and expansion within its natural limits .... Their Lordships do not conceive it to be the duty of this

Board to cut down the provisions of the Act by a narrow and technical construction, but rather to give it a large and liberal interpretation".[13]

The representation issue came up again in the case of Hungary, after the abortive Hungarian up-rising of 1956, the credentials of the Hungarian Government that finally suppressed the 1956 up-rising being challenged and the Hungarian delegation only being permitted to take part in the General Assembly debates on the provisional seating basis envisaged under Article 29 of the General Assembly's Rules of Procedure,[14] this provisional seating procedure being continued for the Hungarian delegation until 1963. In the aftermath of the Congo independence in 1960, the claims of various Congolese delegations, sponsored respectively by the Soviet Union and the United States, were examined by the Credentials Committee of the General Assembly; and what was, essentially, an ideologically-based conflict between rival, Big Power-sponsored political groupings in the Congo, was decided by majority vote of the General Assembly (53 to 24, with 19 abstentions) within the interstices of the General Assembly's procedures when the General Assembly approved the Credentials Committee report.[15]

The issue of South African representation in the United Nations was raised in the Credentials Committee of the General Assembly in 1963, by Algeria, Liberia, and the Soviet Union, on the argument that the South African Government was not representative of the people of South Africa;[16] and it has recurred at regular intervals since that time. General Assembly Resolution 3206 (XXIX), adopted on September 30, 1974, by a vote of 98 to 23, with 14 abstentions, to approve the Credentials Committee report excluding the representatives of the Government of South Africa, is simply the latest expression of General Assembly attitudes in this area.

To recite the history of the "representation" issue in the United Nations and to detail the sustained United Nations practice in this area is to make clear, beyond doubt, that in the Constitutional Law and the history of the United Nations, the "representation" issue has never been coterminous with the "Membership" issue; but developed separately and distinctly from it, forming its own autonomous body of Customary Law principles. The logic of that separate and autonomous Constitutional Law and practice as to "representation" is clear enough, the Law and practice being firmly anchored in the experience of representative, legislative assemblies, – in the Common Law and Common Law-influenced

World not less than in the Civil Law and Civil Law-influenced World. The United States Constitution, for example, in Article I. 5 (1), makes each House the Judge of the Elections, Returns and Qualifications of its own Members: a separate section of the Constitution, Article IV. (3) 1, controls the admission of new States into the Union.

The right to pass on the credentials of one's Members is, it may be submitted, an inherent part of the prerogatives of a representative, legislative assembly, and it would require the existence of express constitutional provisions to derogate from, or take away, that right. Such is clearly not the case with the United Nations Charter: Chapter II (Articles 2 to 6) relates only to the different question of Membership of States in the United Nations, and there is nothing in Chapter IV (Articles 9 to 22) (General Assembly) trenching upon the traditional prerogatives that the General Assembly would have under both Common Law and Civil Law constitutionalism, to pass on the credentials of delegations claiming to represent individual Member-States. Beyond that, the settled, unchallenged, practice of the United Nations General Assembly and the Security Council, since the formation of the United Nations in 1945, has been to confirm, consolidate and extend the principle that the "representative" quality of a Government and its official delegation is a credentials question, – to be determined by the General Assembly, Security Council, specialized agency or other international arena to which the particular Government delegation concerned may seek accreditation, *ex proprio motu*; and not a State Membership question to be decided according to the provisions of Chapter II (Articles 2 to 6) of the Charter. Not to understand and accept the cumulative weight of thirty years of unbroken United Nations Constitutional Law practice, legitimating, if that be needed, the powers to safeguard its own credentials inherent in any legislative assembly is surely to misunderstand the creative element in Common Law and Civil Law constitutionalism and the extent to which, as Dicey proclaimed in relation to English and English-derived Constitutional Law, developing custom and convention amplify and extend positive law principles. [17]

6. U.N. Guide-lines as to "Representativeness" in State Delegations

If the issue of representation, and the ability to pass on and decide the claimed representative quality of any official Government delegation seeking accreditation falls within the competence, therefore, of the Security Council and of the General Assembly, acting each in its own right for purposes of its own acts of accreditation, it is not, nevertheless, something for which no legal guidelines exist as to the actual exercise in concrete cases. As early as October 7, 1950, the General Assembly, upon the initiative of the Cuban delegation, had had submitted to it a draft resolution recommending that the issue of representation be decided, in the future, according to a number of specific criteria. The Cuban proposal was that the General Assembly should make the decision on the legitimacy of the representation of the Member-State in question in the light, variously, of effective authority over the national territory; the general consent of the population; ability and willingness to achieve the purposes of the Charter, to observe its principles and to fulfil the international obligations of the State; and respect for human rights and fundamental freedoms. [18] After considerable discussion, which included a number of amendments and alternative projects of resolution, the General Assembly, on December 14, 1950, adopted a Resolution stipulating that when any difficulties might arise regarding the representation of a Member-State, and in particular when more than one authority might claim to be the government entitled to represent a Member-State in the United Nations and the question thus becomes the subject of controversy in the United Nations, then the "question should be considered *in the light of the purposes and principles of the Charter* and the circumstances of each case"; and that the General Assembly is the organ of the United Nations in which consideration can best be given to the matter. [19] The Legal Opinion of the United Nations General Counsel on November 11, 1970, [20] to which reference was made by several speakers in the debates in the General Assembly in September and October of 1974 on Resolution 3206 (XXIX), so far as it relates to the particular question now being discussed, stems, it is submitted, from an inadmissible assimilation of the United Nations Constitutional Law as to *admission of States to Membership* in the United Nations and those States' suspension and expulsion from Membership which is covered, in terms, in Chapter II (Articles 2 to 6) of the Charter; and of the decision as to the legitimacy of the claims to representative quality, advanced by one or more delegations, in regard to States which have already been admitted to the United Nations under Chapter II (Articles 2 to 6). The latter question, as already submitted, is one which, under well-settled United Nations Constitutional Law practice, is determined by the General Assembly or the

Security Council, as the case may be, acting each of their own accord.

Where the United Nations General Assembly Resolution of December 14, 1950, speaks, in more general terms, of a decision "in the light of the purposes and principles of the Charter", the progressive development of International Law by the United Nations and its main organs since that time offers far more precise criteria for General Assembly and Security Council decision-making on the issue of representativeness. What the distinguished American jurist, Judge Jessup, in his celebrated dissenting opinion in the World Court in the South-West Africa case in 1966 referred to as – "the views and attitudes of the contemporary international commutity", [21] as "proof of the pertinent contemporary international standard", [22] leads not merely to the "accumulation of expressions of condemnation of Apartheid", [23] – a position, indeed, brilliantly restated and developed by the World Court in its Opinion of the Court in the 1971 Advisory Opinion on Namibia. [24] Much more immediately relevant and controlling in regard to issues of the claimed representativeness of Government delegations seeking accreditation to the General Assembly and the Security Council are the principles of the new International Law concerning the Self-Determination of Peoples, beginning with General Assembly Resolution 1514 (XV) of December 14, 1960 on the Granting of Independence to Colonial Countries and Territories, [25] and finding their latest, most authoritative expression perhaps in General Assembly Resolution 2625 (XXV) of October 24, 1970, – Declaration on Principles of International Law concerning Friendly Relations and Cooperation among States in accordance with the Charter of the United Nations. [26] The principle of Equal Rights and Self-Determination of Peoples constitutes today, it might be suggested, not merely a guide-line to decision on the "representation" issue but something in the nature of an imperative principle or *jus cogens* which all competent United Nations organs are obligated to respect in their interpretation and application of the Charter. In the case of the Government of South Africa, the doubts as to the representativeness of its official delegation were compounded at once by its refusal to respect the World Court's 1971 ruling on the *Namibia* issue; and the evident failure, in a plural, multi-cultural society, as amply testified to by successive United Nations Commissions of enquiry, to develop a genuinely inclusive system of political representation that takes proper account of the different constituent communities in that society.

7. Conclusions

The following general conclusions seem to emerge from the present study. First, it is clear that the issue of Membership in the United Nations, covering admission of States to the United Nations and also their suspension and expulsion, is controlled and regulated by Chapter II (Articles 3 to 6) of the Charter, with any decision in this area being made by the General Assembly upon the recommendation of the Security Council. As the Constitutional Law of the United Nations now stands in the light of the World Court Advisory Opinion of 1950, it is doubtful whether the General Assembly can act *ex proprio motu* to overcome a Big Power Veto in the Security Council in Membership cases, exercised after a majority vote in the Security Council in favour of a Membership application; but consideration might be given to a General Assembly request to the World Court for a fresh Advisory Opinion on this point, based upon the dissenting opinions in the 1950 ruling and taking account of the progressive development of International Law since that time.

As a second main point, it may be recognized that, separate and distinct from the issue of Membership of States in the United Nations is the issue of the representative quality of delegations seeking accreditation to the General Assembly or Security Council. This, it is submitted, is a credentials question, falling generally under Chapter IV (Articles 9 to 22) of the Charter, and to be decided by each appropriate United Nations organ in accordance with its own special rules – in case of the General Assembly in accordance with General Assembly Rules of Procedure Articles 27 to 29, and through its Credentials Committee as created under Article 28 reporting directly to the General Assembly for purposes of the General Assembly's decision. In deciding upon the issue of representation, the General Assembly and its Credentials Committee may properly be guided by the new International Law principles like the principle of the Self-Determination of Peoples developed or extended since the adoption of the Charter, and also, *inter alia*, by relevant World Court Opinions bearing on Self-Determination, such as the 1971 ruling on the *Namibia* question. However, infringements of the Charter or rejections of General Assembly or Security Council Resolutions, not going directly to the issue of the representativeness of the delegation seeking accreditation, do not, *prima facie*, seem to bear upon the General Assembly and its Credentials Committee's decisions in this context; though they would undoubtedly be relevant to any Chapter II (Articles 3 to 6) decision by the General Assembly, upon the recommendation of the Security Council, on suspension or expulsion of a State from Membership in the United Nations.

Decisions of the General Assembly, acting upon the report of the Credentials Committee, on the representation question would seem capable of being made by a majority of the members present and voting, in terms of Article 18 (3) of the Charter; though United Nations General Assembly Resolution 1668 (XVI) of December 15, 1961 on the issue of Chinese representation and also subsequent General Assembly practice on the China question treated it as an "important question" to be made by a two-thirds majority of the members present and voting, in terms of Article 18 (2) of the Charter. It would not seem to be necessary, for purposes of any General Assembly decision not to accept the credentials of a particular delegation seeking accreditation, that some alternative, rival or competing delegation be immediately available to claim representation in its place, it being enough that the General Assembly decide that the first delegation be not representative. Finally, any decision of the General Assembly, acting upon the report of the Credentials Committee, not to accept the credentials of a particular Governmental delegation seeking accreditation, could, it is submitted, be either an absolute decision, to operate immediately; or else it could be a temporary one, (with or without provisional seating of the Governmental delegation concerned), subject to re-examination and review in the event of evidence being brought forward, in the future, of a *bona fide* attempt to meet contemporary International Law standards as to the Self-Determination of Peoples. [27]

Chapter IX

CONCLUSION. JUDGE AND COMPANY, AND THE DIALECTICAL DEVELOPMENT OF INTERNATIONAL LAW

1. Judge and Company in International Law-making

Jeremy Bentham's prescription for the early 19th century English Common Law jurisprudence – "The law is not made by judge alone, but by judge and company,"[1] holds true also for the International Law of the last quarter of our present century. The World Court is only one institution among a number of equal, coordinate law-making institutions – the Security Council and the General Assmbly in the first instance, but also lesser or hierarchically subordinate authorities like the office of the Secretary-General. If one or more of these principal U.N. organs becomes clogged or blocked, there will be immediate and correlative political pressures upon the others, in an endeavour to "fill the gap" in effective U.N. policy-making. This happened, for example, in the Korean War crisis of 1950 when the threat of a Big Power Veto, paralysing any Security Council peace-keeping initiatives, led to the adoption by the General Assembly of its celebrated "Uniting for Peace" Resolution. Again, in the Congo Crisis of 1960, Big Power disagreements over the objectives and purposes of the U.N. military force in the Congo persuaded the U.N. Secretary-General to assume personal control over those operations in order to bring them to a successful and speedy conclusion. Neither example cited is, to say the least, free from political controversy. The legality of the "Uniting for Peace" Resolution was strongly contested by Soviet and Soviet bloc jurists as a distortion of the Charter and an attempt to by-pass its stipulations as to the Security Council's powers. The U.N. Congo operations and the Secretary-General's handling of them gave rise to a major political confrontation within the United Nations General Assembly, involving a direct contest before the World Court, a narrowly divided Court ruling on the constitutional-legal merits, and the near paralysis of the work of the United Nations itself for more than a year until the matter was more or less resolved by political compromises.

The point is, however, that in a period of rapid societal change when the World Community itself is undergoing transformation, it is unreasonable to expect the official law-making institutions and processes to be able to stand still. These law-making institutions share a responsibility, in common, for making International Law respond to changing International Society; and if one or more of them cannot function in a major crisis situation because of absence of the relevant technical problem-solving sophistication, or failure to obtain a political consensus on the appropriate wise solution, or even sheer lack of political courage, there will, inevitably, be a correspondingly greater burden on the other institutions. For what is clear, at this particular stage of transition in International Society, is that the World Community cannot tolerate a vacuum as to problem-solving; and that if decision-making powers are not to be exercised by the international institution for which they were originally designed, they will either be exercised by some other institution, or else there will be resort to self-help and direct action.

2. Constitutional Separation of Powers, and the Choice of the Different Arenas of U.N. Problem-solving

The lesson from comparative jurispondence is that the classical conception of a constitutional separation of powers, involving water-tight compartments of governmental decision-making classified on an abstract, *a priori* basis, is no longer a valid description of constitutional law-in-action today. The originally functionally-based divisions and allocations of decision-making have lost their meaning now, when the actual lines of division have become blurred or fused together and when each of the principal governmental organs partakes in measure of all of the governmental functions.

One particular arena of governmental power, rather than another, will however normally seem more appropriate, at any particular time, for particular ventures in international community policy-making, even though there is no reason or need to seek to inhibit it, in advance, by exaggerated emphasis on a functional limitation as to jurisdiction that has long since lapsed into constitutional desuetude.

Why did the World Court become the preferred arena of Third World leaders, in the first half of the 1960's, for international problem-solving as to Southern Africa and for establishment and application there of the principles of self-determination of peoples and of political representation? Partly, no doubt, because, from the opening of the 1950's, the U.N. General Assembly, through its special committees, had given a "legal" connotation to the racial situation in South Africa as a result of the specific Indian Government complaint; and because the Court, as the judicial organ of the United Nations, seemed, on the face of it, the most appropriate arena for determination of what was characterised for official, U.N. purposes as a legal question. Partly, certainly, because of the carry-over to the new International Court of Justice after World War II of the enormous prestige of the old Permanent Court of International Justice and its reputation for political neutrality and intellectual detachment in its approach to great international tension-issues. Partly, to be sure, because of the then Western, somewhat rhetorical and simplistic campaign in behalf of a World Rule of Law which was presumed to be judicially-based, even though principal sponsors, like the United States, were noticeably restrained in the range and extent of their own national acceptance of the compulsory jurisdiction of the World Court. Judicial review, as a community policy-making device, was also at the *apogée* of its constitutional prestige at that time. The archetype constitutional court, the United States Supreme Court, had then only recently rendered its land-mark, legislative decision ending segregation in grade school education; the "reception" of American-style judicial review in the post-War West German and Japanese constitutional systems had been clearly demonstrated as an operational success after a decade of imagination and politically courageous testing on the part of their national judges; and the immense problems besetting Commonwealth Supreme Courts like that of Canada with the emergence of French-Canadian drives for national self-determination, were not yet apparent. In short, there was a great degree of optimism and confidence, at that time, – not necessarily warranted in the special conditions of the World Community – as to the creative possibilities for judicial review in the progressive development of International Law in an era when decolonisation, independence, and self-determination of peoples were becoming so largely consummated.

3. The Creative Possibilities and Limitations Inherent in the Charter: the Charter as a Treaty or a Constitution?

This faith in the judicial process may, as we have suggested, have been somewhat unrealistic at the international level, since failing to take account of the special political and social factors that had combined to make judicial review and judicial policy-making politically acceptable and successful in those few, essentially Western of Western-influenced countries where it had become genuinely operational as part of the constitutional system. It may also have assumed too readily the universality of appeal of judicial legislation, in inter-systemic legal terms: the principal philosophic patrons and sponsors of judicial law-making at the international level, at that time, were Anglo-Saxon, Common Law and Western; where, in contrast, the Soviet Union and Soviet bloc countries were opposed to it in principle, and even the Continental Western European, Civil Law countries had never manifested exclusive support for it. Soviet and Soviet bloc attitudes seem to stem, ultimately, from Vyshinsky's pre-War textbook with its repudiation of any *rôle* at all for judicial legislation in the elaboration of community policy norms, within the Soviet State, under the Stalin Constitution of 1936.[2] Within the United Nations and with particular reference to the World Court, such basic Soviet attitudes were reinforced and accentuated by bitter Soviet memories of their short-lived experience with the old League of Nations, which had voted to expel the Soviet Union from the League for the Soviet Union's part in the Russo-Finnish War of 1939-40, though doing little or nothing, in Soviet eyes, in effective counter to the earlier territorial expansionist policies of Imperial Japan, Fascist Italy and Nazi Germany. A basically defensive Soviet attitude towards international institutions, inherited from the old League of Nations era, was reinforced by the political facts-of-life after 1945 with the new United Nations organisation, in whose principal organs, including the Court, the Soviet Union and its Eastern European allies could expect to be consistently out-manoeuvred and out-voted by the West. Even after the disappearance of the quasi-automatic Western voting majority in the General Assembly, in 1956 with the admission of the first flood of "new" countries from Asia and Africa, such inherently conservative Soviet attitudes to the U.N. organisation and its main agencies, including the Court, persisted. This leads to the conclusion either that there is a bureaucratic momentum of old policy constructs and old ideas in the Soviet foreign ministry, continuing long after the original political and societal facts that gave them their *raison d'être* have disappeared; or else that there is a consistency of principle and sense of strategic, long-range goals for Soviet policy-makers, in comparison to Western, that enable them to put aside temporary tactical advantages in pursuit of ultimate policy objectives.

This long-range Soviet and Soviet bloc doctrinal attitude to the Court is well expressed in the Dissenting Opinion of the Polish jurist, President Winiarski, to the Advisory Opinion on *Certain Expenses of the United Nations*,[3] where the conflict between Soviet bloc and Western (basically Anglo-Saxon) attitudes to the Charter and to the legal principles governing its judicial construction are canvassed in some detail. As President Winiarski commented:

> "The Charter, a multilateral treaty which was the result of prolonged and laborious negotiations, carefully created organs and determined their competence and means of action.
>
> The intention of those who drafted it was clearly to abandon the possibility of useful action rather than to sacrifice the balance of carefully established fields of competence, as can be seen, for example, in the case of voting in the Security Council. It is only by such procedures, which were clearly defined, that the United Nations can seek to achieve its purposes. It may be that the United Nations is sometimes not in a position to undertake action which would be useful for the maintenance of international peace and security or for one or another of the purposes indicated in Article 1 of the Charter, but that is the way in which the Organisation was conceived and brought into being ..."[4]

The Soviet judge, Judge Koretsky, who also dissented in *Certain Expenses of the United Nations*, made the same essential point in his own Dissenting Opinion:

> "I am prepared to stress the necessity of the strict observation and proper interpretation of the provisions of the Charter, its rules, without limiting itself by reference to the purposes of the Organisation: otherwise one would have to come to the long ago condemned formula: 'The ends justify the means'."[5]

Reflected in both these Opinions is the long-term Soviet doctrinal legal position *vis-à-vis* the United Nations that the Charter is merely a treaty – a multilateral treaty – which, for certain limited purposes, may operate to restrict the national sovereignty of its individual national signatories; but that, like all treaties or other international arrangements restricting national sovereignty in any way, the Charter is to be strictly construed, and construed against those arguing that it does operate to restrict national sovereignty in the particular case. Above all, the Charter is not a Constitution; and so there is no ground for arguing for a broad, policy sweep in its interpretation, in the spirit of Chief Justice John Marshall of the United States Supreme Court's celebrated dictum: "Never forget that it is a constitution that we are expounding".

This basic approach to the Charter and its interpretation was taken further by President Winiarski in his Dissenting Opinion in *Certain Expenses of the United Nations*, in reply to the legal argument advanced that the course of actual practice of the General Assembly over the years warranted the World Court's accepting a new legal "gloss" as having been effectively created upon the Charter in supplement to its text:

> "Reliance has been placed upon practice as providing justification for an affirmative answer to the question submitted to the Court. The technical budgetary practice of the Organisation has no bearing upon the question, which is a question of law .... .
>
> It is ... difficult to assert, in the case before the Court, either that practice can furnish a canon of construction warranting an affirmative answer to the question addressed to the Court, or that it may have contributed to the establishment of a legal rule particular to the Organisation, created *praeter legem*, and, still less, that it can have done so *contra legem*."[6]

4. The World Court: "Academy of Jurists" or "Responsible 'Magistrature' "?

The dilemma of policy choice as to the proper *rôle* for the World Court and its individual judges, in the present stage of development by the World Community, in the progressive development and application of International Law is amply indicated in the dichotomy formulated by the Court's sometime American judge, Manley Hudson[7], which was cited with approval by the British judge, Sir Gerald Fitzmaurice, in his Dissenting Opinion to the *Namibia (South West Africa)* Advisory Opinion in 1971.[8]

The differences between a Court *stricto sensu*, as traditionally understood in Common Law and Civil Law legal science, and the newer style of constitutional tribunal, are evidenced in the issues dividing the judges in *Namibia (South West Africa)*[9] and in *South*

West Africa (Second Phase)[10] before that. The more traditional or classic court must satisfy itself that it has a proper jurisdictional base before proceeding to rule on substantive legal issues. The procedural, adjectival law questions must be settled first, simply because they are the essential, preliminary questions upon which any judicial decision-making is predicated. And courts, in deciding upon substantive issues, should escalate slowly to the larger, "constitutional" questions, exhausting the lesser, non-constitutional grounds for decision before doing so. And in the actual decision-making and the opinion-writing in support thereof, courts are obligated to limit themselves to the matters actually raised in the litigation and not to venture into general policy pronouncements or *obiter dicta* not germane to the issues at bar. The individual judges should also respect the collegial character of their office, and cooperate in producing a disciplined and reasoned majority opinion, by avoiding the temptation to redundant or pejorative special opinions whether concurring or dissenting. The Court majority in *South West Africa (Second Phase)*[11], and the Court minority in *Namibia (South West Africa)*[12], fully reflect this basic judicial philosophy and conception of the *rôle* of a court *qua* court; and it is a position of such complete intellectual integrity and intellectual consistency as to dispose of any suggestions of judicial timorousness in the face of great political *causes célèbres* and refute the political charge that the judges concerned were reacting as a "European" tribunal to the general "winds of change" in Southern Africa.

The other approach – the minority position in *South West Africa (Second Phase)*[13] and the majority position in *Namibia (South West Africa)*[14] – has its own *raison d'être* and justification; but it is a different one, and proceeds from its own radically different premises of the proper *rôle* of a judicial tribunal, as one among a number of equal, coordinate institutions of community policy-making, in relation to those other institutions and to society as a whole. The dilemma is one common to modern government, and it is a genuine one on which intellectually honest men may differ. It contains within itself, however, the seeds of public disagreements and conflicts on the part of the judges, where the two strains coexist on the one tribunal at one and the same time. The risks of what, in regard to the work of the West German Federal Constitutional Court, has been called a judicial "Byzantinism"[15], would seem to apply also to a tribunal like the World Court, both because of the relatively frequent changes in its membership having regard to the nine-year elective term for the individual judges, and also because of the lack of continuity in executive leadership within the Court having regard to the limited, three-year term of its presiding officer.

5. Decline in the Court's Business: Contentious Jurisdiction

It would be an error to ascribe to the current differences within the Court as to its proper *rôle* in judicial law-making, the sole or even principal responsibility for the dwindling – almost to vanishing point – of Court business in recent years. The period, between the two World Wars, of the old Permanent Court of International Justice stands out, in retrospect, as a golden era in international adjudication. But it was also a much more compact international community that was served by the old Permanent Court, with far fewer states involved in the Court's work, and with a basic homogenity of legal values and legal thought-ways and legal procedures throughout most of that period that facilitated graceful submission to the Court's jurisdiction in the first place and then equally graceful acquiescence in and acceptance of the Court's final resolution of the dispute involved. It is in this special sense, and this special sense only that the appellation of "European" tribunal applies fittingly to the old Permanent Court: the Court reflected an essentially European family – in Stammler's terms, [16] a "special legal community" that was European in its composition and membership, rather than the larger, more inclusive World Community of the post-World War II period. These have been the essential pre-conditions for succes of judicial review, as a constitutional institution, at the national level. The business of logical exegesis and generic extension if need be of an original constitutional charter can be carried on more or less effectively since recognised by all major interest groups as being within the constitutional rules of the game: community problem-solving can be entrusted to what Max Weber called a system of logically formal rationality, [17] administered by that special group of legal "honoratiores" [18], the judges, because of the pre-existing community agreement on political and social fundamentals. The basic premise or starting point of judicial review, then, is the existence of a more or less coherent and well-defined political society sharing the same basic values. Where an original political consensus no longer exists and has not been replaced by a new one, as has happened with a number of national constitutional systems in recent years; or where the range and degree of political consensus is limited or imperfect, as is perhaps the case with the contemporary World Community, judicial review will operate with great difficulty.

Some of the immediate post-World War II jurisprudence of the new International Court reveals the patterns of Court decision-making for a European society, sharing the same basic values, that characterised the pre-World War II old Permanent Court's work. *Minquiers and Écrehos*, in 1953, [19] is just such an example of a perfectly polite legal dispute between the French and British Foreign Offices, submitted to the Court for neutral adjudication, and equally politely accepted by both parties in its final disposition. *North Sea Continental Shelf* in 1969 [20] in its fact complex, seems generically similar, since involving a dispute within the Continental Western European family: but the adjudication process was complicated by the presence of the "strangers" to the "special legal community" involved – that is, the non-Continental Western European judges participating in the 11 to 6 disposition of the dispute between West Germany and Denmark on the one hand and West Germany and The Netherlands. There was, indeed, some scarcely concealed dissatisfaction, in governmental circles in the countries directly involved, with the part played by several at least of these "stranger" judges, and with their conception of their judicial *rôle* as authorising a more or less personal *tour de force* as to general legal principles, rather than requiring the limiting of oneself to the particular legal issues raised by the parties themselves.

In the result, the Western European countries that once so largely championed judicial settlement of international disputes in the earlier League of Nations and Permanent Court era, and that carried over this enthusiasm into the initial post-World War II, United Nations and International Court of Justice era, are turning elsewhere for the choice of arenas and techniques for their own intra-European "special legal community" problems. France, as we have noted, was so dissatisfied with the World Court's exercise of preliminary jurisdiction in *Nuclear Tests. Interim Protection* in 1973 [21], that it gave formal advice to the United Nations in January, 1974, [22] that France was withdrawing forthwith her acceptance of the compulsory jurisdiction of the Court. The French and British legal dispute concerning the delimitation of the Continental Shelf between themselves, would, in the era of the old Permanent Court, have been happily referred by both parties to the Court for purposes of settlement; and, even in the early years of the new Court, it might, on the example of *Minquiers and Écrehos* [23], have been expected to end up before the Court. Instead, the two parties chose to create their own special arbitral tribunal,[24] with the members necessarily appointed by themselves on a basis of mutual agreement; and to authorise this body to make the final legal disposition.

It may be suggested that the World Court can presently ill afford to have a flight from its jurisdiction on the part of old friends of judicial settlement like France and Great Britain. When it is remembered that the Soviet Union and Soviet bloc countries, for long-standing legal doctrinal reasons, will not accept judicial settlement for purposes of international problem-solving involving themselves; and that the Third World countries, because of their existing political distrust of the Court and, by association, of the international adjudicatory process generally, do not now bring their own disputes to the Court, the prospects, for the immediate future, for the *contentious* jurisdiction of the Court, are bleak. Long-range, the prospects seem hardly better unless there should be some dramatic change in State attitudes to, and expectations of the Court. Other past friends of judicial settlement either, like the United States, maintain a vast "domestic jurisdiction" gap in their acceptance of the Court's compulsory jurisdiction, or else, like Canada[25], have moved in recent years to cut back drastically on their long-standing acceptance of that jurisdiction in disputes involving themselves.

6. The Court's Business for the Future: Opportunities for the Advisory Opinion Jurisdiction

Advisory Opinion jurisdiction is normally frowned upon today in constitutional legal science. The argument is that it lends itself to purely abstract judicial determinations, remote from actual problem-situations; and that legal principles only take on their full meaning in the concrete fact-settings of individual cases. The United States Supreme Court, right from the outset of its work, decided against giving Advisory Opinion rulings;[26] and the new West German Federal Constitutional Court, though it was originally armed with an Advisory Opinion jurisdiction, saw it abolished in 1956 after the Court's politically unfortunate experience, in its first few years, with the European Defence Community controversy.[27]

It is further argued that an abstract judicial finding as to the respective legal rights of contending parties, before their contending legal positions can be examined and weighed against a proper empirical foundation or record, may actually impede or delay the business of political problem-solving by confirming, in one of the parties alone, a sense of legal justification and hence of moral absolutism that is too often fatal to that pragmatic give-and-take and disposition to compromise that is basic to any succesful political accomodation. Such a situation may have arisen, for example, in Canada with the *Ownership of Off-Shore Mineral Rights* Reference of 1968;[28] and it is certainly contended to have been the political consequence of the World Court's majority holding in *Certain Expenses of the United Nations*, in 1962,[29] on Advisory Opinion reference, when the business of the United Nations General Assembly was brought almost to a standstill by the inability of the principal (Big Power) parties to compromise on any pragmatic basis, once the Court had purported to rule definitively in favour of the position of one of them alone.

Nevertheless, in the absence of business arising under its contentious jurisdiction, the Court must, *faute de mieux*, try to maximise its other sources of jurisdiction, and this points more or less inevitably to a Court attempt to encourage and assist, and popularise, resort to its Advisory Opinion jurisdiction. Should the Court, in the exercise of its Advisory Opinion jurisdiction, try to remain within the contours of a regular Court of Law, by assimilating such references as far as possible, – in their preliminary, procedural elements, in particular – to its contentious jurisdiction over actual cases or controversies. Certainly, the Court minority in *Namibia (South West Africa)* in 1971,[30] felt so, in arguing for maintenance of the distinction between "law" and "politics" and for the Court's confining itself to ruling on legal questions *stricto sensu*; and in arguing, also, for proper Court respect for the delimitation of the "*rôles* and missions" of the different principal organs of the United Nations as spelled out in the Charter.

The argument of the minority judges in *Namibia (South West Africa)*[31] is attractive and persuasive in doctrinal legal terms; and it is echoed, with equal intellectual force, in some of the individual specially concurring opinions in *Western Sahara* in 1975.[32] On the other hand, it seems most likely now that the majority positions in both these Advisory Opinion references will prevail for the future. For the majority judges' elaboration of "new" international law doctrine in both those references seems in line both with the main trends in General Assembly declaratory, programmatic law-making Resolutions from 1960 onwards, and also to accord with the publicists' conceptions of the general historical direction in the progressive development of International Law of our times. These judicial expositions, in the majority opinions in *Namibia (South West Africa),*[33] and in *Western Sahara,*[34] are in fact scholarly in their depth of research, and imaginative and innovatory in their intellectual range and outlook. They continue the new emphasis on Law-as-Fact; and on a flexible approach to acceptance of new modes of international law-making, where the new norms are properly evidenced and rest upon an unimpeachable consensus or acceptance of the parties concerned. If it is less a Court in the classical sense, in consequence, and if its judicial opinions become rather more in the tradition of the *responsa prudentium* of Roman Law,[35] the World Court continues none the less to exercise a necessary law-making function in a period of rapid social change. The World Community is not, of course, bound to any static, Western constitutional law models of a Court and of the judicial function. The United Nations' principal organs, including the Court, are living institutions and, as such, have changed in their functions and purposes since the original founding of the United Nations, and will continue to evolve in the future: this is constitutional change through developing constitutional Custom and Convention, and it is an accepted part of the Western constitutional law-making process.

What it all sensibly suggests for the World Court, for the future, is a widening of the range and number of United Nations organs and specialised agencies that may, in terms of Article 96(2) of the Charter,[36] be authorised by the General Assembly to request Advisory Opinions from the Court; and perhaps this can be done on some more general, continuing or permanent basis. It also suggests some intellectually less inhibited approach to the selection of candidates, for filling the judgeships on the Court: if it is unrealistic to expect any diminution in the "political" influences oper[illegible] on the selection of judicial candidates, there is no reason w[illegible] as the contentious jurisdiction of the Court, (involvin[illegible] more States directly pitted against other States, as to t[illegible] interests) atrophies away – that the choices should be c[illegible] the normally more cautious or conservative, appro[illegible] Ministry slates. In presenting the names of candidate[illegible] tries other than their own,[37] could not individual[illegible] tribute to an intellectual break-through by trying to o[illegible] innovators who are not afraid of change in the World C[illegible] or in International Law itself?

Finally, while maintenance of the Court in its more [illegible] *rôle* would necessarily have implied the attempt at executive con-trol, within the Court itself, of the proliferation of separate opinions (both specially concurring and dissenting), and acceptance of collegial responsibility for producing a common, agreed majority statement of the grounds of decision, or *ratio decidendi* in any case, an expanded Advisory Opinion jurisdiction and acknowledgement of a more consciously and avowedly law-making approach for the Court would mean encouragement or tolerance of this spate of separate opinion-writing. What emerges, then, is a species of dialectical development of International Law, with genuine philosophical debate within the Court and also testing of alternative policy constructs for the future, on a trial and error basis in the public *fora*, through their canvassing in individual judicial opinions, whether concurring or dissenting. This would mean a new and different Court, not free from intellectual risks; but still judicial in the best sense of the word and certainly not less politically acceptable to the contemporary World Community than the older-style Court that has seen its working jurisdiction ebb away so completely in recent years.

NOTES TO CHAPTER I

1. As to the "new" International Law, see the discussion between the Soviet jurist, Gregory Tunkin, and Sir Francis Vallat, the Principal Legal Adviser to the British Foreign Office, *The Times*, London, February 25, 1963. The seminal study is, of course, Judge Alvarez' celebrated work, *Le Droit International Nouveau dans ses rapports avec le vie actuelle des peuples* (1959).

2. See generally the author's *The International Law of Détente. Arms Control, European Security, and East-West Cooperation* (1978).

3. Treaty on Principles governing the activities of States in the Exploration and Use of Outer Space, including the Moon and other Celestial Bodies, 1967.

4. *North Sea Continental Shelf, Judgment* (I.C.J. Reports 1969, p. 3, at pp. 228-9 (per Lachs J., dissenting).

5. *Nuclear Tests (Australia v. France), Judgment of 20 December 1974*, (I.C.J. Reports 1974, p. 253, at pp. 269-70 (Judgment)).

6. Compare, Rubin, The International Legal Effects of Unilateral Declarations, 71 A.J.I.L. 1 (1977); and the present writer's response, 71 A.J.I.L. 747 (1977).

7. Compare Tunkin, 95 *Hague Recueil* 1, 23 (1958); Tunkin, [1958] *Sovetskii Ezhegodnik Meshdunarodnogo Prava* 15; *International Law. A textbook for Use in Law Schools*, 12 and 247 *et seq.* (Kozhevnikov, ed., 1957); Krylov, 70 *Hague Recueil* 407, 436 *et seq.* (1947); Lukashuk, SSSR i Mezhdunarodnie Dogovori, [1959] *Sovetskii Ezhegodnik Mezhdunarodnogo Prava* 16.

8. Krylov, 70 *Hague Recueil* 407, 433-7 (1947); *International Law* 280-1 (Kozhevnikov, ed., 1957); Lukashuk, [1959] *Sovetskii Ezhegodnik Mezhdunarodnogo Prava 16.*

9. Tunkin, [1958] *Sovetskii Ezhegodnik Mezhdunarodnogo Prava* 15, 15-29; Tunkin, Remarks on the Juridical Nature of Customary Norms of International Law, 49 *California Law Review* 419, 428-9 (1961); Tunkin, 95 *Hague Recueil* 1,20 (1958).

10. Compare Tunkin, 95 *Hague Recueil* 1, 26 et seq. (1958); Tunkin, 49 *California Law Review* 419 at 423, 428-9 (1961); Pechota, 7 *Casopis pro Mezinarodni Pravo* 97 (1963)

11. See generally *L'élaboration du droit international public* (Mourgeon, ed., (1975)).

12. Compare Dupuy, Droit déclaratoire et droit programmatoire: de la coutume sauvage à la "soft law", in *L'élaboration du droit international public* 132 *et seq.* (1975).

13. *South West Africa, Second Phase, Judgment*, (I.C.J. Reports 1966, p. 6).

14. Strebel, Quellen des Völkerrechts als Rechtsordnung, 36 ZaöRV 301 (1977); and see generally Parry, *The Sources and Evidences of International Law* (1965); d'Amato, *The Concept of Custom in International Law* (1971); Lukashuk, *Istochniki Mezhdunarodnogo Prava* (1966).

15. *Legal Status of Eastern Greenland* (P.C.I.J., Series A/B, No. 53).

16. *Western Sahara, Advisory Opinion* (I.C.J. Reports 1975, p. 12).

17. *Ibid.*

18. See generally Oliver, The Inter-American Security System and the Cuban Crisis, in *The Inter-American Security System and the Cuban Crisis* 23 *et seq.* (Tondel, ed., 1964); Claude, *The O.A.S., the U.N., and the United States* 53 *et seq.* (1964); Chayes, *The Cuban Missile Crisis. International Crisis and the Rôle of Law* (1974).

19. See *Nuclear Tests (Australia and France). Judgment of 20 December 1974,* (I.C.J. Reports 1974, p. 253, at pp. 269-70.

20. Ruda, *The final acceptance of international conventions* (1976), at p. 10: Schachter, Nawaz, and Fried, *Toward wider acceptance of U.N. Treaties* (1971), at p. 124 *et seq.*; and see generally McNair, *The Law of Treaties* (1961), at p. 129 *et seq.*

21. See generally the author's *The Illegal Diversion of Aircraft and International Law* (1975), at p. 36 *et seq.*

22. per Lachs J (dissenting), *North Sea Continental Shelf*, (I.C.J. Reports 1969, p. 3, at pp. 228-9).

23. *Nuclear Tests (Australia v. France), Judgment of 20 December 1974*, (I.C.J. Reports 1974, p. 253).

24. U.N. General Assembly Res. 2625 (XXV), October 24, 1970, (Declaration on Principles of International Law concerning Friendly Relations and Cooperation among States in accordance with the Charter of the United Nations):
"*The principle of sovereign equality of States.*
All States enjoy sovereign equality. They have equal rights and duties and are equal members of the international community, notwithstanding differences of an economic, social, political or other nature.
In particular, sovereign equality includes the following elements:
(a) States are juridically equal."

25. For the discussion that follows, consult *The International Law of Détente. Arms Control, European Security, and East-West Cooperation* (1978), Chs. 3 and 4.

26. See generally Higgins, *The Development of International Law through the political organs of the United Nations* (1963); Asamoah, *The Legal Significance of the Declarations for the General Assembly of the United Nations* (1966); Skubiszewski, A new source of the Law of Nations: Resolutions of International Organisations, in *Recueil d'Etudes de Droit Inter-*

national en hommage à Paul Guggenheim (1968), at p. 508 *et seq.*; Frowein, Der Beitrag der internationalen Organisationen zur Entwicklung des Völkerrechts, 36 ZaöRV 147 (1976).

27. *South West Africa, Second Phase, Judgment* (I.C.J. Reports 1966, p. 6).

28. See, in this vein, Smets, *La conclusion des accords en forme simplifiée* (1969), at p. 17 *et seq*. And compare Wengler, Rechtsvertrag, Konsensus und Absichtserklärung im Völkerrecht, 31 *Juristenzeitung* 193, (April 2, 1976).

29. Compare Münch, Brauch und Missbrauch der normativen Kraft des Faktischen, 15 *Jahrbuch der Albertus-Universität zu Königsberg/Pr.* (1965), p. 29; Doehring, Die Wirkung des Zeitablaufs auf den Bestand völkerrechtlicher Regeln, *Jahrbuch 1964 der Max-Planck-Gesellschaft zur Förderung der Wissenschaften e. V.* (1964), p. 70.

30. And see generally Schwarzenberger, International *Jus cogens*? 43 Texas L.R. 455 (1965); Verdross, *Jus dispositivum* and *Jus Cogens* in International Law, 60 A.J.I.L. 55 (1966); Virally, Réflexions sur le "*Jus cogens*", [1966] *Annuaire Français de Droit International* 1; Nahlik, *Jus cogens* and the codified law of treaties, 33 *Revista "Temis"* (Facultad de Derecho de la Universidad de Zaragoza) 35 (1974).

31. Compare Scelle, Le phénomène juridique du dédoublement fonctionnel, in *Rechtsfragen der Internationalen Organisation: Festschrift für Hans Wehberg* (1956), p. 324.

32. See generally Münch, Die Völkerrechtslehre als Völkerrechtsquelle, 56 *Die Friedenswarte* 349 (1966).

33. See the author's Equity in International Law, in *Equity in the World's Legal Systems. A comparative study dedicated to René Cassin* (Newman, ed., 1973), at p. 581 *et seq.*

NOTES TO CHAPTER II

1. *South West Africa, Second Phase, Judgment*. I.C.J. Reports, 1966, p. 6.

2. *Legal Consequences for States of the Continued Presence of South Africa in Namibia (South West Africa) notwithstanding Security Council Resolution 276 (1970), Advisory Opinion*. I.C.J. Reports, 1971, p. 16.

3. *South West Africa, Preliminary Objections, Judgment*. I.C.J. Reports 1962, p. 319.

4. U.N. General Assembly Resolution 2145 (XXI), October 27, 1966.

5. I.C.J. Reports, 1966, p. 6, at p. 8; and see the analysis by Julius Stone, 52 *Texas Law Review* 187 (1973).

6. I.C.J. Reports, 1966, p. 6, at p. 237.

7. I.C.J. Reports, 1966, p. 6, at p. 323.

8. I.C.J. Reports, 1971, p. 16.

9. S/RES/284 (1970), adopted by 12 to 0, with 3 abstentions (Poland, Soviet Union, United Kingdom).

10. The Soviet Union and the United Kingdom.

11. I.C.J. Reports, 1971, at p. 22.

12. *Ibid.*, at pp. 22-3.

13. *Ibid.*, at p. 23.

14. *Ibid.*

15. *Status of Eastern Carelia*. Advisory Opinion of 23 July 1923. P.C.I.J. Series B, No. 5, p. 7.

16. I.C.J. Reports, 1971, at p. 23.

17. *Ibid.*, pp. 23-4.

18. *Ibid.*, at p. 25.

19. *Ibid.*

20. *Ibid.*, at pp. 26-7.

21. *Ibid.*, p. 12.

22. *Ibid.*, pp. 13-14. (Joint Declaration of Judges Sir Gerald Fitzmaurice, Gros and Petrén).

23. *Ibid.*, pp. 13-14, (Joint Declaration of Judges Fitzmaurice, Gros and Petrén); ibid., p. 14, (Joint Declaration of Judges Onyeama and Dillard).

24. *Ibid.*, p. 3.

25. *Ibid.*, p. 6.

26. *Ibid.*, p. 9.

27. Statute of the International Court of Justice, Art. 17:
"2. No member may participate in the decision of any case in which he has

previously taken part as agent, counsel, or advocate for one of the parties, or as a member of a national or international court, or of a commission of enquiry, or in any other capacity.
3. Any doubt on this point shall be settled by the decision of the Court."

28. I.C.J. Reports, 1971, at pp. 18-19.
29. *Ibid.*, at p. 10.
30. *Ibid.*, at p. 299 *et seq.*
31. *Ibid.*, at pp. 308-9.
32. *Ibid.*, at p. 309.
33. *Ibid.*, at p. 323 *et seq.*
34. *Ibid.*, at p. 324.
35. *Ibid.*, at p. 58.
36. *Ibid.*, at p. 27.
37. *Ibid.*, at p. 28.
38. *Ibid.*
39. I.C.J. Reports, 1950, p. 131.
40. I.C.J. Reports, 1971, at p. 28.
41. *Ibid.*, pp. 31-2.
42. *Ibid.*, p. 45.
43. *Ibid.*, at pp. 299-300.
44. *Ibid.*, at p. 45.
45. *Ibid.*
46. *Ibid.*
47. *Ibid.*, at p. 49.
48. *Ibid.*, at pp. 49-50.
49. *Ibid.*, at p. 27.
50. *Ibid.*, at p. 50.
51. I.C.J. Reports, 1966 at p. 441.
52. I.C.J. Reports, 1971, at p. 50.
53. *Ibid.*, at p. 51.
54. *Ibid.*
55. *Ibid.*, at p. 52.
56. *Ibid.*
57. *Ibid.*, at p. 53.
58. *Ibid.*, at p. 54.
59. *Ibid.*
60. *Ibid.*
61. *Ibid.*, at p. 55.
62. *Ibid.*, at pp. 55-6.
63. *Ibid.*, at p. 58.
64. *Ibid.*, at p. 56.
65. Hudson, *The Permanent Court of International Justice, 1920-1942,* at p. 511.
66. cited by Fitzmaurice J. (Dissenting Opinion), I.C.J. Reports, 1971, at p. 303; and see also Merrils, Sir Gerald Fitzmaurice's Contribution; to the Jurisprudence of the International Court of Justice, (1975-1976) *British Yearbook of International Law* 183.

NOTES TO CHAPTER III

1. See, on this aspect, Goldie, The Nuclear Tests cases: restraints on environmental harm, 5 *J. Maritime Law and Commerce* 491 (1974); and see generally the author's Changing Science and Technology and International Law, 6 *Indiana Law Review* 172 (1972).

2. See, generally, Andrassy, Les relations internationales de voisinage, 79 *Recueil des Cours* 77 (1951). And see also, *Trail Smelter Arbitration*, 3 U.N. Rep. Intl. Arb. Awards 1905 (1949); Schneider, Trail Smelter-Fall, in Strupp-Schlochauer (editors), *Wörterbuch des Völkerrechts*, vol. 3 (1962), p. 447. And see also *Corfu Channel Case (Merits)*, I.C.J. Reports, 1949, p. 22.

3. See, in this regard, the author's *Judicial Review* (4th ed., 1969), especially at p. 233 *et seq.*

4. See, generally, Stone, Problems confronting sociological enquiries concerning International Law, 89 *Recueil des Cours* 61 (1956).

5. See, for example, Pound, *Philosophy of Law* (1930); *Social Control through Law* (1942).

6. See especially Stone, *The Province and Function of Law. Law as Logic, Justice, and Social Control* (1946).

7. Stone, Fallacies of the Logical Form in Legal Reasoning, *The Province and Function of Law* (1946) at p. 149 *et seq.*

8. Cardozo, *The Nature of the Judicial Process* (1921).

9. Stone, Law and Society, *The Province and Function of Law* (1946) at p. 391 *et seq.*

10. *Ibid.*, p. 673 *et seq.* And see also Stone, What price effectiveness?, [1956] Proc. Am. Soc. Int. L. 198.

11. Stone, On the feasibility of Tasks, in Problems confronting sociological enquiries concerning International Law, 89 *Recueil des Cours* 61, 138 (1956).

12. See Freund, Mr. Justice Frankfurter, 26 U. Chicago L.R. 205, 213 (1959).

13. "Courts are not equipped to pursue the paths for discovering wise policy. A court is confined within the bounds of a particular record, and it cannot even shape the record. Only fragments of a social problem are seen through the narrow windows of litigation. Had we innate or acquired understanding of a social problem in its entirety, we would not have at our disposal adequate means for constructive solution." *Per* Frankfurter J., dissenting, *Sherrer v Sherrer*, 334 U.S. 343, 365-6 (1948).

14. Pescatore, Le droit de l'integration (1972), p. 74 *et seq.*; and see also Pescatore (with Donner, Monaco, and Kutscher), Aspects of the Court of Justice of the European Communities of Interest from the point of view of International Law, 32 *Zeitschrift für ausländisches öffentliches Recht und Völkerrecht* 239 (1972); Pescatore, Fédéralisme et intégration: remarques liminaires, in *Federalism and Supreme Courts and the Integration of Legal Systems*, (McWhinney and Pescatore, editors), (1973), 5, esp. at p. 9 *et seq.*

15. See for example, French Nuclear Tests, Comments by Michel Jobert, French Minister of Foreign Affairs, July 24, 1973, (Ambassade de France, Service de Presse et d'Information, New York); Declaration on Disarmament, Statement by His Excellency Louis de Guiringaud, Ambassador, Permanent Representative of France to the United Nations before the General Assembly First Committee, November 1, 1973 (*ibid.*) And see also the comment by the long-time Gaullist leader and former Prime Minister, Michel Debré, in *Le Monde* (Paris) of July 24, 1973 (cited in 78 *Revue Générale de Droit International Public* 793 at 811 (1974): "Si la France n'avait pas fait l'effort de devenir Puissance nucléaire ou si elle cessait de l'être, son siège permanent au Conseil de sécurité de l'O.N.U. lui serait bientôt enlevé."

16. *Livre Blanc sur les expériences nucléaires* (Comité interministériel pour l'information, Paris) (June, 1973), p. 3. And see generally France: nouvelle série d'expériences nucléaires dans le Pacifique (25 juin – 29 juillet 1972), 77 *Revue Générale de Droit International* Public 840 (1973); France: Nouvelle série d'expériences nucléaires dans le Pacifique (21 juillet – 28 août 1973): vives réactions à l'étranger: soumission du problème à la Cour internationale de justice par l'Australie et la Nouvelle Zélande (9 mai 1973); ordonnances de la Cour du 22 juin 1973 relatives à l'indication de mesures conservatoires, 78 *Revue Générale de Droit International Public* 793 (1974).

17. *Ibid.*

18. *Ibid.*, pp. 5-6.

19. *Ibid.*, p. 4.

20. *Ibid.*, p. 10.

21. Nuclear Tests (New Zealand v. France), Interim Protection, Order of 22 June 1973, I.C.J. Reports 1973, p. 135, at p. 164 (Dissenting Opinion of Judge Ignacio-Pinto). And see also *Livre Blanc sur les expériences nucléaires* (Paris, 1973), pp. 65-67, Annexe A. VII, Réunion entre experts scientifiques australiens et français à l'Académie australienne des sciences à Canberra 7 au 9 mai 1973; *Ibid.*, pp. 71-72, Annexe A. IX, Citations de personnalités ou de publications étrangères sur l'innocuité de nos expériences, – Australie, Nouvelle Zélande. And see also France: Nouvelle série d'expériences nucléaires dans le Pacifique (21 juillet – 28 août 1973), 78 *Revue Générale de Droit International Public* 793 at 821-2 (1974): "À la fin des expériences le directeur du laboratoire national des radiations de la Nouvelle Zélande, M. H.J. Yeabsley, déclara le 30 août que des traces de radiation provenant du deuxième essai nucléaire français, celui du 28 juillet, avaient été décelées à Apia, à l'ouest des îles Samoa, les 3 et 4 août, mais que ces traces étaient inférieures au niveau toléré et ne présentaient aucun danger. Le 18 novembre le directeur de l'Institut national d'énergie nucléaire du Perou, M. Walter

Llamosas, confirmait que les radiations constatées dans son pays après les explosions n'atteignaient qu'un degré infinitésimal."

22. Statute of the International Court of Justice, Article 36:
"1. The jurisdiction of the Court comprises all cases which the parties refer to it and all matters specially provided for in the Charter of the United Nations or in treaties and conventions in force.
2. The states parties to the present Statute may at any time declare that they recognise as compulsory *ipso facto* and without special agreement, in relation to any other state accepting the same obligation, the jurisdiction of the Court in all legal disputes ...
3. The declarations referred to above may be made unconditionally or on condition of reciprocity on the part of several or certain states, or for a certain time.
4. Such declarations shall be deposited with the Secretary-General of the United Nations, who shall transmit copies thereof to the parties to the Statute and to the Registrar of the Court.
5. Declarations made under Article 36 of the Statute of the Permanent Court of International Justice and which are still in force shall be deemed, as between the parties to the present Statute, to be acceptances of the compulsory jurisdiction of the International Court of Justice for the period which they still have to run and in accordance with their terms.
6. In the event of a dispute as to whether the Court has jurisdiction, the matter shall be settled by the decision of the Court."

23. Déclaration française d'acceptation de la juridiction obligatoire de la Cour internationale de Justice (20 mai 1966), (M. Couve de Murville, signed at Paris, May 16, 1966): "Au nom du Gouvernement de la République française, je déclare reconnaître comme obligatoire de plein droit et sans convention spéciale vis-à-vis des autres membres des Nations Unies qui acceptent la même obligation, c'est-à-dire sous condition de réciprocité, la juridiction de la Cour, conformément à l'Article 36, paragraphe 2, du Statut, jusqu'à ce qu'il soit donné notification de l'abrogation de cette acceptation, pour tous les differends qui s'élèveraient au sujet de faits ou de situations postérieurs à la présente déclaration, à l'exception: ...

3. – des différends nés d'une guerre ou d'hostilités internationales, des différends nés à l'occasion d'une crise intéressant la sécurité de la nation ou de toute mesure ou action s'y rapportant et des différends concernant des activités se rapportant à la défense nationale ..."

24. See generally Eisenmann, Les effets de la non comparution devant la cour internationale de justice, 19 *Annuaire Français de Droit International* 351 (1973).

25. *Livre Blanc sur les expériences nucléaires* (Paris, June, 1973).

26. See, in this regard, Lacharrière, Cour internationale de justice. Commentaires sur la position juridique de la France à l'égard de la licéité des ses expériences nucléaires, 19 *Annuaire Français de Droit International* 235 (1973).

27. Statute of the International Court of Justice, Article 37:

"Whenever a treaty or convention in force provides for reference of a matter to a tribunal to have been instituted by the League of Nations, or to the Permanent Court of International Justice, the matter shall, as between the parties to the present Statute, be referred to the International Court of Justice."

28. *Livre Blanc sur les expériences nucléaires*, (Paris, June, 1973), at p. 22 *et seq.*

29. *Ibid.*, at p. 23:

"La Cour n'est pas compétente, enfin, parce que l'affaire qui lui est soumise n'est pas fondamentalement un différend d'ordre juridique. Elle se trouve, en fait et par divers biais, invitée à prendre position sur un probleme purement politique et militaire. Ce n'est, selon le Gouvernement français, ni son *rôle* ni sa vocation."

30. *Nuclear Tests (Australia v. France), Interim Protection, Order of 22 June 1973*, I.C.J. Reports 1973, p. 99; *Nuclear Tests (New Zealand v. France), Interim Protection, Order of 22 June 1973*, I.C.J. Reports 1973, p. 135. And see also Goldsworthy, Interim measures of protection in the International Court of Justice, 68 A.J.I.L. 258 (1974).

31. I.C.J. Reports 1973, at p. 106; I.C.J. Reports 1973, at pp. 142-3.

32. I.C.J. Reports 1973, p. 106; *ibid.*, p. 143.

33. *Ibid.*, p. 108; *ibid.*, p. 144.

34. *Ibid.*, p. 108; *ibid.*, p. 145.

35. *Ibid.*, p. 110; *ibid.*, p. 146.

36. *Ibid.*, p. 111; *ibid.*, p. 148.

37. *Ibid.*, p. 115; *ibid.*, p. 149.

38. *Ibid.*, p. 124; *ibid.*, p. 159.

39. *Ibid.*, p. 128; *ibid.*, p. 163.

40. *Nuclear Tests (Austalia v. France), Judgment of 20 December 1974*, I.C.J. Reports 1974, p. 253; *Nuclear Tests (New Zealand v. France), Judgment of 20 December 1974*, I.C.J. Reports 1974, p. 457.

41. *Ibid.*, p. 272; *ibid.*, p. 478.

42. *Ibid.*, p. 312; *ibid.*, p. 494.

43. *Ibid.*, p. 372; *ibid.*, p. 524.

44. *Ibid.*, p. 391; *ibid.*, p. 525.

45. *Ibid.*, p. 273.

46. *Ibid.*, p. 254; *ibid.*, p. 458.

47. *Ibid.*, p. 275; *ibid.*, p. 479.

48. *Ibid.*, p. 276; *ibid.*, p. 480.

49. *Ibid.*, p. 298; *ibid.*, p. 483.

50. *Ibid.*, p. 308; *ibid.*, p. 493.

51. See, for example, per Brandeis J., (specially concurring), *Ashwander v. Tennessee Valley Authority*, 297 U.S. 288, at p. 345 (1936); and see Freund, *On Understanding the Supreme Court* (1949).

52. *Nuclear Tests (Australia v. France), Judgment of 20 December 1974*, I.C.J. Reports 1974, at pp. 271-2.

53. *Ibid.*, pp. 264-6.

54. *Ibid.*, p. 267.

55. *Ibid.*, pp. 267-8.

56. *Ibid.*, p. 268.

57. See, in this regard, Hughes, *The Supreme Court of the United States* (1928), p. 56 *et seq.*; and see generally McElwain, The Business of the Supreme Court as conducted by Chief Justice Hughes, 63 Harv. L.R. 5, at 19 (1949); Frankfurter, The Administrative Side of Chief Justice Hughes, 63 Harv. L.R. 1 (1949); *Of Law and Men, Papers and Addresses of Felix Frankfurter 1939-1956*, at pp. 133-144 (Elman ed., 1956); and see the author's *Judicial Review* (4th ed., 1969), at pp. 217-19 and p. 231.

58. *Nuclear Tests (Australia v. France), Judgment of 20 December 1974*, I.C.J. Reports 1974, at p. 275.

59. *Ibid.*

60. *Ibid.*, pp. 279-80.

61. *Ibid.*, pp. 280-2. And compare *Livre Blanc sur les expériences nucléaires* (Paris, June, 1973) at p. 13 et seq.; *ibid.*, Appendices B.III (Extraits du 168e rapport du Comité des pétitions du Conseil de tutelle), B.IV (Aide-mémoire du Gouvernement australien en date du 9 septembre 1963). B.VI (Loi relative aux essais nucléaires de Montebello, adoptée par le Parlement australien le 10 juin 1952).

62. *Nuclear Tests (Australia v. France, Judgment of 20 December 1974*, I.C.J. Reports 1974, at p. 282.

63. *Ibid.*, p. 285.

64. *Ibid.*, pp. 283-4.

65. *Ibid.*, p. 297.

66. *Ibid.*, pp. 304-5.

67. *Ibid.*, p. 306.

68. *Ibid.*, p. 308.

69. *Ibid.*, pp. 310-11.

70. *Ibid.*, p. 311. Compare, on this point, the specially concurring opinion of Judge Gros, *ibid.*, at p. 284:

> "But there is more than one negative aspect to the want of object of the Australian claim. The principle of equality before the law is constantly invoked, reaffirmed and enshrined in the most solemn texts. This principle would become meaningless if the attitude of 'to each his rule' were to be tolerated in the practice of States and in courts. The proper approach to this matter has been exemplified in Sir Gerald Fitzmaurice's special report to the Institute of International Law: 'The Future of Public International Law' (1973, pp. 35-41)."

71. *Ibid.*, p. 311.

72. *Ibid.*, p. 325.

73. *Ibid.*, p. 262.

74. *Ibid.*, p. 263.

75. *Ibid.*, p. 312.

76. See, in particular, the four Judges' Joint Dissenting Opinion's criticism of the majority Opinion of the Court's reasoning on this point, *ibid.*, p. 325:

> "It is difficult for us to understand the basis upon which the Court could reach substantive findings of fact and law such as those imposing

on France an international obligation to refrain from further nuclear tests in the Pacific, from which the Court deduces that the case 'no longer has any object', without any prior finding that the Court is properly seized of the dispute and has jurisdiction to entertain it. The present Judgment by implication concedes that a dispute existed at the time of the application ....

The conclusion thus seems to us unavoidable that the Court, in the process of rendering the present Judgment, has exercised substantive jurisdiction without having first made a determination of its existence and the legal grounds upon which that jurisdiction rests."

77. *Ibid.*, p. 326 *et seq.*

78. *Ibid.*, p. 329 *et seq.*

79. *Ibid.*, p. 337 *et seq.*

80. *Ibid.*, p. 346 *et seq.*

81. *Ibid.*, p. 372.

82. I.C.J. Reports 1949, p. 22.

83. I.C.J. Reports 1974, at pp. 388-9.

84. I.C.J. Reports 1974, pp. 391-455; I.C.J. Reports 1974, pp. 525-528.

85. There is an historical irony in the fact that *ad hoc* Judge Barwick (nominated by Australia and New Zealand, in terms of Article 31(2) of the Statute of the International Court of Justice, to sit on the Court for purposes of the *French Nuclear Tests* process) had been a key member (Attorney-General, 1958-64; Minister for External Affairs, 1961-4) of the Conservative coalition Government of Australia, that held power at the federal level throughout much of the period of the Australian endorsement of and active cooperation in British and U.S. nuclear tests in the South Pacific region generally or in Australia itself. Appointed Chief Justice of Australia in 1964, directly from federal politics, Chief Justice Barwick had earlier had a distinguished career as an advocate at the Bar, (though never, because of the nature of Australian legal practice, having worked in International Law). See, generally, *Who's Who in Australia* (21st ed., 1974), at p. 85.

86. Declaration on Principles of International Law concerning Friendly Relations and Cooperation among States in accordance with the Charter of the United Nations, UN General Assembly Resolution 2625 (XXV), October 24, 1970: (The principle that States shall settle their international disputes by peaceful means ...:

"Every State shall settle its international disputes with other States by peaceful means, in such a manner that international peace and security, and justice, are not endangered.

States shall accordingly seek early and just settlement of their international disputes by negotiation, inquiry, mediation, conciliation, arbitration, judicial settlement, resort to regional agencies or arrangements or other peaceful means of their choice. In seeking such a settlement, the parties shall agree upon such peaceful means as may be appropriate to the circumstances and nature of the dispute.

The parties to a dispute have the duty, in the event of failure to reach a solution by any one of the above peaceful means, to continue to seek a settlement of the dispute by other peaceful means agreed upon by them."

87. See, in this regard, I.C.J. Reports 1974, specially concurring opinion of Judge Gros, at pp. 279-80.

88. *Ibid.*, p. 293.

89. *Ibid.*, p. 294.

90. *Ibid.*, p. 273.

91. International Court of Justice, The Hague, *Communiqué* no. 74/2, March 26, 1974, *Nuclear Tests (Australia v. France); Annuaire de la Cour* (1973-1974) p. 189. And see also Lacharrière, Cour internationale de justice. Commentaires sur la position juridique de la France à l'égard de la licéité de ses expériences nucléaires, 19 *Annuaire Français de Droit International* 235, at 250-1 (1973).

92. I.C.J. Reports 1974, p. 293.

93. *Ibid.*, p. 294.

94. *Ibid.*, p. 296.

95. *Ibid.*, p. 298.

96. *Ibid.*, p. 273.

97. *Le Monde*, Paris (Sélection Hebdomodaire), January 2-8, 1975, at p. 4.

98. Treaty on Principles governing the Activities of States in the Exploration and Use of Outer Space, including the Moon and other Celestial Bodies, January 27, 1967. 18 U.S.T. 2410, T.I.A.S. No. 6347.

99. U.N. General Assembly Resolution 1884 (XVIII), October 17, 1963. And see U.N. calls on States to refrain from orbiting weapons: Statement by Ambassador Stevenson, 49 *Dept. of State Bulletin* 753 (1963).

100. See, in this regard, Lachs, The International Law of Outer Space, 111 *Recueil des Cours* 1, at 97-9 (1964); Lachs, The Law-making process for Outer Space, in McWhinney and Bradley (editors), *New Frontiers in Space Law* (1969), at pp. 20-23; Lachs, *The Law of Outer Space. An experience in contemporary Law making* (1972) at p. 109.

101. *North Sea Continental Shelf, Judgment*, I.C.J. Reports, 1969, p. 3.

102. I.C.J. Reports, 1969, p. 3, at pp. 229-30, (Dissenting Opinion of Judge Lachs). And see also Goldie, The North Sea Continental Shelf Cases: a ray of hope for the International Court, 16 *New York Law Forum* 327, at 357-8 (1970).

103. "States may obviously change their intentions, conduct and policies, but it would seriously undermine the words of and reliance upon statements made by governments if value-judgments of so important a nature were disregarded or held as not binding upon governments which made them."
I.C.J. Reports, 1969, p. 3, at p. 236, (Dissenting Opinion of Judge Lachs).

104. *Legal Consequences for States of the Continued Presence of South Africa in Namibia (South West Africa) notwithstanding Security Council Resolution 276 (1970), Advisory Opinion*, I.C.J. Reports, 1971, p. 16. See Higgins, The Avisory Opinion on Namibia: Which U.N. Resolutions are binding under Article 25 of the Charter?, 21 Int. and Comp. L.Q. 270 (1972); and compare McDougal, Proceedings of the 67th Annual Meeting, [1973] Proc.

Am. Soc. Int. L. at 293. And see generally Bernhardt, Homogenität, Kontinuität und Dissonanzen in der Rechtsprechung des Internationalen Gerichtshof: eine Fall-Studie zum Sudwestafrika/Namibia-Komplex, 33 *Zeitschrift für ausländisches öffentliches Recht und Völkerrecht* 1 (1973).

105. And compare also Judge Lachs' Declaration, made in the *Appeal Relating to the Jurisdiction of the ICAO Council (India v. Pakistan) (Judgment)*, I.C.J. Reports, 1972, p. 46, at pp. 72-5.

106. *Nuclear Tests Case (Australia v. France). Application by Fiji for permission to intervene*, I.C.J. Reports, 1973, p. 320; *Nuclear Tests Case (New Zealand v. France). Application by Fiji for permission to intervene*, I.C.J. Reports, 1973, p. 324.

107. See generally Pharand, Oil Pollution Control in the Canadian Arctic, 7 Texas Int. L.J. 45 (1971); and compare Bilder, The Canadian Arctic Waters Pollution Prevention Act: new stresses on the Law of the Sea, 69 Mich. L.R.1 (1970).

108. See, in this regard, Cot, Affaires des essais nucléaires (Australie c. France et Nouvelle Zélande c. France): demandes en indication des mesures conservatoires ordonnances du 22 juin 1973, 19 *Annuaire Français de Droit International* 252, at pp. 252-3 (1973), Pinto, La France et la Cour internationale de justice, *Le Monde* (Paris), December 22-3, 1974, at p. 7; Lacharrière, Commentaires sur la position juridique de la France à l'égard de la licéité de ses expériences nucléaires, 19 *Annuaire Français de Droit International* 235, at p. 251 (1973). And see generally Retrait par le gouvernement français de son acceptation de la juridiction obligatoire de la Cour internationale de justice (10 janvier 1974), 78 *Revue Générale de Droit International Public* 822 (1974).

109. "Les ordonnances rendues le 22 juin 1973 par la Cour internationale de justice dans les affaires des *Essais nucléaires* marquent un tournant décisif dans l'attitude de la France à l'égard de la juridiction internationale. Il est inutile de rappeler la tradition française ... Notre pays a joué un *rôle* décisif dans l'institution d'une juridiction internationale. Les contributions d'un Louis Renault, d'un Albert de La Pradelle ou d'un Jules Basdevant illustrent ce long combat de nos juristes, adossé à la ferme volonté des gouvernements successifs. Jamais, lorsque la juridiction internationale a été menacée, la France n'a ménagé son soutien à l'institution. Sur ce point, la Ve Republique, pourtant hostile à toute notion de supranationalité et jalouse gardienne de l'indépendence nationale, est restée fidèle à cette politique. Elle a défendu, au sein des Nations Unies, la Cour internationale de justice et la juridiction obligatoire. Aujourd'hui, le Gouvernement français rompt avec ce passé." Cot, op. cit., *Annuaire Français de Droit International* 252, at 252 (1973).

110. "Les ordonnances de juin 1974 ont provoqué le refus gouvernmental français d'accepter, à partir du 10 janvier 1974, la compétence obligatoire de la Cour internationale de justice dans ses différends d'ordre juridique avec d'autres Etats. Cette décision, prise sans consultation ni débat parlementaire, fait bon marché d'une tradition presque séculaire de notre diplomatie .... Ecartons l'un des motifs du retrait de la France, l'indiscrétion qui a permis au premier ministre australien de connaître le sens de la décision de la Cour et la

majorité obtenue, sans pour autant que des sanctions soient prises, malgré plusieurs démarches officielles, contre les responsables ....
Beaucoup plus grave est le second motif de retrait. Le gouvernement français 'ne peut faire confiance à la Cour actuelle pour se déclarer incompétente dans les cas réservés par sa déclaration relative à la compétence obligatoire de la Cour ....
Les tensions actuelles ont rapproché dangereusement la Cour du point de la rupture. Fallait-il pour autant que la France frappe le coup de grâce sans donner l'occasion à la Cour, par sa présence, de se ressaiser?" Pinto, *op. cit.*, *Le Monde*, December 22-3, 1974. And see generally Waldock, Decline of the Optional Clause, 32 B.Y.B.I.L. 244 (1955-6).

111. *Scott* v. *Sandford*, 19 Howard 393; and see Hughes, *The Supreme Court of the United States* (1928), at pp. 50-1.

112. Compare Lauterpacht, *The Development of International Law by the International Court* (1958), at p. 75 *et seq.*; Fitzmaurice, Judicial Innovation: its Uses and its Perils: as exemplified in some of the Work of the International Court of Justice during Lord McNair's Period of Office, in *Cambridge Essays in International Law. Essays in Honour of Lord McNair* (1965) at p. 24 *et seq.*; Vallat, The Peaceful Settlement of Disputes, ibid., especially at pp. 165-7; Münch, Das Wesen der Rechtsprechung als Leitbegriff für die Tätigkeit des Internationalen Gerichtshof, 31 *Zeitschrift für ausländisches öffentliches Recht und Völkerrecht* 712 (1971); Gross, The International Court of Justice: consideration of requirements for enhancing its *rôle* in the International Legal Order, 65 A.J.I.L. 253 (1971); Fitzmaurice, The Future of Public International Law and of the International Legal System in the circumstances of today, *Institut de Droit International. Livre du Centenaire 1873-1973. Evolutions et perspectives du droit international* (1973), at p. 196, and especially at p. 275 *et seq.*

113. Compare the remarks by Judge Gros, made *before* the French Nuclear Tests case:

> "L'adage 'la paix par le droit' correspondait à un état d'esprit dans une certaine période de l'histoire. Le vaste mouvement d'idées en faveur de l'arbitrage international, parallèlement au désarmement pour créer la sécurité, à la suite des tensions politiques qui culminèrent dans la première guerre mondiale, ne pouvait garder la même influence dans un monde où les conflits sont saisis soit par des organes politiques des Nations Unies, soit par des Etats directement intéressés, dont l'entente réalisée sur des bases politiques, s'avère indispensable pour le règlement de ces conflits." Gros, A propos de cinquante années de justice internationale, 76 *Revue Générale de Droit International Public* 5 at pp. 10-11 (1972).
>
> And see also Judge Gros' further appraisal:
>
> "Une saine autocritique montre les limites de toute amélioration du rôle de la Cour: nous sommes dans un domaine où le lyrisme ne peut voiler la réalité." Gros, Quelques remarques sur la pratique du droit international, *Mélanges offerts à Charles Rousseau. La Communauté Internationale* (1974), 113, at p. 124.

114. See, in this regard, the remarks by Judge Petrén, also made before the *French Nuclear Tests* case:

"It must ... be kept in mind that a party that has raised an objection to the court's jurisdiction to determine a case has the right to expect that the court will not give judgment on the merits therefore, should the said objection be upheld by the court. Would it not then be strange if the court, while upholding the objection to its jurisdiction, were nevertheless to examine the merits of the case, and to declare, for example, that the contentions of the applicant party were well founded in law? And would states not be still more reluctant to accept the court's jurisdiction than they are already today, if they were to learn that valid objections to the court's jurisdiction or to the receivability of an application will not always prevent the court from making statements on matters that the court, by upholding the objection, has found not to be properly brought before it? Petrén, Differences of Procedure between International and National Tribunals, in *Thoughts from the Lake of Time* (Burchard, editor) (1971), 27, at p. 39. And see also Petrén, Quelques réflexions sur la revision du réglement de la Cour internationale de Justice, in *Mélanges offerts à Charles Rousseau. La Communauté Internationale* (1974), 187.

115. I.C.J. Reports, 1974, p. 253, especially at pp. 267-8.

NOTES TO CHAPTER IV

1. *Western Sahara. Advisory Opinion*, I.C.J. Reports, 1975, p. 12. And see Judicial Decisions. Territorial status of Spanish Sahara prior to colonization, 70 A.J.I.L. 366 (1976).

2. *South West Africa, Second Phase, Judgment*. I.C.J. Reports 1966, p. 6. And see the comments by Dr. (now Judge) Elias in *Judicial Settlement of International Disputes* (Mosler & Bernhardt, eds.) 19, at 26-7 (1974).

3. See, in this regard, Pescatore, *Le droit de l'intégration* (1972), at p. 73 *et seq.*

4. See generally Rosenne, *Documents on the International Court of Justice* (1974), at p. 329 *et seq*; Wehberg & Goldschmidt, *Der Internationale Gerichtshof. Enstehungsgeschichte, Analyse, Dokumentation* (1973), p. 18 *et seq.*

5. Wehberg & Golschmidt, *op. cit.*, p. 82 *et seq.*

6. *Rules of Court.* Adopted on 6 May 1946, as amended on 10 May 1972: –

"*Article 33.* 1. The Court shall sit in private to deliberate upon the disputes which are submitted to it and upon advisory opinions which it is asked to give."

"*Article 79.* 1. The judgment shall contain:
... the names of the judges participating;
... the number of the judges constituting the majority."

Resolution concerning the internal judicial practice of the Court. (Rules of Court, Article 33) adopted on 5 July 1968: –

"*Article 6.*

> On the basis of the views expressed in the final deliberation, in the written notes, and in prior deliberations, the Court proceeds to choose a drafting committee by secret ballot and by an absolute majority of votes. Two judges are elected from among those Members of the Court whose oral statements and written notes have most closely and effectively reflected the opinion of the Court as a whole.
>
> The President shall *ex officio* be a member of the drafting committee unless he does not share the majority opinion of the Court as it appears then to exist, in which case his place shall be taken by the Vice-President. If the Vice-President is ineligible for the same reason, the Court shall proceed, by the process already employed, to the election of a third member, in which case the senior elected judge shall preside in the drafting committee ...."

7. *Rules of Court.* Adopted on 6 May 1946, as amended on 10 May 1972: –

"*Article 79.2.* Any judge may, if he so desires, attach his individual opinion to the judgment, whether he dissents from the majority or not, or a bare statement of his dissent."

8. The parameters of permissible disagreement, whether by way of a formal dissent or of a separate opinion not being a dissent, would seem only marginally controllable. *Resolution concerning the internal judicial practice of the Court (Rules of Court, Article 33)*: –

"*Article 7.* (i) A preliminary draft of the decision is circulated to the judges, who may submit to the drafting committee amendments in writing ....
(ii) Judges who wish to deliver separate or dissenting opinions make the text thereof available to the Court after the first reading is concluded and within a time-limit fixed by the Court ....
(iv) In the course of the second reading, judges who are delivering separate or dissenting opinions inform the Court of changes they propose to introduce into the text of their opinions by reason of changes made in the draft judgment."

9. I.C.J. Reports 1975, pp. 12-69.

10. *Ibid.*, pp. 69-77.

11. *Ibid.*, p. 78.

12. *Ibid.*, pp. 78-82.

13. *Ibid.*, pp. 83-102.

14. *Ibid.*, p. 103.

15. *Ibid.*, pp. 104-115.

16. *Ibid.*, pp. 116-126.

17. *Ibid.*, pp. 127-172.

18. *Ibid.*, pp. 173-4.

19. *Ibid.*, pp. 175-6.

20. *Ibid.*, (Opinion of Court), p. 68.

21. *Ibid.*, (Opinion of Court), pp. 68-9.

22. Pound, *Cacoethes Dissentiendi* – The Heated Judicial Dissent, 39 A.B.A.J. 794 (1953). And see generally the author's discussion, Supreme Courts and Opinion-Writing: Specially Concurring and Dissenting Judicial Opinions, in *Judicial Review* 225 *et seq.* (4th ed., 1969).

23. I.C.J. Reports 1975, p. 14.

24. *Ibid.*, p. 13.

25. *Ibid.*, p. 14.

26. *Status of Eastern Carelia, Advisory Opinion of 23 July 1923, P.C.I.J. Series B, No. 5*, p. 7.

27. I.C.J. Reports 1975, p. 24.

28. I.C.J. Reports 1950, p. 65.

29. I.C.J. Reports 1950, p. 65, at p. 71; adopted by the Court in *Western Sahara*, I.C.J. Reports 1975, p. 12, at p. 24.

30. I.C.J. Reports 1975 at p. 27-8.

31. *Ibid.*, p. 28.

32. *Ibid.*

33. *Ibid.*, p. 29

34. *Ibid.*

35. *Charter of the United Nations,*

"Article 96.1 The General Assembly or the Security Council may request the International Court of Justice to give an advisory opinion on any legal question."

36. Statute of the International Court of Justice.

"Article 65.1 The Court may give an advisory opinion on any legal question at the request of whatever body may be authorised by or in accordance with the Charter of the United Nations to make such a request."

37. I.C.J. Reports 1975, p. 12, at p. 19.

38. *Legal Consequences for States of the Continued Presence of South Africa in Namibia (South West Africa) notwithstanding Security Council Resolution 276 (1970).* I.C.J. Reports 1971, p. 27.

39. I.C.J. Reports 1975, p. 19.

40. I.C.J. Reports 1947-1948, p. 61.

41. I.C.J. Reports 1975, p. 19.

42. *Ibid.*, pp. 20-1.

43. *Ibid.*, p. 20.

44. *Ibid.*, p. 29.

45. *Ibid.*, p. 30.

46. *Ibid.*, p. 32.

47. *Ibid.*, p. 37.

48. *Ibid.*, p. 38.

49. *Ibid.*, p. 39.

50. *Ibid.*, p. 40.

51. *Ibid.*

52. *Ibid.*, pp. 41-2.

53. *P.C.I.J., Series A/B, No. 53.*

54. *Ibid.*, p. 45; I.C.J. Reports 1975, p. 12, at p. 42.

55. *P.C.I.J., Series A/B, No. 53*, at p. 46.

56. I.C.J. Reports 1975, p. 12, at p. 43.

57. *Ibid.*, at pp. 43-4

58. *Ibid.*, at p. 45.

59. *Ibid.*, at p. 46.

60. *Ibid.*, at p. 48.

61. *Ibid.*, at p. 49.

62. *Ibid.*, at p. 49.

63. *Ibid.*, at p. 50.

64. *Ibid.*, at p. 56.

65. *Ibid.*, at pp. 56-7.

66. *Ibid.*, at p. 57.

67. *Ibid.*

68. *Ibid.*

69. *Ibid.*, p. 58.

70. *Ibid.*, p. 59.

71. *Ibid.*

72. *Ibid.*, pp. 59-60.

73. *Ibid.*, p. 60.
74. *Ibid.*, p. 61.
75. *Ibid.*, p. 61.
76. *Ibid.*, p. 62.
77. *Ibid.*, p. 63.
78. *Ibid.*, p. 64.
79. *Ibid.*
80. *Ibid.*
81. *Ibid.*, p. 65.
82. *Ibid.*, p. 68.
83. *Ibid.*
84. *Ibid.*, p. 65.
85. *Ibid.*, p. 66.
86. *Ibid.*, p. 67.
87. *Ibid.*
88. *Ibid.*, pp. 66-7.
89. *Ibid.*, p. 68.
90. *Ibid.*, pp. 69-70.
91. *Ibid.*
92. *Ibid.*, p. 72.
93. *Ibid.*, p. 71.
94. *Ibid.*, pp. 69-70.
95. *Ibid.*, p. 72.

96. *Ibid.*, p. 74. The reference was apparently to Vice-President Ammoun, the ground of objection being that he had participated, years before, as a Lebanese national delegate to the U.N. General Assembly, in the debate on Resolution 1514 (XV) of 14 December 1960 containing the Declaration on the Granting of Independence to Colonial Countries and Peoples. An objection on the ground of judicial "interest", though obviously relevant in the case of contentious proceedings, might, *a priori*, seem to be odd or improper in the case of the Court's Advisory Opinion jurisdiction, but the precedent is well established by now. See the *Namibia* affair, where the disqualification of three judges – the President (Sir M. Zafrulla Khan), and Judges Padilla Nervo and Morozov, – was discussed by the Court. *Legal Consequences for States of the Continued Presence of South Africa in Namibia (South West Africa) notwithstanding Security Council Resolution 276 (1970)*, I.C.J. Reports 1971, p. 27.

97. I.C.J. Reports 1975, at p. 74.
98. *Ibid.*
99. *Ibid.*, p. 75.
100. *Ibid.*, p. 76.
101. *Ibid.*
102. *Ibid.*, p. 77.
103. *Ibid.*

104. Judge Gros and Judge Petrén each dissented in the 8 to 6 decision of the Court, on 22 June 1973, to grant interim measures of protection in the *French Nuclear Tests* case, four of the six dissenting judges filing individual

dissenting opinions (Judges Forster, Gros, Petrén, and Ignacio-Pinto): *Nuclear Tests Case (Australia v. France). Request for the indication of Interim Measures of Protection*, I.C.J. Reports 1973, p. 99. In the Court's final judgment of December 20, 1974, rendered by a majority of 9 to 6, four judges who were members of the majority (Judges Forster, Gros, Petrén, and Ignacio-Pinto) filed individual, specially concurring opinions which are sharply critical of the official Opinion of Court and which recur to the basic preliminary, jurisdictional objections raised in their individual dissents in the earlier, *Interim Measures* judgment: *Nuclear Tests Case (Australia v. France)*, I.C.J. Reports 1974, p. 253. And see generally Franck, Word Made Law: The Decision of the International Court of Justice in the Nuclear Test Cases, 69 *A.J.I.L.* 612 (1975); Sur, Les affaires des essais nucléaires devant la C.I.J., 79 *Revue Générale de Droit International Public* 972 (1975).

105. I.C.J. Reports 1975 at p. 106.

106. *Ibid.*, p. 108.

107. *Ibid.*

108. *Ibid.*, p. 109.

109. *Ibid.*, p. 110.

110. *Ibid.*, p. 116.

111. *Ibid.*

112. *Ibid.*, p. 117 (foot-note omitted).

113. *Ibid.*, p. 126.

114. *Ibid.*, pp. 85-6.

115. *Ibid*, p. 86; and see Bedgaoui, *Terra nullius, "droits" historiques et autodétermination* (1975); and see generally Bedgaoui, *Non-Alignment et Droit International*, 151 *Recueil des Cours* 337 (1976), especially at p. 408 *et seq.*

116. *Ibid.*, pp. 86-7.

117. , *Ibid.*, p. 99.

118. *Ibid.*, p.,100.

119. *Ibid.*, p. 101.

120. *Ibid.*, p. 103.

121. *Ibid.*, p. 173.

122. *Ibid.*, pp. 173-4.

123. *Ibid.*, p. 78.

124. *Ibid.*, pp. 79-80.

125. *Ibid.*, p. 80.

126. *Ibid.*, p. 81.

127. *Ibid.*, p. 175.

128. *Ibid.*, pp. 175-6

129. *Ibid.*, p. 176.

130. *Ibid.*, p. 129.

131. *Ibid.*, pp. 137-8.

132. De Visscher, *Théories et Réalités en Droit international public* 431 (1955); I.C.J. Reports 1975, p. 140.

133. I.C.J. Reports 1975, p. 140.

134. *Ibid.*, p. 168.

135. I.C.J. Reports 1953, p. 56.
136. I.C.J. Reports 1975, p. 168.
137. *Ibid.*, p. 169.
138. *Ibid.*, p. 171.
139. *Ibid.*, p. 170.
140. *Ibid.*, p. 170, Foot-note 1.
141. Stylistically, the official Opinion of Court in *Western Sahara* bears all the external evidence of a composite opinion, with two distinct segments, – one concerning the preliminary, jurisdictional issue, and the other the substantive issues of territorial sovereignty and national self-determination – which presumably are the work of different judicial authors. The *Resolution concerning the internal judicial practice of the Court (Rules of Court, Article 33)* adopted on 5 July 1968, provides, as we have noted, for a drafting committee for any matter, chosen by secret ballot of the Court and by an absolute majority of votes, and composed of – "two judges ... elected from among those Members of the Court whose oral statements and written notes have most closely and effectively reflected the opinion of the Court as a whole"; with the President of the Court to be *ex officio* a member of the drafting committee unless he is among the dissenters, and failing the President the Vice-President, and failing the Vice-President a third elected judge with the senior elected judge to preside in the drafting committee in this latter situation. (Article 6).
As adopted, the Resolution on Internal Judicial Practice of the Court would appear to envisage collective, collegial work on the part of the three-man majority drafting committee; but there is nothing excluding the committee's acting as the Privy Council did and having a single strong judicial personality act as *rapporteur* and prepare the final majority Opinion of Court himself. This particular part of the Court's decision-making process is, it has been suggested, veiled in secrecy as to its actual practice. Lillich and White, The deliberative process of the International Court of Justice: a preliminary critique and some possible reforms, 70 A.J.I.L. 28, 35 (1976); though see Rosenne, *The International Court of Justice. An Essay in Political and Legal Theory* (1961), at pp. 416-20. Judge Gros, in a perceptive analysis of the Court's internal decision-making and opinion-writing practice, stresses the influence of the P.C.I.J., in the early, formative years of the Court, as controlling in establishing present day patterns:
"The great jurists of the years 1922-1940 were accustomed to research and to work conducted individually and without either meetings or frequent confrontations. Nothing shews this better than the refusal of the Court, right from its opening session, to institute *rapporteurs*, – a familiar practice in the highest jurisdictions of numerous countries." Gros, Observations sur le mode de délibération de la Cour Internationale de Justice, in *Studi in onore di Gaetano Morelli. Il processo internazionale* 377, at 380 (1975).
142. It is, in this regard, surely rather arch to essay the general comment as to the Court's opinion-writing, without citing any evidence in support thereof, – "Since 1968, however, the President's membership has been of the *ex officio* variety: presumably he does no actual drafting." Lillich and White,

op. cit., 70 A.J.I.L. 28, at 36 (1976). As to the Presidency generally, see Rosenne, *The International Court of Justice. An essay in Political and Legal Theory* (1961), p. 152 *et seq.*; Rosenne, *The World Court. What it is and how it works* (1962), at p. 62 *et seq.*

143. *The Resolution concerning the internal judicial practice of the Court (Rules of Court, Article 33)* adopted on 5 July 1968, though not providing, in terms, for control over the content, form, or tone of separate or dissenting opinions, seems, nevertheless, to envisage some form at least of internal Court scrutiny prior to publication, in stipulating that the text of any such proposed opinions are to be delivered to the Court after the first reading of the draft Opinion of Court is concluded and within a time-limit fixed by the Court (Article 7 (ii)); and that, in the course of the second reading of the Opinion of Court, judges who are delivering separate or dissenting opinions are to inform the Court of changes they propose to introduce into the text of their opinions by reasons of the changes made in the draft Opinion of Court. (Article 7 (iv)).

Anand comments on "discordant notes of varied intensities, [which], it is sometimes asserted, create disharmony and bad taste .... There have also been some complaints about the unseemly use of language and bitter tone of dissents, especially during the *régime* of the International Court, which are full of criticism of the Court's judgments instead of offering 'objective and judicial' exposition of the views of the writer, as was generally the case during the life of the Permanent Court." Anand, The *rôle* of Individual and Dissenting Opinions in International Adjudication, in *Studies in International Adjudication* 191, at 192-3 (1969).

Several members of the Court have, in the past, gone on public record as to the obligation on the part of judges strictly to construe and limit the *rôle* of dissenting opinions, in order to prevent abuses – notably Judge Basdevant and Judge Krylov: Krylov suggested that it is the President's "delicate task" to implement this principle of judicial self-restraint on the part of dissenting judges. Rosenne, *The International Court of Justice. An essay in Political and Legal Theory* (1961), at p. 417. Judge Gros is inclined to blame the Court's own rules to internal judicial practice as having "created a reflex of waiting which does not contribute to the development of a truly collegial justice." Gros, Observations sur le mode de délibération de la Cour Internationale de Justice, in *Studi in onore di Gaetano Morelli. Il processo internazionale* 377, at 384 (1975). As to the Court's practice and procedure generally, see Petrén, Quelques réflexions sur la revision du règlement de la Cour Internationale de Justice, in *Mélanges offerts à Charles Rousseau. La communauté internationale* 187 (1974); Jiménez de Aréchaga, The Amendments to the Rules of Procedure of the International Court of Justice, 67 A.J.I.L. 1 (1973).

144. A criticism that Professor Leo Gross advances in regard to the Court's Advisory Opinion in *Admission of a State to the United Nations (Charter, Article 4)*, I.C.J. Reports 1948, p. 15: Gross, The International Court of Justice and the United Nations, 2 *Recueil des Cours* 313, at 406 (1967). And see also Gross, Election of States to United Nations Membership, [1954] *Proceedings. American Society of International Law* 37. And see also

Sur, Les affaires des essais nucléaires devant la C.I.J., 79 *Revue Générale de Droit International Public* 972, at 1016-1018 (1975).

145. *Statute of the International Court of Justice*, Article 21 (I).

146. *Ibid.*

147. Only one President, J.G. Guerrero of El Salvador, has been re-elected to date and that fact may be attributed to unique circumstances related to the Second World War and the transition, after the war, from the P.C.I.J. to the I.C.J.: Judge Guerrero was the last President of the old Permanent Court (from 1936 to 1946), and the first President of the new Court (from 1946 to 1949), and his nine successors as President have all been limited to a single, three-year term. *Documents on the International Court of Justice* (Rosenne, ed.) 329-334 (1974).

148. *Statute of the International Court of Justice*, Article 13 (I).

149. *Ibid.*

150. The system of the double majority – in the General Assembly and the Security Council – required for purposes of election to the Court, in terms of the Court Statute, Articles 4 (I) and 10 (I) and 10 (3), seems to impose special hazards on the chances of candidates from the smaller or non-affiliated countries. See generally Rosenne, *The International Court of Justice. An essay in Political and Legal Theory* (1961), pp. 136-142; *Documents on the International Court of Justice* (Rosenne, ed.) pp. 337-349 (1974).

At the same time, the increasing politicisation of the processes of election in the aftermath of the Court's one-vote majority decision in the South West Africa case in 1966 clearly implies closer scrutiny than heretofore of the political values or political preferences of the individual judicial candidates. As Dr. (now Judge) Elias comments: "Given the new impetus from 'the third world', there does not appear to be any likelihood of a return to the old order in which Europe dominated the Bench. This is not to say that Western Europe would in future be under-represented. Rather, it is that Western European candidates of the future would stand a far better chance of being elected if they had or were thought to have liberal or progressive views *vis-à-vis* the problems of 'the third world'." Elias, in *Judicial Settlement of International Disputes* (Mosler & Bernhardt, editors), 19 at 26 (1974). Dr. Elias ascribes, in particular, the failure of the Australian jurist, Sir Kenneth Bailey, to secure election to the Court in 1966 in part to the fact that he was considered to be "narrow and conservative", and in part to political back-lash against the Court's 1966 South West Africa decision and the crucial *rôle* played in that one-vote majority decision by the second, tie-breaking vote exercised by the Court's retiring President, Sir Percy Spender, who was of the same nationality as Bailey. *Ibid.*, at 26-7.

151. See generally the author's *Judicial Review* at 217 *et seq.* (4th ed. 1969).

152. See the author's *Constitutionalism in Germany and the Federal Constitutional Court* at 41 *et seq.* (1962); Leibholz, *Der Status des Bundesverfassungsgericht* in *Das Bundesverfassungsgericht* at 61 *et seq.* (1963); Leibholz and Rinck, *Grundgesetz für die Bundesrepublik Deutschland* at 686 *et*

seq. (4th ed. 1971); Laufer, *Verfassungsgerichtsbarkeit und politischer Prozess* at 206 *et seq.* (1968); Laufer, Typus und Status des Bundesverfassungsgerichts in 2 *Die Moderne Demokratie und ihr Recht (Festschrift für Gerhard Leibholz zum 65. Geburtstag.)* (Bracher *et. al.* eds.) at 427 (1966); Kutscher, Die Kompetenzen des Bundesverfassungsgerichts 1951 bis 1969, in *Festschrift für Gebhard Müller zum 70. Geburtstag des Präsidenten des Bundesverfassungsgerichts* (Rittersprach and Geiger, eds.) at 161 (1970).

153. *Status of Eastern Carelia.* Advisory Opinion of 23 July 1923. *P.C.I.J. Series B, No. 5, p. 7.*

154. I.C.J. Reports 1975, p. 24.

155. I.C.J. Reports 1975, pp. 28-9.

156. Compare De Visscher, *Les effectivités du Droit International Public* 151, at 160 (1967); De Visscher, *Théories et Réalités en Droit International Public* at 410 *et seq.* (1955); 1 Verzijl, *The Jurisprudence of the World Court. A case by case commentary* at 50-2 (1967); Lauterpacht, *The Development of International Law by the International Court* at 352 *et seq.* (1958). Gross, The International Court of Justice and the United Nations, 2 *Recueil des Cours* 313 at 412-3 (1967); Hambro, The authority of the Advisory Opinions of the International Court of Justice, 3 I.C.L.Q. 6, at 19-20 (1954); Lachs, Perspectives pour la fonction consultative de la Cour Internationale de Justice, in *Studi in onore di Gaetano Morelli. Il processo internazionale* 423, at 436 (1975).

157. *Nuclear Tests Case (Australia v. France) (Judgment),* I.C.J. Reports 1974, p. 253.

158. *Charter of the United Nations,* Article 96. The earlier warning by Judge Manley Hudson, in the era of the old P.C.I.J., against carrying too far any policy of assimilating the Advisory to the contentious procedure of the Court, lest the advisory opinions come to be regarded as a "species of judgment" and the "advisory jurisdiction ... be regarded as an alternative to obligatory jurisdiction, and this might result in diminishing the frequency of requests for advisory opinions", is presumably counter-balanced, in the case of the present Court, by the stricter political control capable of being exercised over access to the Court's Advisory Opinion jurisdiction, by the Security Council and, especially, by the General Assembly. Hudson, *The Permanent Court of International Justice 1920-1942* at 523 (1943); Gross, The International Court of Justice and the United Nations, *2 Recueil des Cours* 313, at 405 (1967). Judge Lachs notes that the Advisory Opinion procedure has continued to be assimilated to the contentious procedure of the Court: Lachs, Perspectives pour la fonction consultative de la Cour Internationale de Justice, in *Studi in onore di Gaetano Morelli. Il processo internazionale* 423, 426 (1975); while Professor Jennings suggests that the *procedure* of the Advisory Opinion, with its machinery of notice to all interested parties (Statute of the International Court of Justice, Article 64 (2)) – and its possibility of hearing arguments from governments generally as well as the United Nations, is ideally suited to cases "of general constitutional interest", and this may account for its increasing usage. Jennings, in *Judicial Settlement of International Disputes* (Mosler & Bernhardt, eds.) 35, at 45 (1974). For compari-

son of the relative facility of intervention by States in contentious proceedings, (Court Statute, Articles 62 and 63) and in Advisory Opinion proceedings, see Hambro, Intervention under Article 63 of the Statute of the International Court of Justice, in *Studi in onore di Gaetano Morelli. Il processo internazionale* 387 (1975).

159. I.C.J. Reports 1950, p. 72.

160. *Legal Consequences for States of the Continued Presence of South Africa in Namibia (South West Africa) notwithstanding Security Council Resolution 276* (1970). I.C.J. Reports 1971, p. 27.

161. I.C.J. Reports 1975, p. 12, at p. 21.

162. *Peace Treaties* I.C.J. Reports 1950, p. 71; cited with approval, I.C.J. Reports 1975, p. 12, at p. 24. As Gross sums up the "distinguishing", in *Peace Treaties* (1950), of the P.C.I.J. holding in *Eastern Carelia* (1923):

"Seeing itself, as the Court stated categorically in the *Peace Treaties* case, in the *rôle* of organ of the United Nations, albeit a judicial organ, the Court was in principle willing to participate in the activities of the Organisation. It was the Court which made the categorical statement that its Opinions had no binding force, that they were not given to the State but to the requesting organ, and that no State could prevent the giving of an Advisory Opinion which, not the Court, but the United Nations "considers to be desirable in order to obtain enlightenment as to the course of action it should take". The Court maintained that the case before it, the *Peace Treaties* case, was "profoundly different" from the *Eastern Carelia* case. It is suggested that it was rather the perception of its *rôle* which was "profoundly different" from that of the Permanent Court." Gross, The International Court of Justice and the United Nations, *2 Recueil des Cours* 313, at 415-6 (1967); and see also Gross, Expenses of the United Nations for Peace-Keeping Operations: The Advisory Opinion of the International Court of Justice, 17 *International Organisation* 1, at 26-7 (1963).

Judge Lachs has gone on record to the effect that the Court ought to facilitate requests for Advisory Opinions, in order to "breathe new life into Articles 92 and 96 of the Charter": Lachs, Perspectives pour la fonction consultative de la Cour Internationale de Justice, in *Studi in onore di Gaetano Morelli. Il processo internazionale* 423, at 436-7 (1975). And see generally De Visscher, *Aspects récents du Droit procédural de la Cour Internationale de Justice* 195 *et seq.* (1966); Chacko, The possible expansion of the Advisory Jurisdiction of the International Court of Justice, in *Essays on International Law in Honour of Krishna Rao* (Nawaz, ed.) 214 (1975).

163. *The Institut de Droit International* has defined the "general intertemporal problem" as being the "delimitation of the temporal sphere of application of norms", and has gone on to stipulate: –

> "1. Unless otherwise indicated, the temporal sphere of application of any norm of public international law shall be determined in accordance with the general principle of law by which any fact, action or situation must be assessed in the light of the rules of law that are contemporaneous with it."

Institut de Droit International, The Intertemporal Problem in Public International Law. (Resolution adopted at Wiesbaden, August 11, 1975). And see, Le problème dit du droit intertemporel dans l'ordre international (Provisional Report and Definitive Report, Eleventh Commission (Sørensen, *rapporteur*) 55 *Annuaire de l'Institut de Droit International* 1 (1973).

164. Gény, *Méthode d'interprétation et sources en droit privé positif. Essai critique*, p. 74 *et seq.* (1899).

165. This notion seems implicit in Judge Lachs' observations in response to the *Institut de Droit International's* Provisional Report: "A truly appropriate method would consist in taking into consideration at once the conflict of the norms and the validity and the interpretation of the one norm in time: otherwise stated, the intertemporal application of law. This last element appears to me particularly important at an epoch where life evolves so quickly and where certain rules of international law become out-dated in the space of a generation, or must be rethought on new and entirely different bases." 55 *Annuaire de l'Institut de Droit International* 1, at 69 and at 106 (1973). And see also Doehring, Die Wirkung des Zeitablaufs auf den Bestand völkerrechtlicher Regeln, (1964) *Jahrbuch der Max-Planck-Gesellschaft* 70, at 75 *et seq.* and 88-9; Krause-Ablass, *Intertemporales Völkerrecht. Der zeitliche Anwendungsbereich von Völkerrechtsnormen* (1970); Fitzmaurice, The Future of Public International Law and of the International Legal System in the circumstances of today, *Institut de Droit International. Livre du Centenaire 1873-1973; Evolutions et perspectives du Droit International* 196, at 255 *et seq.* (1973); and see generally the Court's Advisory Opinion in *Legal Consequences for States of the Continued Presence of South Africa in Namibia (South West Africa) notwithstanding Security Council Resolution 276 (1970)*, I.C.J. Reports 1971, p. 16.

166. I.C.J. Reports 1975 p. 12, at pp. 16-17.

167. La crise du Sahara occidental rebondit, *Le Monde* (Paris), 18 October 1975.

168. Le Conflit du Sahara occidental. Les positions des partis, *Le Monde*, 4 November 1975; *The Wall Street Journal* (New York), 3 November 1975.

169. La fin de la "Marche Verte": Madrid et Rabat parlent de succès: M. Boumédienne reçoit M. Ould Daddah, *Le Monde*, 11 November 1975; Sahara occidental. Hassan II: la "marche verte" a atteint ses objectifs, *Le Monde*, 11 November 1975; U.N. *rôle* proposed for Spanish Sahara, *The New York Times*, 9 November 1975.

170. La décolonisation du Sahara occidental. Aux termes de l'accord conclu entre Madrid, Rabat, Nouakchott. La présence espagnole prendra fin le 28 février 1976, *Le Monde*, 15 November 1975; Alger: un fait accompli diplomatique, *Le Monde*, 15 November 1975.

171. La crise du Sahara: Le dessous des cartes. 1. Arrière-pensées et intrigues, *Le Monde*, 27 November 1975; and see also Le Maroc et la Mauritanie délimitent leur frontière au Sahara occidental, *Le Monde*, 17 April 1976.

172. La crise du Sahara: Le dessous des cartes. II. Une grande partie de poker, *Le Monde*, 28 November 1975.

173. Sahara occidental: M. Boumédienne obtient l'appui du Colonel Kad-

hafi dans son différend avec le Maroc, *Le Monde*, 31 December 1975; Les risques de l'aventure, *Le Monde*, 31 December 1975.

174. La création de la république sahraouie. La riposte du *Polisario, Le Monde*, 1 March 1976; Sahara occidental: L'ordre marocain règne à El-Aïoun, *Le Monde*, 27 February 1976.

175. Rabat et Nouakchott rompent avec Alger, *Le Monde*, 9 March 1976.

176. La crise du Sahara occidental. La tension entre Alger et Rabat est progressivement retombée, *Le Monde*, 10 April 1976.

177. Sahara occidental. Le Front *Polisario* annonce le déclenchement d'une vaste offensive militaire, *Le Monde*, 26 May, 1976.

178. Phosphate: Taking a Leaf from Oil's Book, *The New York Times*, Sunday, 9 November 1975 (Section F, p. 3). And see also The Big Dispute over the Sahara, *The Wall Street Journal*, 21 October 1975.

179. Per Frankfurter J., dissenting, *Sherrer v. Sherrer*, 334 U.S. 343, 365-6 (1948).

180. The new *Resolution concerning the internal judicial practice of the Court (Rules of Court, Article 33)*, which was adopted by the Court on 12 April 1976, in revision of the earlier *Resolution* adopted on 5 July 1968 and in force at the time of the rendering of the *Western Sahara* Advisory Opinion, seems designed, in part at least, to alleviate the type of judicial dissonance evidenced in the Western Sahara judicial opinion-writing. The thrust of the revised *Resolution* appears twofold: to improve procedures for canvassing of individual judicial positions prior to the actual decision-making stage and so facilitate the achieving of a Court consensus; and to reduce the chances of purely unnecessary judicial disagreements being manifested in the opinion-writing stage by establishing limiting criteria of relevance for separate or dissenting opinions. The first principle seems reflected, in particular, in the revised *Resolution's* new wording in Article 1 (i) and 1 (iii); Article 3 (ii); Article 4 (ii) (b); and Article 5 (i). The second principle seems reflected, in particular, in the new and much more precise wording of Article 7 (iv), which stipulates that, once those judges who wish to deliver separate or dissenting opinions have submitted their first draft opinions to the Court, they may, thereafter, – "make changes in or additions to their opinions only to the extent that changes have been made in the draft decision" [of the Court].

NOTES TO CHAPTER V

1. *Aegean Sea Continental Shelf, Interim Protection, Order of 11 September 1976*, I.C.J. Reports 1976, p. 3.

2. at p. 3.

3. at p. 15.

4. at p. 17.

5. at p. 19.

6. at p. 21.

7. at p. 23.

8. at p. 24.

9. at p. 27.

10. at p. 31.

11. at p. 35 (Judge *ad hoc* Stassinopoulos).

12. *Nuclear Tests Case (Australia v. France), Interim Protection Order*, I.C.J. Reports 1973, p. 99.

13. *Nuclear Tests Case (Australia v. France), Judgment*, I.C.J. Reports 1974, p. 253. And see also Sur, Les affaires des essais nucléaires devant la C.I.J. 79 *Revue générale de droit international public* 972 (1975).

14. *Western Sahara, Advisory Opinion*, I.C.J. Reports 1975, p. 12. And see also Bennouna, L'affaire du Sahara occidental devant la Cour Internationale de Justice. Essai d'analyse structurale de l'avis consultatif du 16 octobre 1975, 1 *Revue juridique politique et économique du Maroc* 81 (1976).

15. *Livre Blanc sur les expériences nucléaires*, Ministère des Affaires étrangères, Service de presse et d'information, (Paris) (June, 1973). And see Lacharrière, Cour internationale de justice. Commentaires sur la position juridique de la France à l'égard de ses expériences nucléaires, 19 *Annuaire Français de Droit International* 235 (1973).

16. I.C.J. Reports, 1976, p. 3, at p. 5.

17. *Ibid.*, at p. 8.

18. *Ibid.*

19. *Ibid.*; and see Merrills, Interim Measures of Protection and the Substantive Jurisdiction of the International Court, 36 *Cambridge Law Journal* 86 (1977).

20. Statute of the International Court of Justice, Article 41:

1. The Court shall have power to indicate, if it considers that circumstances so require, any provisional measures which ought to be taken to preserve the respective rights of either party.

2. Pending the final decision, notice of the measures suggested shall forthwith be given to the parties and to the Security Council.

21. *Nuclear Tests Case (Australia v. France), Interim Protection Order*, I.C.J. Reports 1973, p. 99, at p. 111: *Nuclear Tests Case (Australia v. France), Judgment*, I.C.J. Reports 1974, p. 253, at p. 275.

22. *Nuclear Tests Case (Australia v. France), Interim Protection Order*, I.C.J. Reports 1973, p. 99, at p. 115; *Nuclear Tests Case (Australia v. France), Judgment*, I.C.J. Reports 1974, p. 253, at p. 279.

23. I.C.J. Reports 1976, p. 3, at p. 15.

24. I.C.J. Reports 1976, p. 3, at p. 9.

25. *Ibid.*, at p. 10.

26. *Ibid.*, at p. 11.

27. *Ibid.*, at p. 26.

28. *Ibid.*, at p. 30.

29. *Ibid.*

30. *Nuclear Tests Case (Australia v. France), Judgment*, I.C.J. Reports 1974, p. 253, at p. 267.

31. *Nuclear Tests Case (Australia v. France), Interim Protection Order*, I.C.J. Reports 1973, p. 99

32. I.C.J. Reports 1974, p. 253, at pp. 271-2.

33. I.C.J. Reports 1976, p. 3, at p. 8.

34. *Ibid.*, at p. 10.

35. *Ibid.*

36. I.C.J. Reports 1974, p. 253, at pp. 267-8.

37. I.C.J. Reports 1976, p. 3, at p. 12.

38. *Ibid.*

39. *Ibid.*

40. *Ibid.*, at p. 13.

41. *Ibid.*, at p. 12.

42. *Ibid.*

43. *Ibid.*, at p. 12 and at p. 13.

44. *Ibid.*, at p. 19.

45. *Ibid.*

46. *Ibid.*, at p. 20.

47. *Ibid.*, at p. 33.

48. *Ibid.*

49. *Ibid.*

50. *Ibid.*

51. *Ibid.*, at p. 34.

52. *Ibid.*, at p. 26.

53. Statute of the International Court of Justice, Article 56:

1. The judgment shall state the reasons on which it is based.

2. It shall contain the names of the judges who have taken part in the decision.

54. I.C.J. Reports 1974, p. 253, at pp. 391–455 (Judge *ad hoc* Barwick), the longest individual opinion filed in *Nuclear Tests Case (Australia v. France), Judgment*.

55. I.C.J. Reports 1976, p. 3, at pp. 35–40 (Judge *ad hoc* Stassinopoulos).

NOTES TO CHAPTER VI

1. Editorial, "Scuttle Law of the Sea", *The Wall Street Journal* (New York), July 22, 1977; and see also Martin, "U.S. Somewhat Pessimistic as U.N. Talks on Ocean Exploration face Eighth Year", *The Wall Street Journal* (New York), June 15, 1977.

1a. The substantive legal (policy) problems of the 1978 resumed Geneva session were unhappily compounded by an unexpected procedural problem which arose, necessarily, as the first question on the resumed session's agenda, namely the Conference presidency. The Conference's president, from its inception, Hamilton Shirley Amerasinghe, had been excluded from his own country, Sri Lanka's official delegation to the 1978 resumed Geneva session. (U.N. Press Release WS/860, 31 March, 1978). The first ten days of the 1978 resumed session were occupied in deciding this procedural issue which, obviously, had implications for general United Nations practice transcending the Third U.N. Conference itself. After vigorous opposition by Latin American and Caribbean states, involving a walk-out of the Conference hall by seven Latin American states when the decision was announced, the Conference decided that Mr. Amerasinghe – "was and continued to be its President unless a decision to the contrary were taken by consensus". This Conference decision was taken by a vote of 75 to 18, with 13 abstentions, and with a further 21 countries not participating. The Conference had earlier turned down a motion for a prior vote on a Mexican proposal stating that – "in view of the implications of the problem raised by the legal impediment in the way of Mr. Amerasinghe", any decision should be taken by consensus. (U.N. Press Release WS/861, 7 April, 1978).

2. Editorial, "On to Calcutta", *The Wall Street Journal* (New York), August 29, 1974.

3. See, generally, Stone, On the vocation of the International Law Commission, 57 *Columbia Law Review* 16 (1957).

4. The drafting committee that the Third U.N. Law of the Sea Conference did, in fact, endow itself with, suffered from a number of in-built disabilities that seriously weakened its potential political authority and influence: its membership was unusually large and unwieldy – 23 members in all, yet it was not especially representative in terms of political power, only two of the Permanent Members of the Security Council – the United States and the Soviet Union – being members and no officially francophone state. Beyond that, the committee could neither seize itself of matters of its own volition, nor modify the essentials of documents submitted to it, nor reopen the

debate in depth on any questions, nor initiate its own texts: it existed simply for purposes of referral by the plenary Conference and its three Committees, and thus was reduced, from the beginning, to a purely mechanical and necessarily subordinate *rôle*. See, generally, Vignes, Organisation et règlement intérieur de la III e Conférence sur le droit de la mer, 91 *Revue du Droit Public* 337 (1975).

5. United Nations: Rules of Procedure for the Third U.N. Conference on the Law of the Sea, U.N. Doc. A/Conf. 62/30/Rev. 1, (adopted at the Caracas session, June 27, 1974), Rule 39 (Required Majority); Appendix (Declaration incorporating the "Gentleman's Agreement"), – 13 *International Legal Materials* 1199, at 1205 and 1209 (1974). And see generally Vignes, *op. cit.*, 91 *Revue du Droit Public* 337 (1975); Vignes, Will the Third Conference on the Law of the Sea work according to the Consensus Rule?, 69 *American Journal of International Law* 119 (1975); Lacharrière, Consensus et Nations Unies, [1968] *Annuaire Français de Droit International* 9 (1968); Bastid, Observations sur la pratique du consensus, *Multitudo Legum. Jus Unum, Festschrift für Wilhelm Wengler* 11 (1973); Jenks, Unanimity, the Veto, Weighted Voting, Special and Simple Majorities and Consensus as modes of Decision in International Organizations, *Cambridge Essays in International Law. Essays in Honour of Lord McNair* 488 (1965).

6. Vignes, *op. cit.*, citing Jean Dupuy, 91 *Revue du Droit Public* 337, at 364 (1975).

7. Stone, *op. cit.*, 57 *Columbia Law Review* 16 (1957); Jennings, The Progressive Development of International Law and its Codification, 24 *British Yearbook of International Law* 301 (1947); De Visscher, *Théories et réalités en droit international public* (1953), at p. 177 *et seq.* And see, with particular reference to the Third U.N. Conference on the Law of the Sea, Jennings, *The discipline of International Law* (Lord McNair Memorial Lecture, 30 August, 1976), 5-6 (1978), reprinted in *International Law Association. Report of the Fifty-Seventh Conference (Madrid)* (1978) 620, at 625-6.

8. McDougal and Burke, *The Public Order of the Oceans. A contemporary International Law of the Sea* (1962), seem in this spirit.

9. The literature on the classical Law of the Sea is legion, ranging from that standard, well-respected academic text, – Colombos, *The International Law of the Sea* (4th rev. ed., 1959), to imaginative new, contemporary texts – Dupuy, *The Law of the Sea. Current Problems* (1974).

10. *Friedmann, Selden Redivivus:* Towards a Partition of the Seas?, 65 *American Journal of International Law* 757 (1971).

11. Developed more fully in the author's *The International Law of Détente. Arms Control, European Security, and East-West Cooperation* (1978).

12. Fitzmaurice, The future of Public International Law and of the International Legal System in the circumstances of today, *Institut de Droit International. Livre du Centenaire 1873-1973. Evolution et perspectives du droit international* (1973) at pp. 255-6.

13. See, for example *Anglo-Norwegian Fisheries Case (United Kingdom v. Norway)* (1951) I.C.J. 116.

14. Dupuy, *op. cit.*, at p. 40.

15. Presidential Proclamation 2267, September 28, 1945.

16. Compare Goldie, Where is the Continental Shelf's Outer Boundary?, 1 *Journal of Maritime Law and Commerce* 461 (1970).

17. On the issue of the normative, law-making quality of U.N. General Assembly Resolutions, see Johnson, The effect of Resolutions of the General Assembly of the United Nations, 32 *British Yearbook of International Law* 98 (1955-56); Higgins, *The Development of International Law through the Political Organs of the United Nations* (1963); Parry, *The Sources and Evidences of International Law* (1965); Lukashuk, *Istochniki Mezhdunarodnogo Prava* (1966), at pp. 81-94.

18. Etudes des mesures internationales les plus aptes à prévenir la pollution des milieux maritimes (Andrassy, *rapporteur*), *Annuaire de l'Institut de Droit International*, (1969), vol. 1, at p. 547 *et seq.*; vol. II, p. 255 *et seq.*

19. See, in this regard, the author's study, Changing Science and Technology and International Law, 6 *Indiana Law Review* 172 (1972).

20. United Nations Third Conference on the Law of the Sea: Informal Single Negotiating Text, U.N. Doc. A/Conf. 62/WP. 8/Part I, 7 May, 1975. 14 *International Legal Materials* 682 (1975), (*First Committee* – The Sea-Bed and the Ocean Floor and the Sub-Soil thereof beyond the Limits of National Jurisdiction, *ibid.*, at 682; *Second Committee* – The Territorial Sea and the Contiguous Zone ... *ibid.*, at 710; *Third Committee* – Protection and Preservation of the Marine Environment, *ibid.*, at 743).

21. U.N. Third Conference on the Law of the Sea: Informal Single Negotiating Text. Note by the President of the Conference, 14 *International Legal Materials* 682 (1975).

22 United Nations Third Conference on the Law of the Sea: Informal Composite Negotiating Text from the Sixth Session, U.N. Doc. A/Conf. 62/WP. 10, 15 July, 1977. 16 *International Legal Materials* 1108 (1977).

23. For the decisive *rôle* of these "metajuridical" factors in shaping the development of the renewed Law of the Sea Conference, see Ambassador Rosenne's study, The Third United Nations Conference on the Law of the Sea, 11 *Israel L. Rev.* 1 (1976).

24. 77 *Department of State Bulletin* (no. 1995) 389, (September 19, 1977); 16 *International Legal Materials* 1099 (1977). And see also Editorial, "Scuttle Law of the Sea", *The Wall Street Journal* (New York), July 22, 1977.

25. See, in this regard, the further comments by Ambassador Elliot Richardson of the United States: "I will not support, nor would I commend to the President, a treaty which creates a *régime* for the sea-bed that I cannot honestly defend as offering a reasonable basis for American companies to risk the enormous investments demanded by deep-sea mining.

> "Rather than accept outcomes which we consider wrong for the United States and, we believe, would be wrong for the world community as well, we would reluctantly choose to forego a treaty. The United States does not need a comprehensive treaty more than other nations. Sea-bed mining can and will go forward with or without such a treaty. We have the means at our disposal to protect our ocean interests if the Confer-

> ence should fail, and we shall protect these interests if a comprehensive treaty eludes us".

Richardson, *The Law of the Sea Conference: Is a comprehensive Treaty still possible?* Address by Ambassador Elliot Richardson at the Seapower Symposium of the Cincinnati Council of the Navy League of the United States, Cincinnati, Ohio, January 18, 1978).

26. After the settlement of the preliminary, procedural issue of the Conference presidency, which had occupied the first ten days of the 1978 resumed Geneva session, the Conference was able to agree on arrangements for negotiations during the remainder of that session. Negotiating groups were to tackle seven "hard-core" issues: how to establish the proposed international sea-bed authority; financial arrangements, mining of the sea-bed; access of certain countries to fisheries in the 200-mile economic zone; settlement of disputes over the rights of coastal States in that zone; the continental shelf; and maritime boundaries. (U.N. Press Release WS/862, 14 April 1978).

27. For a cogent reminder of the limitations inherent in the international law-making process, as applied in the Third U.N. Conference on the Law of the Sea, see the Comments by Professor Jennings:

> "The Law of the Sea Conference is not a legislature. The most the Conference can do is to adopt a text of a treaty to be proposed to governments for signature and eventually for ratification .... But certainly the treaty as such could only be binding upon Governments which expressed their willingness to become bound by instruments of ratification or accession .... If 'the vast majority' of the members of the greatly enlarged international community of today were to become parties to a new Law of the Sea Treaty, most of the difficulties would disappear. The situation we ought at least to be prepared for, however, is the more likely one where something significantly less than the 'vast majority' of States, including perhaps some whose interests are 'specially affected', choose not to become parties."

Jennings, *The discipline of International Law* (Lord McNair Memorial Lecture, 30 August, 1976), 6, 10 (1978). And see generally Schwarzenberger, Maritime World Order? Inter-Disciplinary Perspectives, in *The Law of the Sea*, 7 *Thesaurus Acroasium* 1, at 44 *et seq.* (1977).

28. See the further statement by U.S. Ambassador-at-Large Elliott L. Richardson:

> "Deep seabed mining is probably the key to determining whether or not a comprehensive law of the sea agreement can be negotiated that will serve the national interests of the United States. With regard to deep seabed mining, the last session of the Law of the Sea Conference was distressing from both a procedural and substantive point of view ....
>
> The President has decided to support Congressional efforts to develop deep seabed mining legislation consistent with our substantive position .... So long as our legislation is restricted to persons and vessels subject to United States jurisdiction and no exclusive rights to deep seabed areas are conferred, the licensing arrangements are compatible with existing international law ....

The idea of reciprocity grows out of the high seas character of deep seabed mining. It is important to understand that neither the United States nor any other nation can appropriate high seas areas. The deep seabed is, by definition, a high seas area. Hence, the United States must rely upon its jurisdiction over the person or vessel involved to regulate deep seabed mining activities. Since we do not own the area, we have no legal basis to confer exclusive rights on our licensees or permittees that would be valid against persons not subject to our jurisdiction. To preclude any implication that we are appropriating high seas areas, we avoid the allocation of specific areas of the high seas seabed in licenses or permits. Instead, the procedure we support is for applicants to file a work plan which includes details about the proposed location of the work area. Assuming other requirements are met, the administering agency would only approve non-conflicting work plans. The reciprocating state giving the first notice of work plan submissions would be entitled to rely upon other reciprocating states not to approve work plans which conflict ....

Mr. Chairman, some governments have questioned the seriousness of our support for domestic deep seabed mining legislation. They would be mistaken to underestimate our resolve to establish a timely legal *régime* governing deep seabed mining. As I have repeatedly said, the United States much prefers a negotiated, multilateral *régime* .... But if agreement is not forthcoming or negotiations are unduly prolonged, we are prepared to support domestic legislation consistent with our substantive policy goals as the basis for mining by our citizens."

Testimony of Elliott L. Richardson, Special Representative of the President for the Law of the Sea Conference, before the House International Relations Committee Subcommittee on International Organisations and Subcommittee on International Economic Policy and Trade. Washington, D.C., January 23, 1978.

29. The 1978 resumed, Geneva, session of the Third Law of the Sea Conference ended on May 19, 1978, with the delegates so divided over the question of the mining of the deep seabed mineral resources that no votes were taken on any specific issue; but with the conclusion, nevertheless, that still further talks should be undertaken in the future. Progress reports were filed by Chairmen of the Main Committees and Negotiating Groups at the resumed, Geneva, session. The Committee on the Creation of an International Authority to Control the Sea-bed indicated that the main areas of difficulty were the composition of the authority's council (involving the need to balance geographical and special economic interests) as well as the voting system on the council, and the relations between the functions and powers of the council and those of the General Assembly. The Committee dealing with general aspects of the law of the sea indicated that efforts were being made to define more precisely the outer limits of the continental shelf; while the Committee dealing with marine environment, research and technology said that agreement had been reached on changes in the proposed article dealing with pollution from ships. U.N. Press Release WS/866, 12 May, 1978.

NOTES TO CHAPTER VII

1. A/RES/3201 (S-VI) 9 May 1974
2. A/RES/3202 (S-VI) 16 May 1974
3. A/RES/3281 (XXIX) 15 January 1975
4. On the operational legal significance of the distinction between adoption by an international organisation or international legal conference by formal, recorded vote and adoption without vote and informal consensus generally, see Jenks, Unanimity, the Veto, Weighted Voting, Special and Simplified Majorities and Consensus as Modes of Decision in International Law, *Cambridge Essays in International Law: Essays in Honour of Lord McNair* 488 (1965); Lacharrière Consensus et Nations Unies, [1968] *Annuaire Français de Droit International* 9; Bastid, Observations sur la pratique du consensus, I *Multitudo Legum Ius Unum. Festschrift für Wilhelm Wengler;* (Tittel, ed.) 11 (1973); Wengler, Rechtsvertrag, Konsensus und Absichtserklärung im Völkerrecht, 31 *Juristenzeitung* 193 (1976)

For a Legal Realist-style approach to international law-making that emphasises the *fact* of a State's acceptance of a particular legal rule as being binding rather than the more traditional, positivistic-style analysis of whether or not the claimed rule falls into any of the *a priori* categories of formal sources of International Law, see the Dissenting Opinion by Judge Lachs in *North Sea Continental Shelf Cases (Federal Republic of Germany/Denmark: Federal Republic of Germany/Netherlands)*, I.C.J. Reports 1969, p. 3, at pp. 229-30, 236. And see also the Advisory Opinion of the Court in *Legal Consequences for States of the Continued Presence of South Africa in Namibia (South West Africa) Notwithstanding Security Council Resolution 276 (1970)*, I.C.J. Reports 1971, p. 16; *Nuclear Tests Case (Australia v. France)*, I.C.J. Reports 1974, p. 253, at pp. 267-8. And see Franck, Word Made Law: The Decision of the International Court of Justice in the Nuclear Test Cases, 69 A.J.I.L. 612, at 614-5 (1975); Sur, Les affaires des essais nucléaires devant la C.I.J., 79 *Revue Générale de Droit International Public* 972, at 998-9 (1975).

5. It is no doubt historically correct to trace back the campaign for a New International Economic Order ultimately to U.N. General Assembly Resolution 1803 (XVII) of 14 December, 1962. Feuer, Réflexions sur la Charte des droits et devoirs économiques des Etats, 79 *Revue Générale de Droit International Public* 273, 276 (1975). And see also Goldie, Some dilemmas of an Internationalist in a World of State egoism, 2 *Syracuse Journal of International Law and Commerce* 299, 301 (1974); and see generally Schwarzen-

berger, The Principles and Standards of International Economic Law, 1 *Recueil des Cours* 1 (1966).

6. The literature on the old Bipolar model of World Public Order and the mutual interactions of the two blocs and their leaders is now legion: we may cite, variously, Kulski, *Peaceful Coexistence. An analysis of Soviet Foreign Policy* (1959); Hazard, Codifying Peaceful Coexistence, 55 *American Journal of International Law* 109 (1961); Hazard, Coexistence Codification Reconsidered, 57 *American Journal of International Law* 88 (1963); McDougal and Lasswell, The identification and appraisal of diverse systems of public order, 53 *American Journal of International Law* 1 (1959); McWhinney, *"Peaceful Coexistence" and Soviet-Western International Law* (1964); McWhinney, *International Law and World Revolution* (1967); McWhinney, *The International Law of Détente. Arms Control, European Security, and East-West Cooperation* (1978).

7. The intellectual roots of the "new" International Law go back to innovatory Chilean jurist and one-time Judge of the World Court, Alvarez, *Le droit international nouveau dans ses rapports avec la vie actuelle des peuples* (1959). Long before it was embraced by the Third World majority in the United Nations, however, the concept was much canvassed in Soviet and Soviet bloc international law doctrine: see, for example, the debate in 1963 between the celebrated Soviet jurist, Tunkin, and the then Legal Adviser to the British Foreign Office, Sir Francis Vallat, cited in the author's *Conflict idéologique et Ordre public mondial* (1970), at p. 116. And see also Movchan, *Kodifikatsii i progressivnoe razvitie mezhdunarodnogo prava* (1974).

8. This important historical difference in the origins of the two movements is reaffirmed in Kardelj, The Historical Roots of Non-Alignment, 15 *Socialist Thought and Practice* 3 (1975); Hudes, Towards a new international economic order, 2 *Yale Studies in World Public Order* 88, at 95 (1975).

9. Gosovic and Ruggie, On the creation of a new international economic order: issue linkage and the Seventh Special Session of the U.N. General Assembly, 30 *International Organisation* 309, at 311 and 316 (1976); Hudes, *op. cit.*, 2 *Yale Studies in World Public Order* 88, at 99 (1975).

10. Declaration on Principles of International Law concerning Friendly Relations and Cooperation among States in accordance with the Charter of the United Nations, A/RES/2625 (XXV), 24 October 1970. Compare Rosenstock, The Declaration of Principles of International Law concerning Friendly Relations: A survey, 65 *American Journal of International Law* 713 (1971); Sinclair, Principles of International Law concerning Friendly Relations and Cooperation among States, in *Essays on International Law in Honour of Krishna Rao*, (Nawaz, ed.) (1975), at 107; Frowein, Der Beitrag der internationalen Organisationen zur Entwicklung des Völkerrechts, 36 *ZaöRV* 147, 156-8 (1976).

11. Voting *NO* on U.N. General Assembly Resolution 3281 (XXIX) of 15 January 1975 were Belgium, Denmark, West Germany, Luxembourg, the United Kingdom, and the United States; *abstaining* were Austria, Canada, France, Ireland, Israel, Italy, Japan, The Netherlands, Norway, Spain; there were, as noted, 120 *affirmative* votes.

12. See, in this regard, Vignes, Organisation et règlement intérieur de la III e Conférence sur le droit de la mer, 91 *Revue du Droit Public* 337 (1975); Vignes, Will the Third Conference on the Law of the Sea work according to the Consensus Rule?, 69 *American Journal of International Law* 119 (1975). And see also United Nations, Rules of Procedure for the Third U.N. Conference on the Law of the Sea, Rule 39 (Required Majority) and Appendix (Declaration incorporating the "Gentleman's Agreement"), U.N. Doc. A/CONF. 62/30/Rev. 1, at 9 and 17; reproduced in 13 *International Legal Materials* 1199, 1205, 1209 (1974).

13. Feuer, *op. cit.*, 79 *Revue Générale de Droit International Public* 273, 303 (1975); Dupuy, *Mélanges Rousseau* (1974), at pp. 75-87; Hudes, *op. cit.*, 2 *Yale Studies in World Public Order* 88, 114 (1975); Gosovic and Ruggie, *op. cit.*, 30 *International Organisation* 309, 322 (1976).

14. See, for example, the Reservations expressly entered by the United States, U.N. Doc. A/PV. 2229, 1 May 1974, at p. 41; by West Germany, *ibid.* at p. 51; by France, *ibid.*, at p. 73; by Japan, U.N. Doc. A/PV. 2230, 2 May 1974, at p. 17; by the United Kingdom, U.N. Doc. A/PV. 2231, 2 May 1974 at p. 12; reproduced in 13 *International Legal Materials* 744 (1974).

15. "... On s'est alors livré à des exercises véritablement acrobatiques pour rapprocher, fondre, synthétiser tout ce qui pouvait l'être et pour faire entrer dans la Charte, sans souci trop grand de logique ou de réalisme, tout ce que l'on voulait qu'il y entrât. On ne s'étonnera donc pas que la Charte ressemble si fort à l'habit d'Arlequin et qu'on y recontre un déséquilibre, une imprécision, un désordre, une hétérogéneité qui en altèrent quelque peu la cohérence et l'élégance". Feuer, *op. cit.* 79 *Revue Générale de Droit international public* 273, 285 (1975).

16. "Au-delà de ces malfaçons, le document présente un défaut plus grave, qui est d'être ambigu. Et même doublement ambigu .... Derrière une formulation abstraite et générale se cachent des interprétations qui varient d'un Etat à l'autre et dont les discussions a l'Assemblée générale apportent un écho éloquent. Si bien qu'on ne peut rien dire de la Charte qui ne soit susceptible d'être contesté par l'une quelconque des Parties. La tâche de l'interprète ne s'en trouvera pas facilitée". Feuer, *ibid.*, at 285; and see generally Tomuschat, Die Charta der wirtschaftlichen Rechte und Pflichten der Staaten. Zur Gestaltungskraft von Deklarationen der UN-Generalversammlung, 36 *ZaöRV* 444 (1976).

17. Charter of Economic Rights and Duties of States, (U.N. General Assembly Resolution 3281 (XXIX) 15 January 1975), Chapter II, Economic rights and duties of States: —

"*Article 1.* Every State has the sovereign and inalienable right to choose its economic system as well as its political, social and cultural systems in accordance with the will of its people, without outside interference, coercion or threat in any form whatsoever.

Article 2. 1. Every State has and shall freely exercise full permanent sovereignty, including possession, use and disposal, over all its wealth, natural resources and economic activities.

2. Each State has the right:
(a) To regulate and exercise authority over foreign investment within its national jurisdiction in accordance with its laws and regulations and in conformity with its national objectives and priorities ....
(b) To regulate and supervise the activities of transnational corporations within its national jurisdiction and take measures to ensure that such activities comply with its laws, rules and regulations and conform with its economic and social policies ....
(c) To nationalise, expropriate or transfer ownership of foreign property, in which case appropriate compensation should be paid by the State adopting such measures, taking into account its relevant laws and regulations and all circumstances that the State considers pertinent ....

18. Charter of Economic Rights and Duties of States: –
"*Article 32.* No State may use or encourage the use of economic, political or any other type of measures to coerce another State in order to obtain from it the subordination of the exercise of its sovereign rights."
And see, also, additional Charter provisions: –
"*Article 16 (2).* No State has the right to promote or encourage investments that may constitute an obstacle to the liberation of a territory occupied by force."
"*Article 18.* ... In the conduct of international economic relations the developed countries should endeavour to avoid measures having a negative effect on the development of the national economies of the developing countries, as promoted by generalised tariff preferences and other generally agreed differential measures in their favour."

19. "*Article 16.* 1. It is the right and duty of all States, individually and collectively, to eliminate colonialism, *apartheid*, racial discrimination, neocolonialism and all forms of foreign aggression, occupation and domination, and the economic and social consequences thereof, as a prerequisite for development ....

20. "*Article 16 (1)* ... States which practise such coercive policies [i.e. colonialism, *apartheid*, racial discrimination, neo-colonialism ...] are economically responsible to the countries, territories and peoples affected for the restitution and full compensation for the exploitation and depletion of, and damages to, the natural and all other resources of those countries, territories and peoples. It is the duty of all States to extend assistance to them ...."

21. "*Article 29.* The sea-bed and ocean floor and the subsoil thereof, beyond the limits of national jurisdiction, as well as the resources of the area, are the common heritage of mankind ...."

22. "*Article 30.* The protection, preservation and enhancement of the environment for the present and future generations is the responsibility of all States ...."

23. Compare Loewenstein, *Political Power and the Governmental Process* (1957), at pp. 147-9.

24. The logically formal rationality of the "classical", juridically-based system of World Public Order, now being challenged by the campaign for a New World Economic Order, was, of course, itself immediately preceded by a

fundamentally economically-based system, the so-called *Pax Britannica*, which – "rested on the combined might of the City of London and the British Navy. In the last resort needy governments and private entrepreneurs had to take their cue from the City of London on what would-be 'host' countries expected of the borrowers". Schwarzenberger, An evolving Economic World Order, 1 *Rutgers-Camden Law Journal* 243, 246 (1969).

25. The Third World strategy for ending white minority rule in Southern Africa runs the gamut from direct military involvement, as with the sending of Cuban troops to fight in Angola; indirect military involvement, through assistance to guerrilla-type operations, as in Rhodesia; and sophisticated juridically-based operations in official international arenas. And see generally Calogeropoulos-Stratis, *Le droit des peuples à disposer d'eux-mêmes* (1973); Klein, Nationale Befreiungskämpfe und Dekolonisierungspolitik der Vereinten Nationen; zu einigen völkerrechtlichen Tendenzen, 36 *ZaöRV* 618 (1976).

26. *Towards a new international economic order. Report by a Commonwealth Experts Group.* (Commonwealth Secretariat, London) (1975), at p. 49; Hudes, *op. cit.*, 2 *Yale Studies in World Public Order* 88, 178 (1975).

27. Kardelj, The Historical Roots of Non-Alignment, 15 *Socialist Thought and Practice* 3, 44 (1975); and see generally Rubinstein and Ginsburgs, *Soviet and American Policies in the United Nations: a Twenty-Five-Year Perspective* (1971); Frowein, *supra* Note 10, at 161.

28. Compare Castrén, What we expect of International Law, *Essays on International Law in honour of Krishna Rao* (Nawaz, ed.) (1975), at 42; Tunkin, International Law: the contemporary and classic, *ibid.*, 48, at 55 *et seq.*; Petersmann, Die Dritte Welt und das Wirtschaftsvölkerrecht. "Entwicklungsland" als privilegierte Rechtsstatus, 36 *ZaöRV* 492 (1976).

NOTES TO CHAPTER VIII

1. Advisory Opinion of May 28, 1948, (Conditions of Admission of a State to Membership in the United Nations), I.C.J. Reports (1948), p. 57.

2. Advisory Opinion of March 3, 1950 (Competence of the General Assembly for the Admission of a State to the United Nations), I.C.J. Reports (1950), p. 4.

3. Ross, *The United Nations. Peace and Progress* (1966), at p. 93.

4. United Nations Doc. A/AC. 24/SR. 6-14; and see also Draft Resolution of Argentina, United Nations Doc. A/AC 24/15, November 23, 1948.

5. I.C.J. Reports (1950), p. 4.

6. See Alvarez, *Le droit international nouveau dans ses rapports avec la vie actuelle des peuples* (1959).

7. See, for example, McDougal and Gardner, The Veto and the Charter: an interpretation for survival, 60 *Yale Law Journal* 258 (1951), written in reply to Gross, Voting in the Security Council: abstention from voting and absence from meetings, 60 *Yale Law Journal* 209 (1951).

8. A/1123.

9. SCOR, V, no. 1, p. 3.

10. SCOR, V, no. 22, pp. 1-10.

11. United Nations General Assembly Resolution 2758 (XXVI), October 25, 1971.

12. 4 Wheat. 316, 4 L. Ed. 579 (1819).

13. *Edwards v. Attorney-General for Canada*, (1930) A.C. 124, 136 (P.C.).

14. See, for example A/3536, February 13, 1957; GAOR, Annexes (XI) 3, pp. 1-2.

15. GAOR, XV, Plen. pp. 978-9.

16. A/5676/Rev. 1, December 14, 1963; GAOR Annexes (XVIII) 3, p. 2.

17. Dicey, *Introduction to the study of the Law of the Constitution* (1st ed., 1885), at p. 417 *et seq.*

18. UN Doc. A/AC. 38/L. 6; GAOR Annexes (V) 61, p. 5.

19. United Nations General Assembly Resolution 396 (V), December 14, 1950; GAOR, V, Supp. 20 (A/1775), p. 24.

20. A/8160, p. 4.

21. I.C.J. Reports, 1966, p. 3, at p. 325.

22. *ibid.*, p. 441.

23. per Jessup J., ibid., p. 441.

24. I.C.J. Reports, 1971, p. 16.

25. GAOR, XV, Suppl. 16 (A/4684) pp. 66-7.

26. GAOR, Suppl. 28 (A/8028) pp. 122-4.

27. In anticipation, perhaps, of an adverse vote in the U.N. General Assembly's Credentials Committee, the Government of the Union of South Africa was not represented when the Thirtieth Session of the General Assembly opened on September 16, 1975.
Roelof F. Botha (South Africa) said that his country was unlikely to take part in the subsequent proceedings, judging from present circumstances. He added that South Africa was still considering its relations with the United Nations. *U.N. Press Release* WS/728, 19 September, 1975.

NOTES TO CHAPTER IX

1. Freund, *On Understanding the Supreme Court* (1949), at p. 78.

2. Vyshinsky, *The Law of the Soviet State* (1938) (Babb, transl., 1954), at p. 336 *et seq.*

3. I.C.J. Reports, 1962, p. 151.

4. I.C.J. Reports, 1962, p. 151, at p. 230.

5. I.C.J. Reports, 1962, p. 151, at p. 268.

6. I.C.J. Reports, 1962, p. 151, at pp. 230-2.

7. Hudson, *The Permanent Court of International Justice 1920-1942*, at p. 511: –

> "... The Court ... has conceived of its advisory function as a judicial function, and in its exercise of this jurisdiction it has kept within the limits which characterise judicial action. It has acted not as an 'academy of jurists' but as a responsible 'magistrature'."

8. I.C.J. Reports, 1971, p. 16, at p. 303.

9. I.C.J. Reports, 1971, p. 16.

10. I.C.J. Reports, 1966, p. 6.

11. *Ibid.*

12. I.C.J. Reports, 1971, p. 16.

13. I.C.J. Reports, 1966, p. 6.

14. I.C.J. Reports, 1971, p. 16.

15. Von Mehren, The Judicial Process: A Comparative Analysis, 5 *American Journal of Comparative Law* 197, 208-9 (1956); McWhinney, *Constitutionalism in Germany and the Federal Constitutional Court* (1962) at p. 23.

16. Stammler, *Lehre von dem richtigen Recht* (1902).

17. Weber, *Wirtschaft und Gesellschaft* (2nd ed., 1925), at p. 482 *et seq.*

18. Weber, *op. cit.*, at p. 170 and at p. 456 *et seq.*

19. I.C.J. Reports, 1953, p. 47.

20. I.C.J. Reports, 1969, p. 3.

21. I.C.J. Reports, 1973, p. 99: I.C.J. Reports, 1973, p. 135.

22. See generally Retrait par le gouvernement français de son acceptation de la juridiction obligatoire de la Cour internationale de justice (10 janvier 1974), 78 *Revue Générale de Droit International Public* 822 (1974).

23. I.C.J. Reports, 1953, p. 47.

24. France, Grande-Bretagne et Suisse: Accord signé à Berne le 14 janvier 1977 concernant le statut, les privilèges et les immunités en Suisse du Tribunal arbitral chargé de la délimitation du plateau continental entre la France et

le Royaume-Uni et des personnes participant aux travaux de ce tribunal, 81 *Revue Générale de Droit International Public* 934 (1977).

25. See, in this regard, Bilder, The Canadian Arctic Waters Pollution Prevention Act: New Stresses on the Law of the Sea, 69 *Michigan Law Review* 1 (1970); Pharand, Oil Pollution Control in the Canadian Arctic, 7 *Texas International Law Journal* 45 (1971).

26. Freund, A Supreme Court in a Federation: some lessons from Legal History, 53 *Columbia Law Review* 597, at p. 617 et seq. (1953); and see the author's *Judicial Review* (4th ed., 1969), at pp. 181-2 and p. 254 *et seq.*

27. *Constitutionalism in Germany and the Federal Constitutional Court* (1962), at pp. 26-7 and p. 34 *et seq.*

28. 65 D.L.R. (2d) 353 (1968).

29. I.C.J. Reports, 1962, p. 151.

30. I.C.J. Reports, 1971, p. 16.

31. *Ibid.*

32. I.C.J. Reports, 1975, p. 12.

33. I.C.J. Reports, 1971, p. 16.

34. I.C.J. Reports, 1975, p. 12.

35. As to the *rôle* of the *responsa prudentium* in Roman Law and also the special status of the jurisconsults, see Weber, *Wirtschaft und Gesellschaft* (2nd ed., 1925), at p. 456 *et seq.*

36. Charter of the United Nations, Article 96:

> "1. The General Assembly or the Security Council may request the International Court of Justice to give an advisory opinion on any legal question.
>
> 2. Other organs of the United Nations and specialised agencies, which may at any time be so authorised by the General Assembly, may also request advisory opinions of the Court on legal questions arising within the scope of their activities."

37. Statute of the International Court of Justice, – Article 5:

> "2. No [national] group may nominate more than four persons, not more than two of whom shall be of their own nationality. In no case may the number of candidates nominated by a group be more than double the number of seats to be filled."

INDEX